fai child

ISBN: 978-1-63813-527-2

Cover and interior design: Kristi Yoder

Printed in the USA

Third printing: January 2026

Front cover photo: Adobe Stock

Published by:

CAM Books
P.O. Box 355
Berlin, Ohio 44610 USA
Phone: 330.893.4828
Fax: 330.893.4893
cambooks.org

faith child

A story of resilience, redemption, and reliance on a faithful God.

Laura Smucker
with Kaylene (Bontrager) Stoltzfus

Dedication

This book is dedicated to our long-suffering families, who believed in this project enough to put up with skimpy suppers, neglected housework, and distracted wives without complaint.

Contents

Acknowledgment

This book would never have happened if the Bontrager family had not been willing to dig through their many personal archives, both physical and emotional. The process of drawing out this story and sifting through all the details was sometimes humorous, sometimes enlightening, and often tinged with pain. The Bontragers kindly stuck to it with the hope that their story could bring encouragement to many and strengthen the faith of others who have walked through dark valleys.

Author's Note

The dry, windswept Kansas plains slipped away beneath me as my plane soared into the air. Tears pooled in my eyes, blurring my vision. I had just been entrusted with a story I didn't know what to do with. The week I had spent with the Bontragers had overflowed with memories, interviews, and questions. I had arrived on business and left as a friend. But with these new friendships came a responsibility of all they had told me. This was a normal family, wanting nothing more than to live a normal life in a normal community. The story of *Faith Child* demonstrates how their dreams and desires were turned upside down. It also describes their journey to trust in a God who writes different endings than anyone ever imagined. In Eldon and Mary Ellen's lives, we see a clear example of redemption that only comes through forgiveness and brokenness.

How did this nearly unbelievable story become mine to tell? My thoughts went even farther back to how the hand of God had so clearly led the way.

One summer evening in 2018, our church gathered to listen to Grant Bontrager's story. I did not know who he was, and as we drove to church that night, I remember thinking, *What kind of story could a young boy from a Christian home have to tell?* But from his first words, I sat riveted. What a testimony of God's goodness, forgiveness, and mercy!

After the service, I was browsing through Grant's folder of memories when a writer friend came up to me. "This story needs to be written," she said. "Could this be your next book?"

Her words made such an impression on me that I mentioned it to Grant that night, and we made a tentative plan to pursue this project if the rest of his family was willing.

Earlier that summer, just before Grant's trip to my church in Oregon, the Bontrager family had gathered to celebrate fifty years on the farm. A topic of much discussion that week was whether a book should be written. As Grant had become an adult, he had begun to share his story. This was cracking open the lid of silence that had protected him for years, and some of the family thought it was time to put it all into writing.

On the other hand, it was a deeply personal story, and some family members were not sure they wanted to dig out the emotions and feelings that had been tidily packed away for so long. Finally someone suggested looking for an author, but none of them had any idea who to ask.

At the same time, CAM Books sent out an email to CAM employees, asking for story ideas for future book projects. A grandson-in-law to Eldon who worked at CAM suggested Grant's story and was promptly visited by a CAM Books employee. The employee contacted me as a potential author several weeks after I first heard Grant's story.

I sent out some questionnaires to the family—then I waited, waited, and waited, with virtually no response. *Maybe this isn't what God wants me to write,* I thought. I knew I was a stranger to the family, and I didn't want to barge in on a story that wasn't mine to tell.

For several years, the Bontrager family waffled. When I had nearly given up, they contacted me and confirmed they were finally on board. Slowly the completed questionnaires came back. Plans began to fall into place for my husband and me to fly to Kansas in January 2022. But in October 2021, gangsters kidnapped our son Austin in Haiti, along with Grant's cousin Ryan and fifteen others. I remember thinking, *There is no way I can continue pursuing that story with this other upheaval in my life.*

But God had other plans.

Unknown to any of us, God would use Grant's story to help the hostages escape from the gangsters. It was a bizarre yet beautiful confirmation that the story was coming together.

My son came home safely at Christmastime. Now there was no way I could abandon the story. In January, as planned, I made the trip to Kansas and began doing the research and interviews. Grant's cousin Kaylene (Bontrager) Stoltzfus joined me to help provide family details for the story. Little did we know that she would eventually become my co-author. I am forever grateful to her for her attention to the details and for working with the family to get this book as accurate as possible.

I have followed a clear thread of redemption in this book. As with any true story, the writing is a matter of the author's perspective. I have taken the liberty to tweak and add details and conversation to make the story flow. Although the main characters retained their names, several other names have been changed to protect friends and community. Although details may sometimes vary from the actual happenings, my desire is that this amazing story will turn your eyes to the omnipotent God who walked with the Bontragers through their journey. My prayer is that *Faith Child* will bring honor and glory to His name!

–Laura Smucker with Kaylene Stoltzfus

Prologue

The blistering tropical sun beat down on Ryan Korver as he walked circles in the filthy, trash-littered yard. *O God!* he cried inwardly. *You must tell us what to do!*

For eight long weeks in late 2021, a group of missionaries had been held hostage by a Haitian gang. Of the original seventeen people kidnapped, five had been released, but the rest remained in captivity. Ryan and his family were part of this group. It was a perilous situation, but the missionaries knew it was an unparalleled opportunity to share the Gospel. They realized they were involved in daily combat between the powers of light and the powers of darkness. Lately, however, it felt like they were just rotting in the midst of a cesspool of sin. Immorality and witchcraft were all around them, and satanic music blared relentlessly. Weeks had passed since their last communication with the outside world. Had everyone forgotten them?

As Ryan paced, he was gripped with despair and desperation. His three-year-old son Andre was dealing with constant fevers and bellyaches, screaming in pain during the night. Ryan's wife Melodi had a nursing baby, and she was wasting away to a shadow of her typical vigorous self. Still, the group could not agree—should they wait on the Lord for divine deliverance or should they try to escape? Either option had dangerous risks.

Ryan paced and prayed. And then he prayed and paced some more. Melodi sat on the porch watching him, while one of the hostage girls combed out her hair with a plastic fork and then plaited it in a fresh French braid. As Ryan kept pacing, he heard his wife and some of the other hostages chatting about Christmas traditions, reunions, and their extended families.

"Did I ever tell you about Ryan's cousin Grant?" Melodi asked. "It's quite a story..."

As she began to tell the familiar tale, Ryan's thoughts were momentarily distracted from their present crisis. As his mind went to the Bontragers' amazing story, his hope was renewed. *They were also in a crisis, but they were willing to do the right thing—the hard thing.* The more he thought about it, the more he was inspired by this story of resilience, redemption, and reliance on a faithful God...

Part ONE

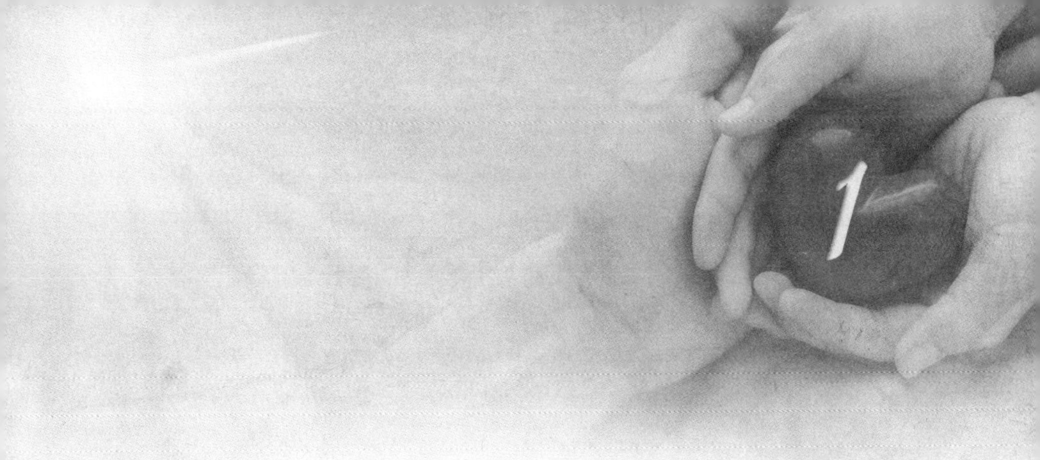

Wedding Day!

The great sun crept over the eastern horizon of the vast Kansas plains. One by one the twinkling stars faded from sight as flowers woke and stretched slender stems toward the warmth of the morning rays. The emerging light filtered down through the leaves of a massive elm tree, illuminating a tall, white Amish farmhouse, the home of Menno Jr. and Elizabeth Yoder.

As dawn descended into the guest bedroom, the clanging of an alarm jarred Eldon Bontrager awake. Reaching over to silence the noise, he became aware of a warm glow spreading through his body. Gradually the feeling enveloped him. Suddenly his eyes opened wide, and he leaped out of bed. "Today is my wedding day!" Yes, today—May 5, 1955—Mary Ellen Yoder would become his bride.

As Eldon got dressed, he thought back over the two years of their long-distance courtship. The many letters carefully tucked away under his bed at home bore witness to the growing relationship that had slowly bound their two hearts together. During the Korean War, he had served at a 1-W base in a Kansas City hospital. His occasional visits to Mary Ellen, riding by train to her home in Hutchinson, had only verified that this was the woman for him. *Every good man has a good woman behind him,* he mused, carefully combing his dark, wavy hair.

Eldon had grown up in Thomas, Oklahoma. Like his bride, he was born to Amish parents—Eli and Delilah Bontrager. His father was a quiet but determined and resourceful man who farmed wheat and raised livestock. Following his father's example, Eldon endeavored to be a good man, striving to be an asset to the community. He moved in quick, logical ways, living modestly and keeping his affairs in order. He did not cause ripples or drama. He conducted himself in a way that there would be no cause for shame or failure. Mary Ellen—with her crisp black curls, quiet smile, and calm, organized ways—seemed a perfect fit for the life he envisioned.

Putting down the comb, Eldon shrugged into his wedding vest, straightening it as he headed downstairs to the Yoders' kitchen. In the early hour, many cooks were already bustling about, preparing for the wedding feast.

Breakfast was a hurried affair with Mary Ellen's parents and her younger brothers, who had been up early to milk the family's dairy herd. The boys snickered behind their hands as Eldon joined them. "Good morning, Eldon *Bohnefadrickah,"* they chorused. The teenage brothers loved to tease their sister about her boyfriend with the funny name. A Bontrager was uncommon in the Hutchinson, Kansas, community, where you were more likely to find a Nisly or a Yoder. So Mary Ellen's brothers had given Eldon this German nickname, which translated to "bean squeezer" in English.

"Good morning," he replied, glaring ferociously at them. Then his face broke into a grin. Eldon had learned to enjoy his fiancée's fun-loving family. But where was his bride?

Mary Ellen was taking special pains before her mirror this morning.

Her eyes shone with an extra sparkle as she meticulously adjusted her dress and arranged her hair. Wedding preparations had absorbed all her time and energy for the last while, but today she knew it had been worth it. She admired Eldon deeply and was awed that he had chosen her. His innovative ambition was a good balance to her own careful, methodical ways. Likewise, her sense of humor and quick, dry comments were a nice counterbalance to his tendency toward workaholism.

As Eldon opened the porch door and strode down the walk, the dry air was uncharacteristically bright and still. *It's going to be a hot one today,* he mused, hooking his fingers on his suspenders as he watched numerous horse-drawn buggies turning in at the lane. *So many special people, all coming just for us!* Eldon's heart swelled as he hurried to greet the guests. Although shy as a child, his confidence had grown as he matured, and now he loved people. A lot of his family lived out of state, but he had spent enough time in the Hutchinson area to connect with the locals.

After the men secured their horses to the hitching rail, the guests made their way to the white round-topped farm shed. It was glistening from the week-long wedding preparations, but Eldon still peeked inside to make sure everything was ready. Doing things well was important to him. Failing was for the unfortunate, and he always felt that with a little forethought, most catastrophes could be avoided.

Finding all in order, Eldon glanced at his watch and headed back to the house, trying to suppress the jitters flaring up inside him. As he crossed the porch, the door opened and there stood his bride, smiling as she stepped back to let him enter.

"Good morning," he said.

"Good morning to you," she answered shyly.

Eldon stuffed down the urge to rhapsodize over the lovely woman standing before him, and instead settled for a more proper compliment. "That's a nice dress," he said, attempting stoicism. Then he grinned.

Mary Ellen laughed nervously. "I'm glad you like it." She smoothed the white organdy apron laid neatly over her copen blue wedding dress.

A heart-shaped prayer cap rested gently on her hair. "I'm a little nervous about all those people out there."

"No need for that," Eldon reassured her. "This is our day, and you look great. I've checked over everything in the shed, and nothing should go wrong."

Mary Ellen's quiet presence calmed him as they walked through the living room and headed upstairs to meet with the ministers before the service. The gray-bearded bishop, John D. Yoder, greeted them as they entered the spare room. "Come in and sit down. We just want to go over a few things with you."

The couple nodded nervously.

"I'm sure it's hard to imagine there could be a time of not loving and caring for each other," the bishop said. "But the vows you will make today are binding until death. Do you understand that?"

They nodded again. Eldon glanced over at Mary Ellen, her hands clasped in her lap.

"How has your courtship been? Have you kept yourselves pure?"

"Yes, we have," Eldon affirmed, while Mary Ellen nodded in assent.

After some more discussion and advice, the ministers drew the session to a close. "We see no reason this union can't take place," the bishop said with a smile. "You are dismissed until the service begins."

Back outside, the couple was joined by their wedding party—Mary Ellen's brother Henry with Eldon's sister Anna Mae, and Eldon's brother Joe with his girlfriend Salina Chupp.

As the procession approached the ceremony in the shed, Eldon reverently took in the scene. Women clothed in dark hues and draped in traditional black aprons sat on the backless wooden benches on the left side of the building. Bearded men with dark trousers and vests and white shirts filled the rows on the right side. Children sat quietly throughout, dressed identically to their parents, boys with their fathers and girls with their mothers.

The congregation began singing the traditional German *Hochzeit Lied* (Wedding Song). Each syllable was drawn out in a chant-like a cappella song:

Will singen euch, im alten Ton,
Ein Lied von Lieb und Treu;
Es sangen's unsre Vater schon,
Doch bleibt's der Liebe neu.

English Translation:

I will sing for you an old melody,
A song of love and fidelity;
Our forefathers already sang it,
Yet it remains new for those in love.[1]

The song trailed off, and that was their cue. The bridal pair led the procession through the door into the shed and to the front where six chairs were arranged in two facing rows of three. Eldon and Mary Ellen took the middle chairs in each row, with Henry and Anna Mae on one side of them and Joe and Salina on the other. There were no flower bouquets at this simple wedding, but the bride and bridesmaids each carried a lacy white handkerchief.

Eldon observed the guests out of the corner of his eye, then took a quick look at his bride. Their eyes met, and Mary Ellen gave him a shy smile as the first preacher rose to begin his sermon. Mary Ellen's uncle Fred Nisly from Kalona, Iowa, had consented to preach the first wedding sermon. The story of Isaac and Rebekah took on new significance as the couple thought of the life they were about to embark on. Like any new couple, they had high ideals of married life.

The local bishop delivered the second sermon. When he finished, he closed his German Bible and folded his hands, surveying the congregation. "No concerns have been raised about this union." He looked at the couple in front of him. "If it is still your desire to be married, you may rise to your feet." Pulling a black book out of his suit pocket, the bishop opened it to the marriage vows.

[1] Translation from https://www.lieder.net/lieder/get_text.html?TextId=122280&RF=0.

Eldon and Mary Ellen stood face to face before the bishop. "Do you promise to love and cherish the person by your side, in health and sickness, in prosperity and adversity, sharing with each other the joys and sorrows of life?"

"I do," Eldon said emphatically.

The bishop turned to Mary Ellen. "I do," she agreed.

After several more questions, the bishop returned the book to his pocket. "You may now join your right hands." Clasping their right hands together, he prayed over the couple and pronounced them husband and wife.

As they sat back down, Eldon beamed from ear to ear. At last! He could hardly believe they were married! He was so caught up in the moment he scarcely heard the disturbance caused by the servers slipping out to help with the wedding meal.

After a time of testimony and announcements, it was time for the closing prayer. Skirts rustled and shoes scuffled as the wedding guests knelt. Church was hardly dismissed when several young men shouldered the backless benches and carried them to the farmhouse to be used for the wedding meal. Eldon and Mary Ellen stayed several steps behind so they could have a few private moments. As they entered the house and walked through the wide doorway to the living room where a special bridal table had been set up, something caught Eldon's attention.

"Do I see an angel food cake?" he gasped, spinning around to look at his new wife.

"Well, today is your birthday, you know," she said, laughing at his astonishment.

Eldon grinned, rubbing his stomach. "I kind of figured no one had time for that today." Mary Ellen was known for her outstanding cooking, and her specialty was angel food cake. Marriage to this woman would have many benefits!

As guests began streaming into the house, Eldon pulled out a chair and seated his new bride. The wedding party sat behind the decorated table where they would wait until all the guests had been served. Other tables

The bridal party on Eldon and Mary Ellen's wedding day, May 5, 1955.
Left to right: Henry, Anna Mae, Eldon, Mary Ellen, Joe, Salina.

were set throughout the house and on the large sunporch. The adults would be served first, then the tables would be reset for the youth.

As soon as the adults were seated, dinner was dished up and served family-style. Chicken and noodles, sweet corn, salad, Jell-O, and dinner rolls sped around the tables, filling empty plates and growling stomachs. As the first course disappeared, ice cream and cake made their rounds as well.

After the meal, the children ran to play as the adults spread out on the wide lawn and visited. Eldon and Mary Ellen mingled with the guests.

"Have a candy bar." Eldon held out a bowl to his groomsmen.

"Just candy?" Joe asked.

Eldon grinned ruefully. "No tobacco from me." Although cigars were often given out at a wedding, that was one tradition Eldon wanted to avoid.

"I guess a candy bar will do," Henry said. He accepted the bar and took a big bite. Chewing thoughtfully, he grinned at his new brother-in-law. "You look awfully pleased."

"Why shouldn't I be?" Eldon smiled at Mary Ellen. "She is exactly what

I need in my life."

Mary Ellen blushed, but her eyes twinkled. She was content to stay by Eldon's side, listening to him socialize with the guests who had come for their special day. While she also enjoyed people, she preferred them in smaller numbers.

As the warm afternoon passed lazily by, guests collected their sleepy children and headed home to tackle chores. Toward dusk, a light evening meal was prepared for the host family and the youth group. The youth boys each chose a girl to accompany to the table, where they sat together as couples. After the meal, they sang from English hymnals until it was time to go home. By the time the last guests had left, the evening had become late.

Hand in hand, Eldon and Mary Ellen climbed the steep wooden stairs to an upstairs bedroom. For the first time the entire day, they were alone. The guests had piled their wedding gifts on the bride's bed, and now the newlyweds took time to open and exclaim over each one.

A fierce thunderstorm ruled the night, sparing Eldon and Mary Ellen from the traditional "bushwhacking" that typically followed a wedding. Youth would surround the house where the bridal couple slept, banging pots and lids together and making a clamorous racket until the bride's father would serve them food, possibly a piece of pie. But even bushwhackers had their limits, and the spring storms of Kansas were enough to give anyone second thoughts.

Eldon felt smug the next morning. "I'm glad we escaped that nonsense."

"Me too," Mary Ellen agreed. "I'm pretty relieved." Conscientious and shy, Mary Ellen had been mortified more than once by the antics of their mischievous youth group.

Over the next few days, the new Bontrager household was established in the small *Daudy*[2] house across the yard from Mary Ellen's parents. As was typical in their culture, the newlyweds spent a lot of time traveling

[2] "Grandpa" in Pennsylvania Dutch.

through the community to visit family and friends during their first year of marriage.

Eldon took his role as provider seriously and was happy to get a job on a local dairy farm. He felt privileged to borrow farmer Fred's pickup truck so he could drive to work. According to the church, Eldon could drive a vehicle as long as he didn't own it himself.

The highlight of his day was coming home to a neat house and a happy wife. Mary Ellen was a wonderful addition to his life and could coax the most delicious food out of their slender pocketbook.

One night Eldon came home to find a secretive smile on Mary Ellen's face. "Eldon, do you know that your math teacher was wrong?"

"Why so?"

"One plus one is about to become three." Mary Ellen laughed at his shocked expression.

"Well, well!" Eldon was delighted with the news. "I think we should thank God for such a gift." His heart nearly burst as he asked the blessing for their evening meal and for this new stage of life they were entering. He felt certain that if they continued to live quietly and conscientiously, their married life would be happy and blessed.

2 A Bitter Blow

On April 26, 1956, nearly a year after Eldon and Mary Ellen were married, the air was rent with the cries of a beautiful baby girl. Lynette Kaye had joined the Bontrager home, and her parents were thrilled to meet this tiny miracle.

"She looks just like her mama," Eldon declared. "Look at those curls! She is just the cutest little thing. Lynette, you have made me a proud papa!"

Mary Ellen smiled as she held her newborn baby, her weary face shining with the wonder of motherhood. "She will make us pleased, but I hope she will never make us proud." Pride was considered a sin in the church, and being of a sensitive nature, Mary Ellen wanted to live humbly.

The days passed quickly with all the exhausting intensity of caring for a newborn. As Lynette grew, Mary Ellen watched eagerly for that first smile, but it seemed a long time in coming.

"Oh, well," she consoled herself. "Some babies are just slower than others."

And fussier too, she decided. With a baby in the house, it was hard to get anything done. Lynette did not sleep well and was often hard to soothe. Caring for her was exhausting, but Mary Ellen had heard stories of this stage from friends.

"It will get better soon!" they assured her. "Mine was colicky too!"

But as Lynette neared six months of age, Mary Ellen had a dark knot in her stomach. Her years of maid work for other moms had acquainted her with normal milestones—and Lynette was not hitting them. So far, Mary Ellen's suggestions to Eldon that not all might be well had fallen on deaf ears. He was optimistic that Lynette would catch up soon. But eventually Mary Ellen noticed that he too looked concerned as he watched their little daughter lying on the floor, stuck in an infant stage.

After another Sunday of watching other babies at church, Mary Ellen felt sure something was wrong. "Lynette is too unresponsive," she told Eldon on the way home. "Other babies are cooing and focusing and responding in ways she isn't."

"But what could be wrong?" Eldon asked. He scrutinized the gravel road as the buggy rattled along. "Her birth was normal, and she looks perfectly fine..."

A few evenings later, Perry and Judy Miller from church came to visit the new parents and their baby girl. They had three boys of their own, and Linford, the second-born, had cerebral palsy. As the visitors held Lynette, the friendly conversation trailed away and their eyes grew grave and concerned.

"Is she always this... this listless?" Judy finally asked.

Mary Ellen gulped and nodded.

"Have you considered seeing a doctor?" Perry's question was kind, but it came as a blow.

"Do you think something is wrong?" Eldon asked sharply.

"I don't know," Perry said softly. "But it wouldn't hurt to check." He turned to his wife. "What do you think?"

Judy nodded. "Taking a baby to the doctor is a hard thing for parents to do, but if something is wrong, you'll be glad you did." Her eyes shone with unshed tears as she remembered their own journey down this road.

After more strained conversation, Perry and Judy gathered up their children to leave. Eldon walked out to the buggy with them. "We will be praying for you," Perry said, grasping Eldon's shoulder.

As the visitors' buggy rattled away, Eldon stood on the steps, gazing across the fields with unseeing eyes. It was time to confront the reality his fears had been denying. Perry and Judy's encouragement to visit a doctor was unexpected, even frightening. In this community, people preferred natural treatments. Doctors were only consulted for the worst diseases. Was his young family facing something that serious? Perry and Judy seemed to think so.

Inside the house, Mary Ellen's thoughts raced as she rocked Lynette to sleep. Having her fears validated by someone else brought both trepidation and a strange sense of relief. Maybe now they could find some answers. Perhaps there was a cure for the unknown problem that had been haunting her.

When Lynette finally dropped off to sleep, Mary Ellen laid her carefully in her bed and went out to the porch to find Eldon. Even in the darkness, she could see that his face was drawn. She dropped down beside him on the steps, and together they gazed at the stars that twinkled so cheerfully, oblivious to their inner agony.

"What are you thinking?" she finally asked.

Eldon shook his head. "I don't know what to think. I still had hopes she would snap out of it..." He turned to face her. "But I agree it's time we check things out. Maybe it's nothing to worry about..." He trailed off again, doubtfully. "What do you think?"

"Yes, I think it's time."

Quietly they discussed their next step. When the hour grew late, they went to bed with heavy hearts.

The time leading up to Lynette's appointment both sped and crept by. Finally the day arrived. Early in the morning, a driver picked them up and took them four hours away to Kansas City to see Dr. Baird, an osteopathic physician. After many questions and a thorough examination, Dr. Baird sat back in his seat. "Mr. and Mrs. Bontrager..." He removed his glasses and placed them on his lap. "Your baby is quite behind in her motor skills. She is not holding her head, her eyes don't track, and she's not focusing like she should. Is that what you have observed?"

Mary Ellen nodded. "Yes. I kept hoping she would catch up, but she seems to be getting farther behind."

Eldon took a deep breath. His worst fears were coming true. "What do you recommend, Doctor? Is there any hope for a normal life?" His eyes were desperate. "Are there exercises we can do to help her?"

Dr. Baird was silent for a moment. He gently stroked the baby's cheek and peered into her eyes. "From what I can see, she is mentally handicapped. I am sorry. There is really nothing I can do. Take her home and show her love and care. She will always be your innocent baby."

Heads bowed low, Eldon and Mary Ellen stumbled out of the doctor's office. They wrapped Lynette in her baby blanket and headed for the car that would take them home. The despondent couple almost wished they would not have to face their family and friends, but they knew word would travel quickly through their close-knit community.

Word did get around. It wasn't long before they began to notice sidelong glances and were bombarded with many questions and well-meaning advice. But through their deep grief, they spotted a ray of hope: Dr. Hulse. He was a cranial doctor who lived in Iowa, and the success stories they heard about his treatments were impressive.

"I heard of two girls who were helped by his treatments," a friend told Mary Ellen. "Today they are living normal lives."

Another friend said, "The legs of Eli Bontrager's seven-year-old son were so twisted they couldn't get his trousers on. Now he goes to school and makes good grades."

There was no doubt in anyone's mind that Lynette would be perfectly normal after this doctor treated her. Eldon and Mary Ellen decided they had nothing to lose, so they took the train to visit Dr. Hulse. After an examination, the doctor was optimistic about helping Lynette. "I have worked with over eleven hundred children, many worse than your child. She has a good chance of complete recovery."

In high spirits, Eldon and Mary Ellen traveled back home to pack up and move to Kalona, Iowa. If this doctor could help Lynette, they felt it would be best to live close by. Happily they settled into their new home, a two-story house they loved immediately.

Since the Amish community in Thomas, Oklahoma, was dispersing, Eldon's family relocated to Kalona as well. They moved into a nearby house so Eldon and Mary Ellen would not be alone. Both families had intentions of making the move permanent.

Eldon found a job on a local hog and cattle farm. He worked with George, the manager of the large operation.

Iowa had rolling hills, unlike flat Kansas. Eldon was so glad he could still work on a farm, with the sun in his eyes and the wind in his hair. And it was a blessing to have a job so close to his new home that he could walk back and forth and be there to help Mary Ellen with Lynette in the evenings.

Lynette was often fussy, and it became increasingly difficult to comfort her. It seemed she was often in pain. At her next appointment, Dr. Hulse examined the top of her head. "I believe her soft spot closed too early, leaving no room for her brain to grow as she develops. It is causing pressure in her head."

At the next visit, he put her to sleep and performed a skull reconstruction. "I was able to widen her soft spot," he said cheerfully after the surgery. "This will give her brain a good chance to begin growing again.

She should be walking and talking in seven months." These comforting words increased their hope. "But just a warning, she may be extra fussy for a while."

During each visit, the doctor gently massaged the top of her head in an effort to keep the soft spot open with more room to grow. The treatments relaxed Lynette and helped her sleep, but Eldon and Mary Ellen were disappointed that it was not helping her in any other way. Her disability remained unchanged.

The doctor also seemed puzzled. "Perhaps if you had come sooner, I would have been able to help her." Once more, devastation crashed upon them.

At home that evening, Mary Ellen rocked the fussy baby as Eldon paced through the house in frustration. "Well, it looks like we came too late." He threw his hands in the air. "Oh, why didn't we come sooner?" The question hung in the air as they both remembered the difficulty of accepting that their baby needed help. Mary Ellen said nothing, and eventually Eldon calmed down and sat on the couch beside the rocker.

"Did we make a mistake in trying Dr. Hulse?" he asked. "It has taken almost all my earnings. And what have we gained?"

"Well, she is less fussy," Mary Ellen encouraged. "I think we should at least finish the treatments. Besides, Dr. Hulse has helped so many other children. Maybe he will still be able to make a difference."

There was something else on Eldon and Mary Ellen's minds—and had been for some time. They were expecting another baby. While this was exciting, they felt apprehension as well.

"How will we ever cope if this child isn't normal either?" Mary Ellen worried.

Eldon tried to be optimistic. "Surely the next one will be fine."

On April 19, 1957, a week before Lynette's first birthday, Carolyn Jean made her appearance, a bundle of energetic, vivacious health. Eldon and Mary Ellen could see immediately that she was quick to respond to their eager attention. In no time at all, she passed Lynette in her development.

Carolyn's charming spirit was a balm to Eldon and Mary Ellen's dashed hopes and dreams, and they reveled in her normalcy. "I'm afraid we spoil Carolyn," Mary Ellen wrote to her mother back in Kansas. "But it is such a joy to watch her grow."

While Carolyn was still quite young, Lynette came down with measles. Her high fever made her parents uneasy, and there were many sleepless nights. Mary Ellen cared for the newborn while Eldon held Lynette.

As the disease came to a climax, Lynette became increasingly listless and weak. Her fever was high, her breathing sounded rattly, and her body broke out in a rash. Dr. Hulse came to the house to examine her. "Yes, she certainly has measles," he said worriedly. "She is extremely sick! With her weakened state, I'm not sure she'll make it through the night."

It was a long, arduous night. Eldon and Mary Ellen pushed their weary bodies to the limit as they cared for their desperately sick daughter and newborn baby. "I believe Lynette finally feels a bit cooler," Mary Ellen said in the morning hours. "I guess her mission here on earth isn't over yet."

"Praise the Lord," Eldon breathed as he collapsed on the couch. "I think she might make it."

That night marked the turning point, and Lynette slowly returned to health. Carolyn continued to thrive as Lynette finished her cranial treatments. Although disappointed that the treatments had not helped their daughter, Eldon and Mary Ellen did their best to provide for their growing family.

Eldon worked hard to make a living, but it wasn't easy. Although he had loved farming in Kansas, it didn't agree with him in Iowa. The more he worked outdoors, the more he battled headaches and other health issues. Several times he was ill with pneumonia. Despite his hard work and good character, the meticulous young Amish man was finding adulthood more of a struggle than he had expected. *Why is life suddenly so difficult?* he wondered.

3

Dashed Hopes

Scratch, scratch, scratch. Mary Ellen's hoe made its way down the long row of tiny carrots as the early morning sun brightened the sky above her. She breathed in deeply, absorbing the delicious earthiness of green plants and freshly turned soil. Working quickly, she finished one row and moved to the next. This was a favorite part of her early morning ritual; it soothed her soul to see the straight, tidy rows.

Mothering her babies was fulfilling but wearying, especially as she continued to reconcile her dreams for her firstborn with the reality of Lynette's profound disabilities. But in her garden world, her little plants grew and flourished happily, just the way she liked them to do.

This summer was unseasonably hot and dry. Mary Ellen looked at the empty sky, straining to find any signs of rain. If it didn't rain soon, her garden would suffer, and that would be a disaster. With Eldon's meager wages as a farm laborer, her family could use everything she grew.

A faint sound from the house caught her attention, and she cocked her head, listening carefully. *Lynette's awake. So much for weeding the garden.* It was time to return to sticky fingers and diapers.

Once inside, she found Lynette fussing in her bed. "Good morning," Mary Ellen crooned. Scooping up the child, she placed Lynette in her special bouncy chair, which helped her sit up slightly and gave her a change of position. Setting a kettle on the stove, Mary Ellen heated water for some cream of wheat. Lynette was unable to eat anything that was not of a pureed consistency. *It kind of feels like my cooking skills are wasted once the food has gone through the blender.*

As she stirred the cereal, she watched Lynette's eyes. *Is she following my movements? No, I think it's just my imagination.* Sometimes Mary Ellen and Eldon thought their daughter was making slight improvements, but nothing seemed to last.

Pouring the cereal into a bowl, Mary Ellen pondered how different life would be if Lynette were developing normally like Carolyn. Her second-born was active every day, cooing as she rolled onto her stomach and then to her back. She cruised all over the floor, entertaining herself with her rambunctious play, smiling and giggling at any attention that came her way. Lynette had never done those things and probably never would. Mary Ellen's mother heart wept at the life Lynette would never know.

A deep, hacking cough signaled Eldon's return that evening. His latest round of pneumonia just kept hanging on. Stepping up to Lynette's chair, he handed his firstborn a rattle. She gripped it and put it to her mouth to chew on. "Mary Ellen, look at this!" Eldon exclaimed. "I wonder if she's not getting better. She never used to do this before!" His voice rang with optimism.

Mary Ellen sighed. "You think so? I think we just need to accept that she won't ever be normal. We've worked so hard and gone to so many appointments, and nothing has really changed. The last while I thought maybe she was tracking better with her eyes, but that has gone away too." She turned back to her simmering soup.

Eldon said nothing. After a quick supper, he headed outside, his steps leading to the barn out of habit. Leaning over the fence, he watched the milk cow chewing her cud. Accepting the truth cut against every fiber of his being—the daughter he had fathered would never even recognize him. It smote him to the core.

There has to be something we can do! He could fix any equipment that broke down, yet for his poor, twisted daughter he could do nothing. Eldon grabbed a pitchfork and viciously attacked his chores, trying to subdue the pain in his heart.

When he returned to the house, it was late. Mary Ellen had already tucked the children into bed and was settled comfortably in her chair, devouring a book a friend had lent her. She glanced up briefly as Eldon came in, then turned back to her reading.

Eldon paused in the doorway, watching her, then headed to the bathroom to take a shower. He knew it was pointless to try to get her attention now. Burying herself in a book was Mary Ellen's escape from the hard reality of Lynette's care.

Mary Ellen was up early the next morning. Esther, the hired maid, was there to help with the laundry. Mary Ellen was a traditional homemaker and preferred using a wringer washer over an electric washer. After a scrub and a rinse, the clothes glided through the wringer and were ready for the clothesline.

As the women hung up the damp clothes, Mary Ellen inhaled deeply. *Ah, there is nothing like the smell of clean laundry.* She grabbed another clothespin and hung up another piece. The laundry fluttered in the hot breeze, drying quickly. Hanging up clean laundry brought her a measure of joy, knowing her family would be well-clothed for another week.

"I'm going to check the garden," Mary Ellen told Esther when they had finished hanging out the clothes. Although the garden seemed dry as tinder, she still clung to the hope of a life-giving rain. Surely it wouldn't stay dry forever.

While Mary Ellen worked in the garden, Esther stayed inside with Lynette. She carefully cut matching dresses for Lynette and Carolyn out of a green puckered nylon that had been given to Mary Ellen. Fabric was precious for a small farming family, and she didn't want to waste a single inch.

Before she left that night, Esther gathered in the laundry from the line, and Mary Ellen set to work folding it. Each piece was meticulously creased into a perfect square. Carefully Mary Ellen carried the stacks of clothes back to their drawers and tucked them neatly inside. The pile that needed to be ironed had to wait for another day.

When Eldon came home, he admired the fabric pieces ready to sew into little dresses. "And I hope you make that light blue dress for yourself," he said generously. "I like when you have new clothes."

Mary Ellen laughed. "I think you like my new clothes better than I do."

Eldon flashed a sheepish grin. "Well, there's no reason to look shoddy." He washed his hands for supper, thinking about how lovely his wife would look in her new dress.

The morning dawned with a barren sky suggesting yet another scorching day. *O Lord, send us rain,* Mary Ellen prayed fervently over her breakfast dishes. Her morning hour in the garden had been discouraging. Leaves hung limply on the stalks. If it didn't rain soon, she would lose all her plants.

Later that afternoon, Mary Ellen glanced out the window and spotted a thundercloud forming in the west. She watched it anxiously, her spirits rising as the cloud grew larger and darker—almost too dark. By the time Eldon got home from the farm, rain was pounding on the roof, and it was so dark they nearly had to light a lamp.

"There's the rain for your garden," Eldon whooped as he pulled off his wet shoes.

"I just hope it doesn't flatten everything!" Mary Ellen wasn't a farmer's daughter for nothing; she knew a storm like this could do more harm than good.

"Oh, it's an ill wind that blows no good," Eldon said, his voice not worried. "I expect everything will be fine." That evening when thcy went to bed, the music of the rain played in their ears.

In the morning, Mary Ellen dressed quickly and headed outside to check the garden. The dawn was delightfully cool, and the plants waved happily in the damp morning air. In several days they would be back on track again. "Thank you, Lord," she breathed, stroking leaves and straightening corn stalks that had blown crooked in the storm. Her family needed every vegetable she could put up for the winter.

The dry summer wasn't the only thing distressing the young Bontrager family that year. Because of a growing concern about the direction some of their church friends were taking, Eldon and Mary Ellen set out on a search for something different. After trying several area churches, they decided on Sharon Bethel Amish Mennonite. The church was small and the fellowship close, helping to make Kalona feel more like home. If only the climate would agree with Eldon's health.

The next two years brought two healthy sons to their family. Joseph LaVon arrived on August 7, 1958, a strong, healthy boy they chose to call by his middle name. Myron James was born on July 28, 1959, a plump ten-pound bundle of joy.

Taking care of four children ages three and under left little time for fun. Lynette's disability made it especially difficult to get away from home. But one Saturday evening, Eldon and Mary Ellen decided it was time to do something special. Grandma Bontrager agreed to care for Lynette while they were gone.

The rest of the family drove to a small local park to eat supper. The beautiful evening had drawn quite a crowd. To the children's delight, some nearby pens housed raccoons, bears, and monkeys. The family made their way through the people to watch the entertaining animals. The bears showed off, shaking their heads from side to side. They rose on their hind legs, then dropped down on all fours and paced around the cage. Two-year-old Carolyn squealed with delight.

The monkeys held onto the bars of their cage with their hands and feet. "Ooo! Ooo! Ooo!" they called. LaVon clapped his hands and copied their antics.

After watching the animals for a while, the family boarded a zoo train that took them around the park grounds. "This is the best train in the whole world," proclaimed Carolyn, jumping up and down on the seat.

"Careful there," Eldon chuckled, wrapping an arm around her waist. "You might jump right out of the train the way you're carrying on."

"It's so good to see our children having fun," Mary Ellen remarked. "I just wish Lynette could enjoy things like this with us."

Eldon turned his head away, wrestling with his thoughts. Although he felt a twinge of guilt for feeling like this, the prospect of bringing his handicapped daughter into public was difficult to get excited about. He hated being a spectacle. The times they had taken Lynette on shopping trips had resulted in too many stares.

As the train slowed to a stop, he shrugged off his feelings and helped his family clamber off with the rest of the riders. Before them was a pony carousel. "Oh, Eldon, look at that!" Mary Ellen exclaimed, her eyes twinkling like they often had when they were first married. "A merry-go-round!"

Eldon grinned. On a whim, he asked her, "Do you want to take a ride?"

Mary Ellen was quiet for a moment, then admitted, "Well, I've always wanted to ride a merry-go-round."

Eldon chuckled. "You might as well do it then. You've earned it with all the work you do. Children, shall Mama ride a pony?"

Carolyn nodded decisively, so Mary Ellen smiled and got on a pony. It took her round and round. Each time around she waved at her children.

"Whee!" Carolyn called. "I want a ride too!"

"Sorry, Carolyn." Eldon patted her head. "The tickets cost money—and you are almost too small. So let's just let Mama have a turn." LaVon was happily entertained by the moving carousel, and Myron was too young to have an opinion about the ride.

All too soon the fun evening was over, and Eldon and Mary Ellen loaded their tired, happy children back into the car. On the way home, Eldon glanced at Mary Ellen. "What would you say about moving back to Kansas?"

She studied his face. "Well, I can't say I'd be against it. It sure would be nice to live close to my family again. Why do you ask?"

"You know, I really like the church here and it seems my parents and siblings have settled in well, but I'm getting tired of these health issues I'm dealing with. Before too long, we'll be heading into another winter, and I just know I'll get pneumonia again. I think I've gotten it every year since we've moved here. Even during the summer, it feels like my head is always under pressure. It's so hard for me to concentrate; it just makes me long for the clear air of Kansas. I hardly ever got sick there."

Mary Ellen nodded, turning her gaze out the window. "Your health has really taken a beating here in Iowa. I can understand why you are ready for a change."

"Although I'll miss living close to my parents, it seems our main reason for being here is gone. As much as he tried, Dr. Hulse really didn't bring any lasting changes for Lynette. It just makes me wonder if it's time to go back to Kansas." Eldon tried to keep the disappointment out of his voice. To give up on his daughter had been almost more than he could do, but he was now resigned to accepting that Lynette would never progress beyond her current state.

"Moving is pretty expensive," Mary Ellen pointed out. "Do we have enough saved up?"

Eldon chuckled a bit. "Well, despite all the doctor's bills, I've managed to save up some money in the last several years. It's still not enough to make the move, but we're getting close."

Over the next few weeks, they continued their discussion. When Mary Ellen's dad notified them about a house for sale in Kansas, it was too good to pass up. They carefully drafted a letter in reply:

> Dear Dad and Mom,
>
> We are no longer doctoring Lynette here in Iowa. Because of Eldon's health problems, we do not see any future for our family in this community. We would like to move to a farm back home, but we are not finding any farms for sale. However, since you let us know the Whiteside house is for sale, we are considering buying it.
>
> We might need some financial help. We don't like to burden anyone, but we also know we could not borrow with so little collateral. We would rather make house payments than pay rent all the time. Would there be any chance of you being able to help us out?
>
> Love, Eldon and Mary Ellen

They waited anxiously for a reply. One week, two weeks, a month passed. Finally a letter arrived from Mary Ellen's parents. She tore it open and scanned it quickly. "Daudys are going to help us move to Kansas," she told her children.

Their eyes opened wide. Carolyn clapped her hands and LaVon hopped up and down. Although Iowa had always been the children's home, they were delighted to see their mother happy.

Mary Ellen's heart surged with excitement. She was going back home to Hutchinson.

4

Back to Kansas

Packing up over three years' worth of living was no small task. It was especially difficult with four children, one of them a baby. Fortunately for Eldon and Mary Ellen, an acquaintance who was traveling to Kansas offered to take Carolyn and LaVon on ahead to Mary Ellen's parents. This helped to relieve some of the stress of moving.

"It sure is quiet around here without those two," Mary Ellen said after they were gone.

"Yeah, I miss them," Eldon replied. "Thankfully, we'll see them again in a few days."

"But their absence makes the packing easier," Mary Ellen added. She was glad her sister Clara Mae would be at her parents' place to help take care of the children. That relieved her mind.

The alarm clock jangled early on the morning of January 2, 1960. Eldon and Mary Ellen had worked hard the evening before to load up all their belongings, and after a hurried breakfast they were finally ready to go. Lynette was settled in the back seat with Mary Ellen, wrapped in blankets so she wouldn't get cold. The miles flew by quickly. They were eager to get to their new home, so they wasted no time stopping or sightseeing along the way.

Finally, as the day ended, they pulled in at their new house. It was a significant moment. For Mary Ellen, there was joy in being back among the people she had grown up with. For Eldon, there was pride in seeing his first major purchase. The house was new but cheaply built, and the inside had never been finished. But the realization of the enormous work ahead didn't deter him. This would be home.

The family got settled into the basement in the days ahead while Eldon and his father-in-law trimmed out the upstairs, getting it ready to occupy. Another thing Eldon did was plant a fast-growing hedge to divide the property from their close neighbors, the Becketts. He preferred privacy. Hopefully, if they were quiet and respectful, there would be no problems between them and their neighbors.

Upon their return to Kansas, the Bontragers attended the newly formed Center Amish Mennonite Church. This church was part of the Beachy constituency and was similar to Sharon Bethel back in Iowa. The members were primarily from the Amish church Eldon and Mary Ellen had attended previously. Center Church was a church with godly teaching and faithful members, and it proved to be a good choice for the young family.

Moving back to Kansas brought another big change for Eldon. Although farming ran deep in his blood, he didn't have enough land of his own and opportunities on neighboring farms were scarce. Somehow Eldon had to get a job to support his family, and an alternate option soon came up. Detroiter Mobile Home Factory, where his friends Ora and Harley Nisly worked, was hiring. Eldon's friends offered to let him carpool with them to save gas on the twenty-mile drive.

The very first day on the job showed him the magnitude of the change he had made.

"Well, here we are," Ora remarked in his slow drawl as they turned off the road. A foreboding chain-link fence gate swung open to let them drive through.

Eldon cringed inwardly as the heavy gate slammed behind them. "Feels more like a prison than a factory."

"Yeah," agreed Harley. "And that gate won't open again till quitting time."

A buzzer blared, hurrying their steps across the parking lot. Eldon glanced back over his shoulder as they entered the building. *Goodbye to the sun, goodbye to the wind.* Nothing smelled like a farm in this factory. The scowling foreman assigned him a spot on the assembly line, and Eldon fell into step with the other men.

Working in the factory was grueling. No matter what the output, the workers were always pushed faster and harder. The foreman watched every move they made and was quick to bark out criticism. Eldon was thankful for the good work ethic he had been taught and for the quick, nimble fingers God had blessed him with as he installed the plumbing in bathroom after bathroom. But despite these advantages, there were still times when the mobile home he was working on moved down the conveyor belt before his team had completed their assigned tasks.

"Hey, my drills are on there!" Eldon exclaimed one day when this happened again.

"You need to work faster!" the foreman hollered.

"He makes me so mad," another worker said, swearing under his breath.

"Just do the best you can," Eldon encouraged, plunging into the new job in front of him.

The foreman sneered at them. "Can't keep up, can you? Well, if I make you mad, you work quicker, and we get more done." He snickered at his joke.

Eldon bit his lip so he wouldn't say the wrong thing. *Lord, keep my mouth closed.*

Quitting time was a relief. The workers filed out of the building, where a security guard stood at the door leading into the fenced parking lot. "Lunch box," he barked at each man as they passed.

Eldon was next. Wearily he opened his lunch box and showed it to the guard. "I'm an honest man," he said respectfully.

The guard glowered at him. "Anything in your pockets?"

Eldon searched his overall pockets and came up empty. He would not take any tools out of the factory, and the guard knew it. But other workers did. They stole, drank, cursed, smoked, and took advantage of the factory in every way they could.

The guard opened the door and let him through. "We could use more men like you," he said in a calmer tone. Eldon nodded quietly and went on his way.

The ride home was often subdued as Eldon and his friends pondered the day. "It sure isn't the easiest work I've ever done," Ora remarked in his typical understated fashion.

"I would gladly work from dawn till dusk on a farm instead of this," Eldon agreed fervently. "But work is work, and we should do our best."

He pushed himself hard, but he could feel the stress of having to perform every day. The routine but mind-numbing pressure wore him down as the months rolled by.

That November, Phyllis Eileen was born. Eldon and Mary Ellen's third daughter was quiet, sweet, and content. She favored her sister Carolyn but had less hair and a lighter skin color.

Her parents were sad to see that her beautiful blue eyes were profoundly crossed. They were also concerned when she suffered from odd rashes and asthma. But as for her mental development, only time would tell.

Although the Detroiter company drove its employees hard, it could throw a fantastic Christmas party. On December 7, the Bontrager family timidly entered the Hutchinson Sports Arena, the children gazing in awe at the huge Christmas tree strung with glittering lights. Underneath were nestled piles upon piles of fascinating gifts and packages. Along a wall sat numerous tables laden with mountains of food.

The family followed the line through the buffet, filling their plates. "So much food," Carolyn breathed, standing on her tiptoes to look at the many options. The children had never seen such a variety. They felt like royalty, able to pick whatever they wanted.

When the meal was over, the president of the company walked to the front of the room. The children sat spellbound, watching him hand out the gifts that had been under the tree. All the employees got a roasting turkey and fifty-dollar bill for a bonus. Eldon carefully placed the bill in his pocket. No one realized how much he needed this cash. He would take it home and use it to finish up some projects in the house.

Then it was time for the children's presents. Each age bracket received a different gift. Lynette got a bathinette and a doll that looked just like a newborn. Carolyn got a nice doll like all the other three-year-old girls. LaVon got a big transport truck—one that could haul cars. His eyes shone when he saw the two cars and the pickup on it. Myron got a pickup truck toy as well, and Phyllis got a teddy bear that was bigger than she was.

Each child was allowed to write his or her name on a slip of paper and drop it into a box for a drawing. Mary Ellen helped Carolyn print her name in her neatest handwriting. Carolyn was ecstatic when they called her name for a prize. She hustled up front, grinning as the president presented her with her very own bike. The children went home feeling rich and happy. Although they received no other gifts for Christmas, this was enough. They treasured and played with those gifts for years to come.

As Phyllis passed her first month, Mary Ellen watched her carefully as she played with her hands. She brought her fist to her mouth as a normal baby would. She cooed and smiled easily. She was content. The knot that always tightened in Mary Ellen's heart with the birth of each child began to relax. Even though Phyllis had some health issues, and her eyes were crossing more each day, she was a normal child. *Thank you, Lord. I don't think I would have enough energy if Phyllis were like Lynette.* Mary Ellen knew without a doubt that the Lord had given her a special strength and grace to handle Lynette's disability. Still, it was a heavy load to carry.

She glanced up as Myron pushed open the door and tramped inside. His eyes were sparkling, and he held a treasure in his tightly clenched fist.

"Frog!" he beamed, showing his prize to LaVon.

"Ooh! Can I have it?" LaVon eagerly reached for the little critter.

"No!" Myron yanked it away. "Mine." His voice rang with finality as he tightened his grip on the frog. He was ready to fight like a banty rooster if needed.

LaVon reluctantly went back to his toys. Myron could keep his frog to himself. He knew that starting a fight would turn out badly for them. Mary Ellen had little time for squabbling children, and he also knew frogs would not be tolerated for long in her house. Myron would need to take it back outside soon anyway.

At times, Phyllis seemed to have trouble breathing. "You don't suppose she's allergic to baby powder, do you?" Mary Ellen asked Eldon one evening. "Sometimes it seems she can hardly breathe when I powder her after changing her diaper. Maybe I should quit using it for a while."

"It's worth a try," Eldon said. "Sometimes she seems so miserable."

When Mary Ellen quit using the powder on her daughter, Phyllis's breathing quickly improved. The rash she was battling disappeared as well. But her eyes were as crossed as ever. Eldon cringed inwardly nearly every time he saw them. It was bad enough having a mentally handicapped daughter—now there was a cross-eyed one as well. People would soon start thinking something was wrong with all of them!

Thankfully, Lynette was extra calm during this busy time with so many little ones. In the evenings, she cried to be held, but she was more content during the day. With Phyllis teething, Mary Ellen was thankful Lynette wasn't crying all the time.

Time flew by, and soon the Bontragers had been at the Whiteside house for two years. There was never a dull moment. Eldon spent many evenings and Saturdays remodeling the basement, adding wiring and putting in ceiling lights. Myron was usually by his side, getting his tools and asking questions.

"Thank you, Myron," Eldon praised him one evening after the boy handed him a tape measure.

Smiling, Myron disappeared up the stairs. When he returned, Eldon looked up in surprise. Myron had donned one of his dad's everyday hats and one brown glove.

Eldon smiled. "What are you doing now, Myron?"

"I'm Daddy's helper."

"Indeed, you are," Eldon said, chuckling. "I don't know what I would do without you boys."

One Friday evening Eldon called all the children to sit down in the living room for their evening devotions. They quickly did as they were told. "Story, story," Myron smiled, clapping his hands.

"What story do we have this evening?" Eldon asked as he opened the Bible storybook. "Oh, this is a story you will like, Myron. It's a story about a boy who was good at using a slingshot." Myron nodded eagerly.

Eldon read the story of David and Goliath. When he was finished, he said,

"Now, children, stand in front of the bookcase in a row and we will sing."

Their childish voices sang out: "Jesus loves me! this I know..."

Then they all knelt and prayed together:

Now I lay me down to sleep.
I pray thee, Lord, my soul to keep.
If I should die before I wake,
I pray thee, Lord, my soul to take.

The end of prayer signaled bedtime, and most of the children traipsed off toward their rooms. But as usual, three-year-old LaVon wasn't ready. He was a clown and could never pass up a good audience. He goofed around, stalling for time.

"LaVon," Eldon finally said sternly. "It's time for bed."

LaVon took off running for his basement bedroom and—*wham!*—ran right into the arm of the rocking chair. Blood spurted from his ear, and his wails echoed through the house.

"Do you think we should take him in?" Mary Ellen asked, pressing a cloth to his head.

"Let's clean him up and see what it looks like," Eldon said. They were almost afraid to look at the cut because they knew LaVon was a tough little boy. If he cried this hard, it must be bad.

A tentative peek revealed that the cut ear would indeed need stitches. Eldon loaded up LaVon and headed for the hospital. LaVon's toughness came in handy as he bravely sat still while the surgeon put in five stitches.

On the way home, the boy was sober. Finally he stirred. "Dad?" came a meek voice.

"Yes, LaVon?"

"I'll go to bed now."

Eldon grinned despite himself. "I'm sure you will. And the next time, go the first time we tell you, all right?"

"Yes, I will!" LaVon's voice was emphatic even in his sleepiness. His breathing grew more and more relaxed and soon he was snoozing. When they arrived home, Eldon carried him inside and carefully put him in bed with his stitches facing the ceiling so he could sleep comfortably.

The next morning, a weary Eldon shut off the alarm and stumbled out of bed. The night had been far too short, and he dreaded the day ahead. He knew the company had ten trailers on the schedule, each with one and a half baths. The extra stool and lavatory would double the work on the line.

Groggily he poured himself a cup of coffee and sat down to eat a quick breakfast. Amid his fog, he heard the pitter-patter of feet. He looked up to see two little boys standing in the doorway, rubbing sleep from their eyes.

"What are you boys doing?" Eldon smiled, feeling pleased that his sons wanted to have breakfast with him.

"We heard you and thought maybe you needed us," LaVon said in a grown-up voice.

Eldon chuckled. "How did you know? Today is going to be a big day at the factory, but I'm afraid you can't be much help there." He patted the chairs on each side of him. "Here. Sit down with me and have a few bites of breakfast and a sip of coffee."

The boys grinned and crawled up beside their daddy. Quietly they sampled his breakfast and sipped some of the bitter drink.

Eldon turned to LaVon. "How does your ear feel?"

LaVon gingerly touched the bandage. "It hurts. But not too much."

"Ouch," Myron said, pointing to LaVon's ear.

Mary Ellen came in from hanging laundry on the line. She had started her laundry at 4:00, trying to have it hung out before the children were up.

"Boys!" she said in surprise. "You're up early!"

LaVon thrust out his chest. "Daddy needed us to have breakfast with him," he said importantly.

Eldon winked at Mary Ellen over the tops of their heads. His boys sure brightened the morning. "Well," he said, grabbing his lunch box, "I'd better be going. Help your mom today, boys." He ruffled their hair, then headed out the door.

He had found the perfect burst of energy he needed for his long day.

5

Another Blow

On May 12, 1962, little Faith Darlene arrived. She was a sickly baby, and though she wasn't as fussy as Lynette had been, she took lots of care.

Mary Ellen holding baby Faith, 1962.

As always, Mary Ellen watched with worried eyes as her baby grew. Would she hit the expected developmental milestones? Sometimes Faith responded well, and Mary Ellen's hopes rose as she told herself she was just too anxious.

The load on her shoulders was already almost too hard to bear. God would surely not send them another child like Lynette. How could they ever cope? But still she watched carefully, not convinced that all was well. All indications were that Faith would be like Lynette.

Because of Lynette's needs and baby Faith's poor health, Eldon and Mary Ellen missed many church services and other activities. They tried hard to have a normal family life, but the level of care their children needed, even in their own home, turned any outing into a monumental ordeal. However, they did their best to stay connected in the limited ways they could, and one rare Sunday, they invited a church family for lunch.

Five-year-old Carolyn was old enough to feel the lack of social life, so she was thrilled to have a little girl her age coming to visit. She watched shyly as Eldon and Mary Ellen welcomed their guests into the house.

Young Andrea sniffed the air. "Your house stinks," she remarked loudly.

"Andrea!" her mother rebuked. "Don't say that."

"Well, it's true," Andrea said.

Carolyn's face grew red. She had not noticed that, despite her mother's hard work, odors from the mounds of diapers that accumulated each day were tainting the air. Noticing the warning look in her mother's eyes, Carolyn determined this would not ruin her special day.

After lunch, she tried her best to entertain her friend. "Do you want to play with dolls?"

"Dolls are for babies," Andrea stated.

"Well, we can go outside and ride my bike. I got a bike at a Christmas party the other year."

"I can't ride a bike by myself," Andrea sniffed.

Carolyn's face fell. Entertaining company was difficult! Dejectedly she took her friend to her bedroom, and they sat idly on the bed. Suddenly Andrea took her fingernail and began scratching paint off the headboard. Carolyn was horrified!

"Oh, stop, please!" she pleaded.

"Well, you just have retarded sisters," Andrea scoffed. "Why would you care about a nice bed? Especially when your house smells bad."

Carolyn's eyes stung. Every fiber of her being wanted to call for her mother, but she knew Mary Ellen had no patience with tattling. Instead, she jammed her fingers into her ears so she couldn't hear the scratching of Andrea's nails.

Soon Mary Ellen came in to see what they were playing. "What was the noise in here?" She looked sharply at Carolyn. Then she saw the loose paint, and her eyes narrowed. "Who scratched up the bed?"

Carolyn shrugged miserably, not wanting to tell the truth.

"It wasn't me!" Andrea declared loudly.

Andrea's mom popped through the door. "What's wrong? Did something happen?"

Andrea shoved her hands behind her back. "They're trying to say I scratched the paint off the bed, but I didn't!"

"Can I see your fingernails?" her mother asked, approaching her.

Andrea slowly brought out her hands from behind her back.

"I see paint here, under your nails," her mother said. "You need to tell Carolyn you are sorry."

"Sorry," Andrea parroted, her apology clearly insincere.

"Now, I don't want you to do that again," her mother admonished. "Come now. It's time to go home."

Carolyn followed the little girl to the front door. Quietly she put her hand in her mother's as they watched the car drive out the lane. Her little heart was crushed.

After the visitors were gone, the dam broke. Carolyn's tears came hot and fast. "Mama, Andrea was mean," she sobbed. "She scratched the paint off my bed! And I don't think she was even very sorry." In broken words, the whole story came flooding out as her parents listened.

"Oh, Carolyn," Mary Ellen murmured, quietly stroking her hair, her own heart bleeding to see her daughter's hurt. "I hope this can be a lesson to you to always treat others kindly. Other children don't understand how those things can hurt."

Eldon stood nearby, watching the scene. His fists were tightly clenched, his nails cutting into his palms. Willing himself to relax, he stepped up and put his hand on Carolyn's shoulder. "Don't take it personally, Carolyn. She didn't mean to be uncaring. People just don't know how things like that affect us." His words sounded hollow even to his own ears.

Quickly excusing himself, he headed outside. The gravel road beckoned, and he started out at a rapid pace, his thoughts hammering in his head as he walked. *"Your house stinks. Why would you care about a nice bed? Your sisters are retarded."* He felt like covering his ears to block out the jeers his child had received. *How could anyone be so cruel?*

And deep down, a bigger question haunted him: *Is this what everyone else is thinking?* The American culture around them viewed mental handicaps as an embarrassment, and sometimes he caught fleeting glimpses of that view in his own church. The quickly averted glances, the ignoring of their many absences—Eldon's heart cried out for fairness. *God, you know I hate being a spectacle. All my life I've worked hard to avoid shame and reproach.* Now it had entered his own home, and there was nothing he could do about it.

Eldon's agitated steps quickened even more. He loved his family, but being unable to fix its brokenness smote the deepest part of his soul. Sometimes he suspected that some flaw in himself might have caused his daughters' handicaps. But this thought was too painful to entertain, and he always stifled it. He would just have to carry on and prove that he could take care of his family like the man he meant to be.

God, what are you trying to teach us? He thought of baby Faith and the many questions they still had about her. Surely this wouldn't happen to them twice. *God, I want to just put her in your hands. If there is something wrong, we know you can heal. Please let her be okay!* If only there was something he could do for his daughters.

Slowly a Scripture he had read that morning worked its way into his thoughts. He repeated it out loud: "God is our refuge and strength, a very present help in trouble."[1] His steps began to slow. *Thank you, Lord. Even if I can do nothing for my family, I know you can, and you will be with us.*

Although his heart still ached, peace began to soothe his agitated thoughts. Eldon turned around, surprised to see the sun already descending on the Kansas plains. Great swaths of dark purple clouds filled the western horizon, punctuated with glittering bands of bright gold. His breath caught in wonder. The glory of the sunset soothed the wound in his heart. Surely the God who created such beauty cared about his every struggle. With faith in his heart, Eldon straightened his shoulders and gathered the strength to head back home.

In the house, Mary Ellen was struggling as well. Her instructions to Carolyn had been proper and kind. But after Carolyn tearfully lay down for a nap, Mary Ellen attacked the dishes with an uncharacteristic vengeance. Questions rolled through her mind. After all the sacrifices she had made to make this day happen, was this how they were to be repaid? Her mind saw the blatant destruction of property and heard the taunting, mocking words. Fighting back tears, she slammed the plates through the sink.

If she were my daughter... she steamed inwardly.

Suddenly she recognized the quiet voice of her Lord. *You must forgive, my child.*

Oh, I'll forgive her all right, Mary Ellen thought. *But that behavior is just not acceptable!*

The quiet voice came again. *As I have loved you, so you must love each other.*

Her anger crumpled. *O God, I do want to serve you. Please help me to love as you do. It's just so hard to see my children suffer.* A tear trickled down her cheek, and she felt suddenly weary.

Mary Ellen finished clearing the table and settled into the recliner. Reaching for her book, she flipped it open to her marker. As she began to read, the hurt in her heart slowly faded to the background, and she entered her world of escape.

---

[1] Psalm 46:1

Monday dawned bright and clear. The troubles of the day before were forgotten amid the flurry of activity that always accompanied a Monday. As usual, Mary Ellen had done her laundry early in the morning before the children were up. Now, as she washed dishes, she kept an eye on Faith lying on the living room floor. Was she or was she not developing properly? Unlike Lynette, she ate well and was gaining weight. But she was becoming fussier and fussier. On top of that, it seemed her eyes did not work well. They rarely followed motion, although they sometimes followed the sound of a voice. This morning over breakfast, Mary Ellen and Eldon had finally decided it was time to contact Dr. Hulse again. If there was something wrong, they would rather treat it sooner than later.

When the dishes were done, Mary Ellen breathed a silent prayer as she sat down at the phone for another difficult call. Dr. Hulse listened to her concerns and asked many questions. He felt that Faith's symptoms indicated a pinched optic nerve. Unfortunately for the Bontragers, he was now practicing in Arizona, but he would gladly help Faith if they wanted to come that far.

When Mary Ellen relayed the information to Eldon that evening, he showed no hesitation. If this would help Faith, he would do whatever it took. Immediately the discussion shifted to the logistics of such a trip. With Lynette and four other children to care for at home, a babysitter would have a huge load.

The next day Mary Ellen made another phone call, this time to her mother Lizzie. She told her about the doctor and how they would need to take Faith to Arizona.

"We'll gladly stay with the children," Lizzie said. Her understanding voice filled Mary Ellen with relief. "If you think it would help Faith, the sooner you get there, the better."

"Thank you," Mary Ellen said around the lump in her throat. "We will start making plans as soon as Eldon can make a weekend work."

"I think that's a good idea. And please don't worry about the children. Clara Mae will help, and I know we will be just fine."

"I don't know how we can ever thank you," Mary Ellen said.

"We're here for you, Mary Ellen."

"We appreciate it," Mary Ellen replied brokenly. "And, Mom, please keep this to yourself. We don't need a lot of unnecessary talk and sympathy. But please pray with us about this, will you?" She felt uncertain how the community would respond. And above all, she didn't want rumors flying around before they were certain of what they were dealing with.

"Dad and I are always praying for you," Lizzie said, her voice kind.

Mary Ellen's eyes misted with tears. Her parents' support comforted her. Though she didn't understand why she and Eldon had been chosen for this difficult journey, she treasured the support they received from both sets of parents.

Several days later, as Mary Ellen began packing for the trip to the doctor, Carolyn took a break from watching the babies and ran outside for a bike ride. Up and down the road she pedaled, the wind blowing through her hair. The bike she had won was still her most prized possession.

After a while she grew thirsty. Leaning her bike against a tree, she ran inside to get a drink. As she sprinted up the steps, she saw Myron ambling around the corner. Stopping short, she eyeballed her innocent-looking brother.

"Myron," she called warningly. "Leave my bike alone!"

He grinned at her mischievously. After she had entered the house, Myron glanced around. Seeing no one else outside, he dashed across the driveway and knelt by the rear wheel of the bike. Pushing the valve on the tire with his finger, he let the air leak out.

Quickly he returned to his previous spot across the yard and strolled along casually, whacking the bushes with a stick. Carolyn came out and climbed back on her bike. As she tried to pedal forward, the rear wheel wibble-wobbled. Looking down, she saw the flat tire. "Myron!" She glared at him from across the yard. "I told you to leave my bike alone!" She parked it again and stomped into the house. "Mom!" she hollered. "I came in to get a drink, and Myron let all the breeze out of my tire."

Mary Ellen was bent over a suitcase but her shaking shoulders gave away her silent laughter. Battling for composure, she followed her daughter outside. Carolyn triumphantly marched ahead and led her to the offending boy.

"Myron," Mary Ellen said reprovingly. "Did you let the air out of your sister's tire?"

Myron's mischievous face turned serious. "I'll fix it," he said, turning toward the garage where his dad was working.

"You'd better. And I don't ever again want to hear about you doing such a mean thing, okay?"

It was fun, though, Myron thought. "No, Mom, I won't," he said out loud.

Mary Ellen turned quickly before her laughter betrayed her. As she resumed packing, her grin remained. *God knows we need some humor during this time,* she thought.

She watched through the window as Eldon helped Myron pump air back into the tire. Soon Carolyn was happily riding her bike again.

Once everything was packed into the '52 Pontiac, they headed down the highway toward Arizona. Mary Ellen's dad, Menno Jr., had joined them to help with the driving. Mile after mile slipped beneath the tires. Mary Ellen's mind filled with memories of their many trips to the same doctor with Lynette. *Wouldn't it be wonderful if this time Faith's problem could be an easy fix!* She tried hard to picture a positive ending, but the knot in her stomach refused to untangle.

It made for a long day to drive the 950 miles to Globe, Arizona, where they found a motel. Though they were weary from the long trip, their sleep was fitful as they thought about the upcoming appointment and what it might mean for their family.

After eating the light breakfast they had brought along, they drove to Dr. Hulse's office.

"Hello, Mr. and Mrs. Bontrager," he greeted with professional confidence as he ushered them into his office. "I'm so glad you came, although I'm sorry it is under these circumstances. Since you brought your second daughter sooner, I believe it will give us a good chance of correcting what is wrong. Let's have a look at Faith." Mary Ellen carefully held the four-month-old baby as the doctor shone a beam of light into Faith's eyes. "Just as I expected," he said cheerfully. "Her optic nerve is pinched, which takes her vision practically to zero. I will treat her, and it should all be taken care of."

The load on Mary Ellen's shoulders shifted slightly but did not lift. She wanted so badly to believe the doctor's optimistic words. She knew many children had been helped by his expertise, but the Bontragers had heard similar promises when he had treated Lynette, and nothing had changed.

"Bring her back tomorrow and I will treat her eyes," Dr. Hulse added. "She shouldn't need any more treatment after that."

With hope in their hearts and a prayer on their lips, they returned the following morning.

"Yes, her eyes are all that are affected," Doctor Hulse repeated confidently after another careful examination. Quickly and skillfully, he treated the pinched nerve, then he assured them she should have no more difficulties. Eldon and Mary Ellen thanked him, left the office, and loaded up for the long trip back home.

The three adults traveled in silence for a while.

"Well," Mary Ellen finally asked from the back seat, "dare we hope the doctor is right?"

Eldon shrugged. "I just don't know. He sounds so sure, but that's how it was with Lynette too. Hopefully since Faith is so young . . ." His voice trailed off.

"Let's just pray he is right," Mary Ellen said. "How can we ever care for another child like Lynette?"

"I'm sure God would give us the grace," Eldon said. "We just don't know yet what plans He has for Faith. I believe we should do all we can with doctoring, but God is still the Healer. He controls her future."

The trip was long. Worn out from the treatment, Faith slept most of the way home.

Soon after they were home, they made an appointment for a second opinion with Dr. Stout, their family doctor. They had a lot of trust in his judgment and knew he would be honest with them.

Dr. Stout examined Faith very carefully. After a long time, he sat back on his stool and looked into the hopeful eyes of Eldon and Mary Ellen. "I'm very sorry to tell you this," he said regretfully. "I do think her eyes are doing better, but Faith will never be normal."

Although they had tried to brace themselves, the news was a shock almost too hard to bear. They had no questions for the doctor; they knew far too well what was ahead of them. Numbly they gathered their tiny baby and headed back home to a life that had just become even more difficult.

When they arrived home, Mary Ellen sat down in the living room with her mother Lizzie. With tears in her eyes, she passed on the doctor's crushing diagnosis.

Lizzie's heart ached for the heavy load her daughter was being asked to bear. "You know we are here for you," she comforted. "We will do all we can to help you through this." Hearing a squabble in the kitchen, they listened as Clara Mae's cheerful voice refereed the children. Lizzie stood, laid her hand briefly on Mary Ellen's stooped shoulder, and left the room, allowing the young mother a few minutes to gather her composure.

Soon Mary Ellen headed to the kitchen as well and stopped in surprise when she saw her counter filled with neat rows of canned peaches. "Where did these come from?"

"Fannie from church canned them for you," Lizzie said. "She brought them all over this morning. She said they are praying for you."

"We sure appreciate it," Mary Ellen said. "There's no way I can ever repay her for this."

"She wanted to do something," her mother said. "Friends do care, Mary Ellen. They just don't always know how to show it."

Mary Ellen nodded. "It can be hard to remember that. I feel so disconnected from the community with hardly being able to go to church. It's easy to start thinking no one cares. But I know that's not true. Please thank her if I don't get the chance."

"I will," her mom promised.

"Another thing—now that the doctor has diagnosed Faith, I feel like the community should know her condition. If we let people know, we won't be carrying the weight all alone. I admit though, it is discouraging to think that I brought another child into the world to suffer all her life."

Her mom squeezed her shoulders. "We don't understand God's plan, but I think Faith is here for a purpose. Do you believe that?"

Mary Ellen bowed her head. "I'd like to. It's just hard to remember that in the daily grind. Especially when Faith cries and cries and there is nothing I can do. Eldon almost can't handle it anymore."

Clara Mae spoke up. "We will do all we can to help."

Having no eyesight had made Faith nervous and tense. Now, with her improved vision, she became a little calmer. But otherwise, there was no change.

"If I felt these sleepless nights would be helping her somehow, and that she would someday be a healthy child, I would never complain," Mary Ellen said wearily one morning as she sat at the breakfast table. "But I know that unless God performs a miracle, she will always be this way."

"It's so hard to understand why God is allowing this," Eldon replied, resting his elbows on the table. "But your dad told me to remember God's ways aren't our ways. And I do believe that." He rubbed his tired face as he rose and headed out the door for work.

Mary Ellen willed her fatigued body to get up and start the dishes. In the next room, LaVon and Myron were playing with the transport truck LaVon had gotten from the Detroiter Christmas party. As she washed, she heard the little voices begin to rise.

"Myron," LaVon said firmly, "this is mine, remember? You can play with your pickup truck."

"But I want to play with the big truck too!" Myron sniffled. "If you don't share with me, I'm going far away."

Mary Ellen looked up from the sink as he stomped resolutely through the kitchen, carrying a handful of toys. "Where are you going, Myron?"

"To Daudys in Iowa. I'm going to walk all the way, like this." He stuck out his thumb the way he had seen hitchhikers doing along the road.

Mary Ellen's mouth twitched. "We'll sure miss you," she said, wiping her hands on the hand towel.

Myron paused a moment. Then, dumping his toys onto the floor, he ran to her and buried his face in her skirt. "Maybe I'll just stay here! I would miss you too. And LaVon too, even though he doesn't share his truck with me."

"Oh, I'm glad you're staying," Mary Ellen said. "I wouldn't know what to do without my little Myron."

6

The Neighborhood

The fast-growing bushes Eldon had planted to divide their yard from the Becketts were now six feet tall. LaVon and Myron spent hours outside, living many fantasies in this leafy home. With a little imagination, the shrubbery became forests and fortresses. Of course, every good fort needs some enemies, and the Becketts filled this role nicely. In fact, they were pretend enemies so often that the boys almost forgot they weren't real foes.

Carolyn and Phyllis were banned from the boys' empire, but they didn't mind. They just moved to the back of the property and created a playhouse in the shrubs back there. Using their kittens, they played house, mothering and nurturing their tiny, furry children.

One morning Phyllis despondently came inside for breakfast. "My favorite kitty is gone," she mourned, stirring her oatmeal floating in milk and brown sugar.

"Those Beckett children probably shot and killed her," LaVon said knowingly.

"Now, don't jump to conclusions," Eldon cautioned, trying to prevent troubled waters. "I'm sure the kitten will show up soon." But it never did.

Several days later, Mary Ellen heard a knock at the door. She opened it to see Mrs. Beckett.

"Come in!" Mary Ellen invited.

Her neighbor looked uncomfortable. "May I use your phone? Ours isn't working."

"Of course!" Mary Ellen led her to the phone in the dining room. Then she hurried back to the kitchen, giving Mrs. Beckett some privacy.

A few minutes later, Mary Ellen glanced up as Mrs. Beckett came out of the dining room. "I hope you got through."

"Thank you. I did." Mrs. Beckett gave her a small smile and walked out, closing the door behind her. Suddenly the door reopened slightly, and Mrs. Beckett's nervous face peeked back in. "I'm afraid my boys killed one of your kittens," she admitted. "Honestly, I had no idea they would do that. I'm so sorry." Her eyes looked frightened.

Mary Ellen could see the woman was lonely and unhappy. "It's okay," she said kindly. "We forgive you and would like to be friends with your family."

"It won't happen again, I promise," Mrs. Beckett said. "And we'd like to be friends too. Maybe you could come over to visit sometime."

Mary Ellen's heart filled with regret. She had been so busy with her own life that she hadn't taken the time to reach out to her neighbor. "We will," she promised.

The next day, Mary Ellen baked some fresh pies and decided to take one over for Mrs. Beckett. She walked around the hedge, and there sat a propane truck, delivering gas to the Becketts. She was just in time to see the neighbors' big black dog lunge at the driver as he filled up the tank.

"Hey!" the driver yelled, spraying the dog with a bit of gas to deter him. "Get out of here!"

Mrs. Beckett yanked open her front door. "Don't hurt my dog!"

The driver whirled around to see who was yelling. "Ma'am," he called, "if this dog bites me, I'll kill him."

Mrs. Beckett slammed the door shut.

Mary Ellen walked around the truck hesitantly. *What am I getting into here? Is that dog going to lunge at me too?*

Watching over her shoulder, she hurried to the front door and knocked. Thankfully, the dog had disappeared. After a moment, the door creaked open, and Mrs. Beckett peered out suspiciously. "Oh, hi," she said when she saw who it was.

"I brought you a pie," Mary Ellen said hurriedly, again glancing anxiously over her shoulder. "I hope your family will enjoy it."

Mrs. Beckett gave her a quick smile. "Thank you," she said simply. "Watch out for the dog when you leave. He can be a little cantankerous. We should tie him up again."

Mary Ellen smiled as she hurried home on light feet. The dog was still nowhere to be seen. She felt satisfied she had done the right thing in reaching out to her neighbor.

The Becketts were not their only neighbors. Houses lined the road, and the Bontrager children always had friends to play with. Bikes, trikes, and dogs roamed the street. It was a safe environment, and the children loved their playmates.

Hoping to provide more responsibility for their children on the small property, Eldon bought a pony named Judy and a saddle and bridle. The children and their friends spent many happy hours clip-clopping Judy up and down the dusty country road.

"You would think we live in town," Eldon complained. "I wish my children could be on a farm. I don't think the influences here are all good. Some of the families have television and aren't Christians."

But the children were quite happy with where they were. One highlight was the railroad that ran along the back of the property. It was a busy freight line; lots of trains went by every day. As soon as the children heard a whistle, they beelined for the back fence, where they would climb up and watch the familiar locomotives go by. "One, two, three..." counted Carolyn. "Do you think this one will be pulling a hundred cars?"

The children loved seeing which train had the most cars. ". . . ninety-eight, ninety-nine, one hundred exactly!" Carolyn yelled as the caboose clanged by.

The mail train, the *Imperial,* was always on time, its whistle blowing at 1:00 sharp every afternoon. The children tried hard not to hear that one because it was a signal to Mary Ellen. "Time to climb into bed for some quiet time," she would call from the back porch. The children watched the caboose until it was out of sight, then they dragged themselves into the house to lie down for a nap. Mary Ellen was always glad for this hour when the house was quiet. It helped calm her nerves.

The Bontrager children became more and more aware that their "babies" were different from other babies. (Even as Lynette and Faith grew older, they were still called babies.) Both Lynette and Faith sat in special recliner chairs, held in place by straps across their shoulders and pillows placed beside them. At a young age, the children learned to help with the added responsibilities of the handicapped girls. It was bonding for the family to work together on the unique difficulties in their home.

Every evening, although he was often tired from the grueling work at Detroiter, Eldon helped Mary Ellen as much as he could. He washed dishes, folded laundry, and vacuumed.

Mealtimes, especially, were ordeals. Before the rest of the family ate, the two babies were fed. Eldon held "Kaye-Kaye," a nickname fashioned from Lynette's middle name, and Mary Ellen held Faith. The living room couch and an additional big chair both had very wide arms, perfect for supporting the girls' arms and with enough room for a bowl of food. It took a long time to feed the girls, and there was often a big mess when they were done. Once everything was cleaned up, the two parents ate with the rest of the children at the table. The meals never really felt complete with Lynette and Faith in their seats in the living room. But that was just how it had to be.

"Carolyn," Mary Ellen said one day, "I think you are old enough to help feed the babies."

"Sure, Mom," six-year-old Carolyn replied. She already helped with a lot of the work and took care of the children at home when Mary Ellen made quick trips to the grocery store about three miles away.

Growing up in a family with two handicapped daughters meant Carolyn had to grow up quickly. She was a willing worker and assumed more and more responsibilities. Hard work was just part of life in the Bontrager home.

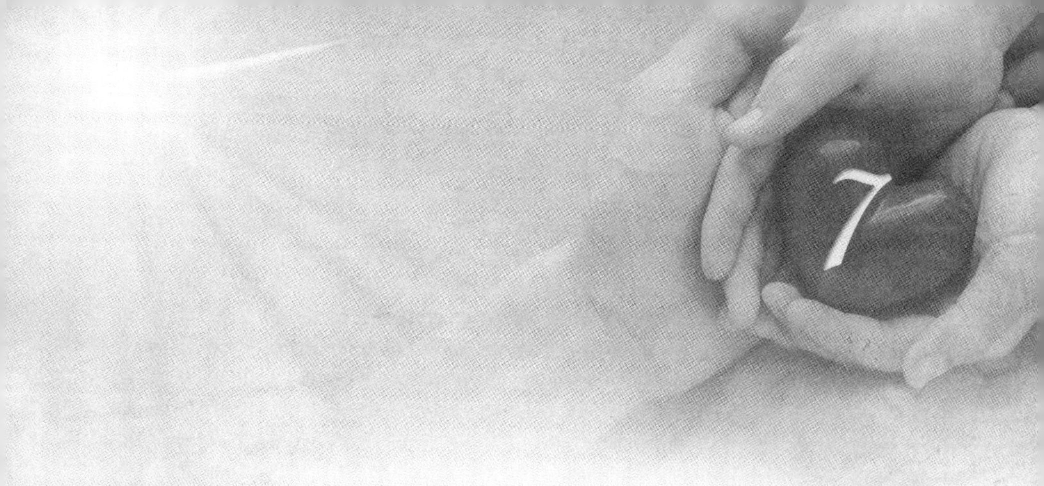

7

Facing the Stigma

The sun was setting as Eldon's Dodge pickup came to a stop in the driveway. Stepping from the vehicle, he heard the familiar sound of a child crying in the house. *Faith seems to be sick almost every day.* The one-year-old had been crying that morning when he left, and by the sound of things, she hadn't improved much.

He sagged back against the truck, his head in his hands. *O God, I just don't know how long I can take this.* The everlasting crying was almost more than he could bear. Sometimes he wondered if he was losing his mind. But what was there to do? Faith had become so miserable lately that Eldon and Mary Ellen had begun to pray that God would just take her home rather than allowing her to suffer.

Wearily Eldon gritted his teeth and walked to the door.

Inside, he found every bit of the disorder he was expecting. Supper was cooling on the back of the stove as LaVon wandered past to set the table, carrying plastic cups on his head. Myron and Phyllis had erected a blanket house in the living room, nearly obscuring Carolyn, who was feeding Lynette in the corner. Mary Ellen was nowhere to be seen. Eldon assumed she was with Faith, who was still wailing from somewhere in the depths of the house.

When Mary Ellen heard him talking to the children, she emerged from the hallway, looking discouraged.

"Has she been like this all day?" Eldon asked.

"Yes, I'm afraid so," Mary Ellen sighed. "Nothing I do seems to help."

Eldon sank into a chair, removed his shoes, and hurled them into a corner in frustration. "That's just it! I feel so bad for her. I would do anything to help, but nothing does any good!"

As they ate supper, Faith's crying was grim background music for the meal. As usual, her wails continued the entire evening. At midnight, when she finally fell asleep, Eldon groaned aloud, "How can we go on like this?" Flopping into bed beside his wife, he fell asleep immediately—and dreamed.

In his dream, Eldon saw little Faith Darlene dressed in a white robe like an angel. She looked like any other perfect little girl—healthy, happy, and walking. He couldn't believe his eyes. She was beautiful and completely whole.

Eldon awoke with a start and lifted the alarm clock. To his surprise, only fifteen minutes had passed since he had lain down. Heart pounding, he ran to Faith's crib to see if she was still alive.

Her tiny chest rose and fell as the exhausted child slept. Eldon breathed a sigh of relief. Bending over his beloved daughter, he tenderly whispered in her ear, "Our heavenly Father must have a bigger purpose for you." He kissed her cheek. "Oh, Faith, I'm so sorry you must suffer like this. One day you will be whole."

As Eldon climbed back into bed, his former weariness was replaced with a sense of wonder. He thought of a favorite verse about heaven: "And God shall wipe away all tears from their eyes; and there shall be no more death, neither sorrow, nor crying, neither shall there be any more pain: for the former things are passed away" (Revelation 21:4).

Thank you for the reminder that all our suffering is confined to this world, he prayed. *With your help, God, we will try to be faithful.*

That spring Faith was stricken with boils that covered much of her body. She was in so much agony that her parents wondered again if she would live. Their family doctor refused to make a house call, and Faith was too sick to be moved.

"I just don't understand why the doctor won't come see her," Mary Ellen lamented, feeling abandoned.

"I don't understand it either," Eldon said, helplessly watching his daughter suffer. "Maybe he feels powerless to do anything."

Daily they watched little Faith become weaker and thinner. Finally she weighed only eleven pounds. Her waist was seven inches around and Eldon could encircle it with his hands. All the poor child could do was turn her face from side to side. At times it was hard to detect any breathing from her frail body.

One night, when all seemed hopeless, Eldon and Mary Ellen knelt together beside their daughter's bed. "Dear Lord," Eldon prayed. "We beg you to relieve Faith of her suffering somehow. If it means taking her to heaven, we are willing to release her from our family, knowing she would be healed and whole. But if you choose to lend her to us here, we want to accept your divine will for us. It's a hard journey, but we want to be faithful. In Jesus' name. Amen."

Tears rolled down their cheeks as they got up from their knees. A peace stole over them as they found rest in once again accepting God's will for their family and daughter.

Faith continued to waver between life and death. Eldon longed to stay home with his wife and sick child, but he had no choice but to go to work. At every breaktime and lunch hour, he hurried to his foreman's office. "My baby is still so sick," he would say. "Can I please use your phone again?" The foreman would push the rotary phone toward him, and Eldon would quickly dial the number and wait with bated breath. Finally Mary Ellen would answer, and he would find out if Faith was still alive.

One day it seemed she finally turned the corner. Though not in a dramatic way, God restored partial health to Faith. How thankful they were, even though her care remained as relentless as ever.

Caring for the girls took twenty-four hours a day, seven days a week, twelve months a year—without any break. Eldon and Mary Ellen missed many church functions. Friends and church people tried to support them with a day of help here and a meal or two there. While this was certainly a blessing, it did little to relieve the pain and exhaustion a caregiver feels with no reprieve in sight.

Eldon and Mary Ellen with their young family in June 1963. Left to right: Carolyn (6), Myron (3), Eldon holding Lynette (7), LaVon (4), Mary Ellen holding Faith (1), and Phyllis (2).

Crowds bothered the girls, and they became restless and irritable when they were away from home. It seemed going to church was especially difficult for them. Eldon and Mary Ellen often used the classrooms in the basement of the church, which held extra cribs for babies who needed more privacy. The girls liked it better down there—it was quiet and they could relax while the rest of the family enjoyed the service in the sanctuary above. Mary Ellen's ears were always tuned downstairs, however, and she frequently went down to check on them.

One time as she came down the stairs, she heard laughter from the room. Then she heard Faith cry out and Lynette scream. *Oh, no! What's wrong?* Her thoughts raced as she ran down the remaining steps. Hurrying across the basement, she yanked open the door—and her eyes bulged in disbelief.

Two naughty boys, each with a pile of juniper berries, were pulling back their suspender straps like slingshots and shooting berries at Lynette and Faith. "Boys!" Mary Ellen scolded, stepping inside. "Whatever are you doing?"

Guiltily the boys grabbed the rest of their berries and scampered out the door. Mary Ellen hurried to the cribs, talking softly to the girls until they settled down. Straightening her back, she turned toward several young mothers sitting at the other end of the room. Their faces were carefully averted as they tended their own babies.

"Didn't you see what they were doing?" Mary Ellen asked, raising her normally mild tone. "Why didn't you stop them? They were shooting those berries at my helpless babies!"

"Sorry," one mother mumbled. "But it's not like they were shooting them very hard."

"The girls were crying! Do you think they don't have feelings?" Mary Ellen tried to stay calm. "Just because they can't protect themselves and tell you what's going on doesn't make it right to allow your children to mistreat them. You wouldn't allow them to treat other children like that." She felt hot with indignation.

The mothers looked unconcerned. "You know our boys didn't mean anything by it," another lady said. "Boys will be boys."

Mary Ellen couldn't believe her ears. She turned so she wouldn't say something she would regret. This could have been used as a teaching moment, but instead the mothers were defending their boys' behavior.

That night, after the girls were tucked in bed, Mary Ellen told Eldon what had happened. "I don't feel like making all the effort to take them to church if they face this kind of thing," she sighed, feeling weary and defeated.

Eldon was silent, but his tightened lips gave testimony to a struggle within. He had always wanted to live a quiet, peaceful life, but now his own flesh and blood were falling victim to cruel pranks and mockery. He felt the sting of the juniper berries hit his own heart, carelessly splattering onto his dreams and desires.

After that incident, the Bontragers rarely took the girls to church. They knew that society in general viewed disabled children as a shameful embarrassment rather than as persons created by God, but they had not expected to find this attitude among their church friends. It hurt them deeply when others felt their daughters were not worthy of basic kindness.

Mary Ellen usually stayed home with the girls. Although in many ways this was easier than trying to take them along to church, the loneliness and discouragement took its toll. Mary Ellen rarely saw her church family, and it became even easier to imagine nobody cared.

Every Monday, her sister Clara Mae came to visit her. She washed up the dishes as she told Mary Ellen what the sermon was about, who had visited church, and what the latest news was in the community. Mary Ellen never complained about staying home from church, but she was glad to hear what was going on around her.

Despite the stigma they faced, Eldon wanted to support the church. He was even elected for church offices, such as Sunday school superintendent and midweek planning committee, but that required attending meetings in the evenings. As much as he hated the thought of not continuing to be involved in such church responsibilities, he felt he was more needed at home.

Jonas, a preacher friend from another local church, often showed empathy for the Bontrager family. One day he dropped in, taking time to hear their deepest struggles. "How do you feel about your responsibilities in the church?"

"You know we are church supporters," Eldon said. "I don't want to shirk my duty. But Jonas, the Lord knows I'm telling the truth when I say I have my hands full here with my family. I need to be here in the evenings to help my wife. Although I want to do what I can for the church, having this role makes life hard for me. But neither do I want to be a slacker."

Jonas nodded in agreement. "I doubt the church people have any idea how much strain this puts on you. I don't feel at all like you are slacking off. If you will allow me to, I will request that you be freed of your church responsibilities for a time."

"I sure would appreciate that," Eldon said gratefully. "I'm often on the verge of exhaustion."

"I sensed as much," Jonas said. "Do you get many visits from church people?"

"A few here and there," Eldon replied. "Mostly family, though. I think it makes people uncomfortable to come to our home. We want to be understanding of that, but we need encouragement as much as anyone else."

One Sunday when the Bontragers were absent, Jonas visited Center Amish Mennonite Church. He took the opportunity to bring their need before the church. An overwhelming majority of the church agreed with him, and Eldon's church responsibilities were lifted.

The family was so thankful for the advocate Jonas had been. They wouldn't have been brave enough to speak up for themselves. Although being relieved from other responsibilities didn't take away the burden of caring for the girls, it helped.

Having support from others was so encouraging.

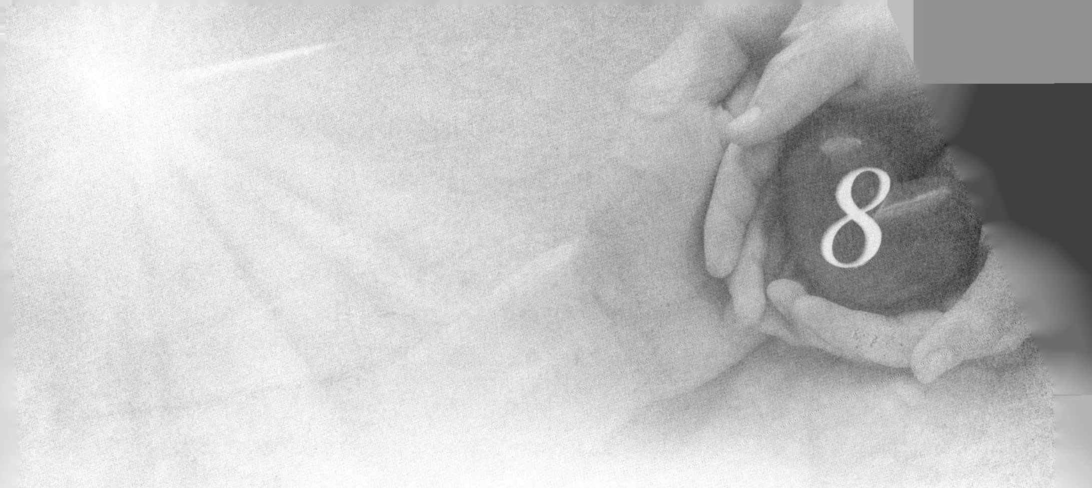

8

Wash Peddler, World Affairs, and Prison Whistle

"Mom!" Carolyn cried one morning, dashing into the house. "The wash peddler is coming!"

"Oh, no," Mary Ellen exclaimed, grabbing the telephone to warn Mrs. Beckett that she would be next on his route. "Today of all days, I have no time to listen to his long-winded spiel. I have no money to spend on his stuff anyway." Into the receiver, she said, "The Watkins man is here!" Hanging up the phone, she scooped up Faith from the floor. "All right, children. Story time in the basement!"

The children grabbed some books and headed downstairs. They felt a bit disappointed that they wouldn't get to watch the peddler open his magical suitcase to show all his wonderful spices, cleaning supplies, medicines, and salves. But they knew money was tight, and they could not afford the extras the Watkins man had to offer. They also knew that once he started on his sales pitch, it was hard to get him to leave unless they bought something.

In the basement, Mom began to read the children a story as they all snuggled close. Listening to stories was a rare treat for the Bontrager children since Mom rarely had time for such leisure.

Upstairs, they heard the Watkins man knock on the door. There was a long pause, then a louder knock. Eventually they heard his footsteps fade away as he headed back out the sidewalk. Soon they heard his car start, and when it purred out the drive, story time was over.

"Mom, don't you feel a bit deceitful?" Carolyn asked as they headed up the stairs, her young conscience smiting her. "We acted like we weren't here, but we actually were."

"You do have a point," Mary Ellen said, pausing at the top. "I hadn't thought about it like that. Maybe I just need to open the door, listen to him for an hour, then send him on his way without buying anything. Do you think that would be more kind?"

Carolyn looked thoughtful as they headed for the kitchen. "I'm not sure. It sure wouldn't be a nice job to be a peddler! Do you think anybody buys from him?"

"Oh, they must, or he would quit coming around."

Carolyn still felt sorry for the thwarted salesman. "But maybe he's poor and needs money."

"I think a lot of peddlers just don't like to work," Mary Ellen replied. "They want a life of freedom, adventure, and the opportunity to earn money based on how smooth they can talk. I don't think they are poor. I think they make a decent living."

"Well, I'm glad to hear that. I like the wash peddler. Wouldn't it be fun to have a job where you could travel all over the world?"

Mary Ellen chuckled as she piled dirty breakfast dishes into the sink. "You would like that, wouldn't you?"

"Yes," Carolyn said, standing at the window with a faraway look in her eyes. She wanted to see the whole world as soon as she was old enough.

That night Eldon came home from the factory in better spirits than he had been for a long time.

"Good evening," Mary Ellen smiled. "You look like you had a good day."

"Yes, I did," Eldon said, grinning as he plopped his lunch box on the counter. "One of the regular workers had surgery on his hand, so they moved me to a different location on the line. Instead of the grueling work I'm used to, I was building vanities, chests of drawers, valances, and nightstands. I liked this lighter work so much better that I was brash enough to tell the foreman I would like this job permanently. He indicated he might be able to work that out!"

"Oh, wouldn't that be nice!" Mary Ellen exclaimed.

"Yes, I don't think I would mind my job so much if I could work on cabinets."

Mary Ellen hoped for her husband's sake that he could keep this new position. It seemed to suit him much better than the stress of plumbing on the production line. She had often felt sorry that he needed to work at a job he disliked so much, even though he rarely complained. It would be almost too good to be true if he could do something he enjoyed.

While Eldon and Mary Ellen were struggling to care for their disabled girls, the rest of the world was struggling too. For the past few years, the Cold War had loomed at the forefront of everyone's mind. As the Berlin Wall went up to keep people in East Germany from moving to freedom, Christians all over the world were praying about the impending crisis. Would they soon be exchanging their earthly cares for a heavenly home?

Since Russia and the United States remained at loggerheads, the fear and tension across the world was palpable. As the communist world powers and the democratic world powers faced off, it seemed clear no one could win this war. Eldon prayed with his family, trying to keep their faith strong no matter what happened.

When President Kennedy gave an order to Russia's leader Khrushchev to remove his missiles from Cuba, six long, tense days followed. The world held its breath until Khrushchev finally complied and a devastating nuclear war was averted. People everywhere sighed with relief, many still wondering if Khrushchev would change his mind and blow up the entire planet. Many Christians in America lived in constant awareness that their freedom to worship was safe only if Russia remained the enemy, not the conqueror.

Refusing to live in fear, Eldon prayed that peace would last. He prayed for harmony between the world leaders. Most of all, he prayed that his family could be part of God's kingdom forever. He didn't know how the affairs of the world would affect his family in the future, but he knew he wanted to be faithful to Christ and raise his children to be faithful too.

One Saturday morning, Eldon was in the backyard building a henhouse for Mary Ellen's chickens. The little boys were helping as best they could. Suddenly a long, piercing whistle rang out across the prairie. "Why are they blowing that whistle again?" LaVon asked, slapping his hands over his ears. "It always scares me when I hear it."

Myron covered his ears as well. "Me too," he said, squeezing his eyes shut.

"Someone must have escaped from the reformatory again," Eldon said, looking out over the blowing grasses. A maximum-security penitentiary sat only seven miles away. When a prisoner escaped, the prison blew a loud whistle that could be heard for miles.

"Keep an extra close eye on the children today," Eldon told Mary Ellen, stepping into the house with one eye on the backyard. "I don't want to be fearful, but prisoners on the loose are usually evil men."

Mary Ellen had reason to take his warning to heart. Just the week before, four other prisoners had escaped. They had stolen a car from a nearby home and robbed another family. So far they had not been recaptured. She hoped the escapees today would head in a different direction.

At midmorning, Mary Ellen took a break from her work to check on the development of the henhouse and to refresh the warm workers. "It always makes me uneasy when that whistle blows," she told Eldon as he sat on a pile of wood drinking the cold lemonade.

"Me too," Eldon said, wiping his forehead. "Escaped prisoners are dangerous, maybe even desperate." He took another long drink. "But this stuff sure hits the spot!"

"It's a small price to pay for doing this job for me." Mary Ellen smiled, then grew pensive. "Sometimes I wish we wouldn't live so close to the penitentiary. Have you ever thought about that?"

"Yes, I have," Eldon said, taking another sip. "But I don't know what to do about it. Do you think we should look for a farm for the children to grow up on?"

She gazed across the fields. "I would love that. Learning more responsibilities would be good for the children."

"That's my dream too," he confided. "We don't have the money yet, but I hope someday we will."

"God knows our dreams," Mary Ellen said, taking his empty glass. "Let's keep our ears open. Maybe a farm will come up for sale within our price range."

"I could walk away from Detroiter tomorrow and never miss it," Eldon declared. "My heart is still in farming."

"Either your heart is in farming or farming is in your heart," Mary Ellen laughed. "It's kind of hard to know where one stops and the other starts." Smiling, she returned to the house.

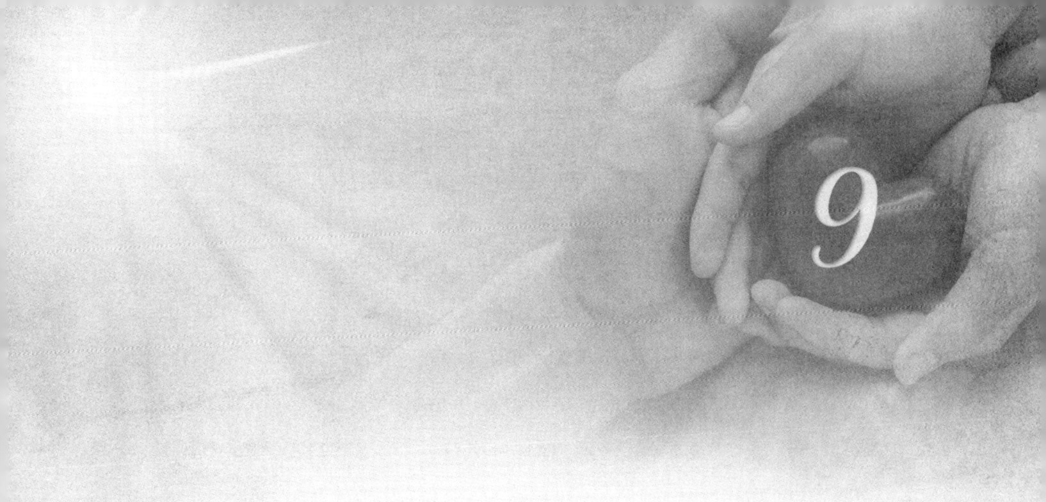

9

Burdens Too Heavy

Although his new role as a cabinetmaker at Detroiter was a great improvement over his previous position, it was with a sigh of relief that Eldon punched the time clock there for the last time. He had found a job at Prairie Construction, building sheds and doing remodel work with other men from the church. Even though this new job wasn't the farming he loved, he did enjoy it. The atmosphere among the crew was pleasant, and the relationships were friendly. The only dark spot was the long hours, which increased the heavy load on Mary Ellen.

Riiing! Eldon punched the button on the alarm with an exhausted finger. He sank back into bed, every bit as tired as he had been the evening before. He shuddered as he recalled their exhausting evening. As was all too common, Lynette and Faith had screamed from the time he came home from work until long after he wanted to be in bed. Now this morning, Eldon felt as if his bones were screaming for more rest. Even though it was Saturday, he had to get up. There were things to do.

He and Mary Ellen had recently turned to sedatives for the girls, hoping this would relieve the constant pain their daughters struggled with. Even so, sleep seemed elusive for the girls and, consequently, for their parents. But no matter how brutal the night, morning always arrived, forcing Eldon and Mary Ellen to get up and start another day.

Eldon pried himself out of bed, pulled on his homemade trousers and short-sleeved shirt, then sat back on the bed to tug his shoes on his feet. Mary Ellen pushed herself up beside him with a groan.

"If this doesn't stop," Eldon mumbled, "I'm afraid I'm going to lose my mind."

Mary Ellen yawned, dark circles framing her eyes. "Me too. I can hardly care for the other children when I'm so tired. Every night I think maybe they'll sleep better, but it never happens. I don't know what else to try." She staggered after Eldon to the kitchen. "How are we going to keep on?"

Eldon put an arm around her, pulling her close and kissing her forehead. "Something needs to change, but I don't know what. I guess we just need to pray for strength for today." Grabbing his straw hat from a hook, he opened the door to go check on their animals.

"Hurry back," Mary Ellen called after him as he stepped outside. "Breakfast will soon be ready." The children were still sleeping, and she decided not to wake them for breakfast. They could eat later. She and Eldon needed a bit of time alone to collect their thoughts.

She put the coffee on to perk, then mixed up the biscuits and popped them into the oven. On the stovetop, she stirred flour and milk together over the heat to make gravy. Then she set the table for two.

Soon the back screen door slammed and Eldon came in, hanging his hat back on the hook. Pulling out a chair at the table, he unlaced his shoes and set them out of the way. As he scooted his chair to the table, Mary Ellen poured him a cup of steaming coffee and dished up the biscuits and gravy. Placing them on the table, she sat down beside him.

As they bowed their heads, Eldon prayed aloud. "Dear heavenly Father, thank you for your daily provisions in our lives. Thank you for the health and strength you give us for this day. Lead us and guide us as we care for our family. Thank you for this food. I ask your blessing on our day. In Jesus' name. Amen."

He took a biscuit, ladling it with gravy. Taking a deep breath, he said decisively, "We can't keep functioning with only two to three hours of sleep per night." Hesitantly he glanced at Mary Ellen for her reaction.

The weary lines on her face deepened. "So what is the answer?" She knew how much the girls' crying grated on his nerves.

"I wish I knew," Eldon said, his certainty crumbling in the face of their helplessness. "Faith was crying again early this morning, and I had barely fallen back asleep when the alarm went off. There's never a break for our nerves. If we can't calm down the babies, it sometimes seems better for me to just go someplace where I can't hear them cry."

"I know what you mean," Mary Ellen said, taking a sip of coffee and staring at her plate. Although she had somewhat resigned herself to the strange, unbearable normal their life had become, the stress still wore on her. But she knew it was even harder for Eldon.

"If there was just something we could do." Eldon stabbed at his breakfast. "But nothing helps."

Mary Ellen cleared her throat. "I hesitated to go shopping last night because I know they get on your nerves. But I really needed to buy some things..."

"You had to go," Eldon replied. "And yet, after you left, I knew I couldn't handle it all evening, so I just went outside and mowed the lawn." His admission held both guilt and frustration.

Mary Ellen registered no surprise at his confession. She knew he was not coping well. Although Eldon's tendency to escape the incessant crying by going outside to work increased her own burden, she never complained about it. Nor did she complain about the care their babies required, though it was just as exhausting for her as it was for Eldon—probably even more so. Mary Ellen knew she had her own way of coping by escaping into her books.

She knew Eldon loved each member of his family every bit as deeply as she did. This knowledge helped Mary Ellen through the difficult hours she spent alone with the children. And although at times the constant stress and lack of sleep frayed their nerves—causing small irritations to fester and brood—they were still a team, secure in their trust in each other.

Not all was depression and weariness at the Bontrager home. As the days slowly ticked by, Carolyn at last awoke to her first day of school. She bounded out of bed at the crack of dawn and rushed through her preparations in eager anticipation.

"When will the bus come?" she asked for the umpteenth time as she danced past the window, lunch box in hand.

"I sure hope all your school mornings will be like this," Mary Ellen said, chuckling. "I almost need to hold on to you so you don't race out the door ahead of time."

"I don't want to miss the bus," Carolyn said, watching eagerly out the window.

"Oh, you won't," Mary Ellen assured her daughter. "In fact, there it is!"

Like a shot, Carolyn ran out the door and down the sidewalk to the yellow bus waiting at the driveway. Before boarding, she turned and waved. "Bye, Mom!"

"Have fun!" Mary Ellen called from the open door. "Obey your teacher!" The smile on her face was a good cover for the lump in her throat. Gently she closed the door left open in her daughter's haste.

How can it be that Carolyn is old enough to go to school? Her hand still on the knob, Mary Ellen thought about the past six years. How long the days had been, but how quickly the years had flown.

Walking into the living room, she saw seven-year-old Lynette lying on the floor. A pang went through Mary Ellen at the thought that Carolyn's big sister would never go to school with her. Reaching down, she smoothed Lynette's hair.

"Lynette, I wish you could go to school too." The huge lump in her throat threatened to choke her. For a moment, a wave of pain washed over her as she saw her daughter miss out yet again on a delightful milestone. Straightening her back, Mary Ellen pushed away her sad thoughts and returned to the waiting breakfast dishes.

The day sped by as Mary Ellen worked busily, trying to make up for her missing helper.

"Where is Carolyn?" little Phyllis asked at lunchtime.

"She went to school, remember?" Mary Ellen pulled the almost three-year-old onto her lap. "Now she will learn how to read and write."

"I hope she's not naughty." Phyllis arched her eyebrows and pursed her little lips.

Mary Ellen tried to compare mischievous Phyllis with mature-for-her-years Carolyn. The contrast made her laugh. "I'm sure she will be just fine."

She held Phyllis close and took a moment to look into her eyes. A patch covered one eye to help her learn to focus with the other. Her eyes did look straighter than before, but deep in Mary Ellen's heart, she was almost certain the child would still need surgery. She knew the surgery would be another hard thing to face, but as Eldon often said in the mornings, "We only need grace for today." Mary Ellen wanted to rest on that truth.

At 3:30 that afternoon, Carolyn bounced into the house. As the first grader slammed the screen door behind her, Mary Ellen asked, "How did you like school?"

"It was so much fun," bubbled Carolyn. "Our teacher is so nice. She said we will learn to read and write and do arithmetic." She put her lunch box on the table. Beaming, she held out a paper with all her numbers written from one to ten.

"That looks good," Mary Ellen praised. "Your numbers look perfect." Her heart swelled as she watched her daughter glowing in this new stage.

What a blessing it was to watch a child grow! Mary Ellen hoped Carolyn would make friends in her class to help fill the social void in their world. Even though Carolyn was attending a public school, there were other students there from plain families as well.

All through supper, Carolyn regaled the family with stories and facts about school. She found a rapt audience in her younger siblings.

"I can't wait till I can go to school," LaVon remarked enviously.

Mary Ellen chuckled at his eagerness. "Next year you can go."

LaVon pondered this as he finished the meal in silence. A whole year sounded like a long time to him.

After supper was over and the dishes were washed, the family sat in the living room. Tonight they fed the girls after their evening meal. Eldon fed Kaye-Kaye, as Lynette was often called, and Mary Ellen fed Faith. The other children played on the floor as the two girls spat and waved their arms and legs, spilling food everywhere.

"You must be full," Mary Ellen said to Faith. She wiped her clean, then handed the towel to Eldon so he could clean up Lynette.

Afterward Eldon sat on the couch and took both girls on his lap. They leaned against him, content for the moment. Looking at the other children, he asked, "Shall I tell you a story?"

Their little tousled heads jerked up, and the children abandoned their toys to crowd around him. They loved stories, and their father was the best storyteller.

Eldon cleared his throat as he looked at his first grader. "Carolyn, today was your first day of school. I remember something that happened when I was a little boy in first grade."

"Did you have a nice teacher?" Carolyn asked.

Eldon smiled. "Yes, she was nice. She was very kind."

"Go on," LaVon put in eagerly. "What happened?"

"Well, sometimes it got really cold in the schoolhouse. Down in the basement, there was a wood-burning stove, and beside it was a box of old wooden shingles we used for kindling. One day in January we had the stove so roaring hot that those shingles caught fire."

The children gasped. "What happened then?" LaVon bounced up and down.

Eldon continued his exciting tale. "The teacher smelled smoke, so she asked a sixth-grade boy to go down to the basement to check it out. Pretty soon he came running up, shouting, 'Fire! Fire!'

"My family lived just down the road, and my dad heard the commotion. He saw smoke and came running with two empty milk pails, one in each hand." Eldon looked around at the huge eyes surrounding him.

"Were you scared?" Myron asked, concern written on his face.

"Oh yes, I was scared. All of us children were scared. Our knees were trembling as the teacher herded us outside. My dad tried hard to fill the buckets with water but the pump wouldn't work. So we just stood there and watched the schoolhouse burn down. The flames devoured everything."

Carolyn released her held breath. "I hope that doesn't happen at our school."

"I hope not, either," Eldon said. "We need to remember to respect fire and be careful. But we won't worry about things like that tonight. Let's have our Bible story, then we need to get our schoolgirl to bed."

Soon the children were snuggled in for the night. But the day wasn't over for Eldon and Mary Ellen. Lynette and Faith both cried until late once again, wailing in pain as their parents held them, trying in vain to soothe them. Deep into the night, both parents finally sank into a fitful sleep for a few short hours.

The school year flew by. Thanksgiving came and went, then Christmas. Spring brought warmer weather, and with it came Carolyn's seventh birthday.

"May I have some friends over?" she asked Mary Ellen two days before her birthday.

“I think that’s a good plan,” Mary Ellen agreed. “Why don’t you invite one of your school friends? She can come after school and stay until bedtime.”

“Oh, I can’t wait!” Carolyn exclaimed. “I’m going to invite Rachel.”

“Invite her tomorrow, so she can check with her mom first.” Mary Ellen was glad Carolyn had a friend to invite over. She wanted her children to have the chance to do things other children did.

“I will,” Carolyn said. Then her face clouded. “I hope Rachel will like our house,” she added dubiously.

“Are you thinking of Andrea?” Mary Ellen asked. “Try to forget how her words hurt you, Carolyn. Not everyone will act like she did. Rachel is a nice girl, and I think she’ll be understanding.”

After school on Carolyn’s special day, the two first-grade girls burst through the door. Mary Ellen had baked her signature chocolate angel food cake, and it was cooling on the table.

“Look at that yummy cake,” Rachel exclaimed, admiring it.

Mary Ellen smiled. “Do you want a piece? It should be cool by now.”

The girls scrambled onto the bench at the table while Mary Ellen sliced a generous piece for each. She topped the cake on their plates with a dip of ice cream. The girls savored the treat to the last bite as they chatted about their day. When they finished the snack, they jumped up and ran through the living room. Stopping short, Rachel looked a bit startled at the sight of the girls sitting in their recliners. Even though she knew Carolyn had disabled sisters, she hadn’t been around them much. Beside her, Carolyn looked nervous.

“This is Kaye-Kaye, and this is Faith.” Carolyn pointed to each one as she introduced her sisters hesitantly.

“Mama said you had sisters like this,” Rachel said. When she ventured closer, Faith flapped her arms in excitement. Rachel pulled back in confusion. “What did I do?”

“It’s all right,” Carolyn said. “She’s just excited.” Rachel looked a little perplexed, but she reached out and gently rubbed Faith’s hand.

Not wanting to talk more about their babies, Carolyn led Rachel out the front door to play in her favorite hideaway. Soon the hedge enveloped them like a little cocoon. They sang songs they had learned at school and brainstormed about how to make money. The two friends stayed there until Mary Ellen called them for supper.

The evening breezed by, and after supper Rachel's mom came to pick up her daughter.

"Bye!" Carolyn called to her friend. "See you tomorrow!"

As Mary Ellen cleaned up the supper dishes, she asked, "How did your evening go?"

"Good," Carolyn said, beaming. "Rachel was so kind to Faith. Did you see what she did? She rubbed Faith's hand!"

"Yes, I saw," Mary Ellen replied, smiling back. "It warmed my heart too."

10

Surgery

One Sunday evening a year later, Eldon felt a bad case of cabin fever descending after a long day of dealing with fussy babies. "Let's go on a drive," he proposed to Mary Ellen.

Her tired face lit up. "Sure, the babies like drives. It might settle them down a bit."

Phyllis overheard the conversation and came running. "Are we going on a drive?" she asked excitedly. "I'll pack my doll and my purse. Can we take the kittens along too?"

Her parents laughed. "The doll can go, but I think the kittens need to stay here," Mary Ellen chuckled.

After a flurry of loading, the Bontragers settled into the car and started down the road. Although a drive through the countryside might seem like a minor outing to many, for the often-housebound Bontragers it was a treat. Even LaVon sat quietly, not teasing anyone for a change, and Phyllis's small nose was pressed to the window. "It's fun to go on a drive, but it makes me tired when I try to look at everything." She rubbed her eyes with her fists.

Mary Ellen glanced at Eldon. "Those eyes just aren't fixing themselves, are they?"

Eldon sighed. "No, they aren't. I wonder if it's time to do something about them. Why don't you see if you can get an appointment to check them out?"

Mary Ellen agreed, and the conversation died away as they filled their souls on the blessed quietness in the car and the brilliant sunset over the prairie. Wistfully Eldon checked out the growth of the wheat in the fields they were passing. The green rows beckoned to him. *Someday I'm going to farm again.*

All too soon dusk had descended, and it was time to head back home. Mary Ellen yawned as they pulled into the driveway. The night ahead would likely be as difficult as always, but the short reprieve had been soothing for her weary nerves.

Eldon grinned at her in the semi-darkness. "Did you have fun?"

"Yes, I did," she said emphatically. "We should do this more often. I feel better when I get out of the house for a bit. And I think the girls do too."

"I needed a change of scenery as much as you did," Eldon admitted. He stepped out of the car, stretched his arms toward the starry sky, then turned to start unloading the sleepy children.

June arrived, bringing four-year-old Phyllis's first appointment with Dr. McCoy in Hutchinson. His quiet, kindly demeanor quickly won their trust as he carefully shone a flashlight into her little blue eyes.

"Yes, her eyes are definitely crossed," he said when he finished the examination. "The technical term for her condition is strabismus. Her eyes don't look at the same place at the same time, which makes it hard for her to focus. The typical cause of this is poor eye muscles. Have her eyes been crossed since birth?"

"Yes, they have," Mary Ellen answered. "We thought maybe as she grew, they would fix themselves." She rubbed the back of her neck.

"And sometimes they do," Dr. McCoy reassured her. "But if a child hasn't outgrown it by three years old, she will probably need surgery." He laid down his flashlight. "The good news is this surgery is usually successful. It should straighten out her eyes permanently."

Eldon and Mary Ellen nodded. They had been expecting surgery, so the news did not come as a surprise to them.

"When would the surgery be?" Eldon asked. "We would like to get her fixed up soon."

"Well, if it works for you, I could do it next week. Then she will need to stay in the hospital for a day or two. I want to make sure no pressure builds up in her eyes and that no infection develops." At their nods, Dr. McCoy pulled out his schedule book to write in the appointment.

The next week, they took Phyllis to Grace Hospital in Hutchinson for her scheduled surgery. Even though the little girl was outwardly calm, Mary Ellen could tell by her tense face that she was terrified. Mary Ellen herself felt nervous as they sat in the waiting room.

Finally the double doors to the hallway opened, and Dr. McCoy stepped through. "Good morning, Phyllis," he smiled.

Phyllis stifled a sob and buried her face in her mother's shoulder. Mary Ellen willed herself to relax so she could reassure her fearful daughter.

The doctor explained the surgery again, then turned to Phyllis. "Now it's surgery time. Are you ready to be able to see better?" She did not reply but got up and walked stiffly over to him. Mary Ellen breathed a sigh of relief as they disappeared through the doors without a fuss. Quietly she and Eldon prayed as they waited.

Before an hour had passed, the doctor came back through the doors. "Well, the surgery went well." Pausing before them, he smiled at their relieved expressions. "At this point I foresee no complications; I think you can expect a full recovery. But we will be able to tell better once she wakes up." He headed back toward the doors, beckoning. "I'll take you to her room and you can sit with her while she comes out of anesthesia."

Eldon and Mary Ellen followed him into the room and sat beside the big bed holding a quiet little Phyllis. Since both eyes were covered with bandages, it was hard to tell if she was asleep or awake. They jumped when she finally croaked, "I'm thirsty. May I have a drink?"

"Well, hello Phyllis!" Eldon jumped up and headed for the door. "I'll ask the nurses to get you a drink."

He soon returned with a bottle of soda. "Would you like some root beer?" he asked, and he was rewarded with a sleepy smile. He put the straw to Phyllis's mouth, and she took a sip before lying back to rest.

That evening, when the doctor was making his rounds, he stopped by to check on his patient. "Phyllis, shall we get rid of these bandages?"

She nodded, and he carefully removed the wrappings while Eldon and Mary Ellen held their breath. Finally the little eyes were uncovered. Sitting on the bed beside her, the doctor asked, "Can you see?" Phyllis nodded again and smiled. Dr. McCoy carefully shone a flashlight into her eyes. Although they were watery and bloodshot, he seemed happy with the results. "It looks good," he reported, sitting back and switching off his light. "I think she should be ready to go home tomorrow."

True to his word, Phyllis was released the next morning. She was still weak but was glad to be home. It didn't take her long to return to her usual lively self. For a while, a sticky overnight discharge meant she couldn't open her eyes in the morning, and this always caused a bit of panic. "Somebody take me to the bathroom," she would cry as soon as she woke up. Carolyn would take her to the bathroom and help her wipe her eyes gently until they opened and she could see.

Every day Phyllis's vision and focus improved. Soon she could see as well as any other little girl. For Eldon and Mary Ellen, it was encouraging to go through a medical experience that brought such obvious and measurable results after all the futile doctoring they had experienced with Lynette and Faith.

As Phyllis was recovering from surgery, Kansas was hit with the torrential rains that caused the Mississippi River Flood of 1965. "I've never seen so much rainfall," Eldon exclaimed one day as he sloshed up the steps into the house. "I hear that the town of Newton is in awfully bad shape, with people sitting on their housetops waiting to be rescued by boat. That's only thirty miles from here! And even as far away as Denver, Colorado, there are flash floods with walls of water fifteen feet high moving into the city."

"This is so unreal," Mary Ellen agreed. "Normally we are wishing for rain, not trying to deal with such a deluge. What would it be like to lose your home like that?"

With the Arkansas River rising fast, Hutchinson began preparing for the worst. Eldon helped the other men of the town pile sandbags in front of businesses to keep out the water. "I'm afraid those dikes won't hold," he told Mary Ellen when he got home. "But it's all we can do to keep out the water."

Day after day the rain continued. The river kept rising, and true to Eldon's prediction, it flooded its banks and broke through the sand dikes they had built throughout the city. It was the worst flood anyone could remember, even though the damage in Hutchinson was minimal compared to other areas of the state. Even so, major highways were closed and flash-flood warnings were issued.

"I heard that more than eight hundred homes were destroyed in Dodge City," Eldon told Mary Ellen one night. Wistfully he added, "I would love to go help with the cleanup." But even as he said it, he knew it would never happen. He was needed at home.

"Let's drive out and see the high water," LaVon suggested.

They all climbed into the car and headed out the lane. It was quickly obvious they weren't the only ones who were curious. Along with many other sightseers, they crept bumper to bumper onto the bridge over the Arkansas River. Peering out the windows, they gazed in trepidation at the dirty water raging just inches below the bridge.

LaVon's scared voice came from the back seat. "What if the bridge collapses?"

"Oh, I think it's strong enough," Eldon reassured him.

Thankfully the storm eventually passed, and the water receded. The businesses cleaned up their buildings and life continued. The farmers breathed a sigh of relief at the timing of the storm. The June flood hadn't ruined the crops, since they wouldn't be ready to harvest until September. Still, it was an experience the locals would never forget.

The Mental Institution

Although crying babies had been a fact of life in the Bontrager home for years, the tension finally mounted to an unendurable level. Lack of sleep sharpened tempers until it became easy to let hot words fly and allow injured feelings to smolder. The almost endless fussing from the girls ranged from discontented grunts to prolonged screaming sessions. Eldon and Mary Ellen felt they might literally lose their minds in the face of the constant need and clamor of caring for the girls along with the rest of their lively tribe.

The Amish and Mennonites always encourage caring for their own people, but the exhausted parents of Lynette and Faith were dangling at the end of their slender connection to sanity. Very few other options were available except for a good mental institution. They finally gave that option some attention. Although everything in them recoiled against what seemed like the ultimate betrayal, Eldon and Mary Ellen knew they were reaching their limit. Something needed to change.

In 1966, Eldon and Mary Ellen heard of Winfield State Hospital, a large home for severely disabled people in Winfield, Kansas, about a hundred miles from their home. The hospital's goals for helping mentally disabled children live in society were ahead of the times, although overcrowding of the facility had challenged their ambitions. At this point, the organization was mostly centered on providing custodial care. The huge facility housed up to fourteen hundred children at full capacity, with many levels of conditions among various wards.

After Eldon and Mary Ellen heard about this institute, they began to feel encouragement from others to check it out. Well-meaning friends said maybe it would be a good place for Lynette and Faith.

"It would be easier to follow Lynette and Faith's caskets to their graves than to see them go there," Eldon muttered one night as he lay in bed, exhausted and defeated. "How could we ever admit them to a mental institute?"

"I can't even let myself think about it," Mary Ellen said, staring at the ceiling as she lay beside him. "And no one is saying that we must, although there have been enough hints." There was a short pause as she grappled with the decision they were facing. Hesitantly she added, "I heard Lucille Yoder has been admitted there and is doing well."

"Do you think we should make an appointment to see what they have to offer?"

"I suppose we could at least do that, but that doesn't mean we have to send them there."

Eldon rolled over to face the wall. "No, we don't have to send them there. But I think it's time to look at options. We just can't do this much longer. Especially now that we're expecting another baby."

They made an appointment and were soon on their way with the girls for a visit and an evaluation. As they neared Winfield, they spotted the hospital grounds on a hill. Smoke rolled out of chimneys protruding from the tops of the tall block buildings.

Mary Ellen shivered. "It looks like a prison," she observed warily as they drove closer.

Eldon felt the same. *Is this place the answer we're so desperately praying for? Or are we giving in to the temptation of abandoning our children?* The bombardment of alternating hope and guilt was overwhelming.

They parked close to the entrance. With feet of lead, they got out of their car, removed the girls from the back seat, and carried them up the sidewalk to the front entrance. The ominous doors swung open to admit them, then clanged shut behind them as they walked through. The loud bang reverberated down the bare block hall toward the office.

Mary Ellen closed her eyes for a moment. She did not want to see the many cribs and disabled children. *How can we even consider leaving our babies at a place like this?*

Standing inside the doors, they nearly lost their courage. They were both almost ready to turn around and run away, but desperation prompted them to start walking. Suddenly a door down the long hall swung open, and a lady stepped out. "You must be the Bontragers," she said warmly. "I'm Helen Wright. Come this way." Eldon and Mary Ellen, still carrying the girls, followed her into a sparsely furnished office.

Mrs. Wright introduced them to all the administration members who oversaw the care of the patients. Eldon and Mary Ellen asked many questions and listened carefully to the options available for the girls. "We'll do our best for them," the administrative staff assured them. "Would you mind if we did a more in-depth evaluation? This would give us an idea of the extent of their mental damage. It would also help us know which ward to put the girls in and what kind of treatments they will need."

The parents agreed, watching pensively as a few staff members placed their babies in special chairs and wheeled them away. After a time, they were returned. "Here you go," a nurse said cheerfully, depositing the girls back into their parents' laps. "We'll take some time to discuss the results among ourselves, then we'll meet with you in a few hours."

After a long wait, Mrs. Wright called Eldon and Mary Ellen back to her office, inviting them to sit down. "We think we can help your daughters," she said. "And we don't have a waiting list right now. If you are willing, we would like to admit the girls next week."

Mary Ellen gasped. "I was not expecting to make such a decision today."

Eldon cleared his throat. "This does seem rather fast," he agreed. "We thought there would be others ahead of us, and that we could think over the next step awhile."

Mrs. Wright smiled understandingly. "The decision is yours, of course. But the sooner you get your daughters registered, the sooner they can get care, and the sooner you will have rest."

"We'll think about it," Eldon promised her.

As they carried the babies out to the car, Mary Ellen was almost in shock. "How can I put my girls in an institution?"

Eldon sighed. "I never thought we would need to make this decision. But to be honest, Mary Ellen, I feel like we have no other options. We've worn ourselves out, and we have our other children to live for." His words were determined, and his face was sad.

The decision weighed heavily on the parents all night. They prayed for wisdom as they tossed and turned. But by morning, they were surrounded by peace and hope. Despite the lumps in their throats, they knew what would be best for their family. Eldon placed the call, telling the hospital they would admit Lynette and Faith the following week.

The next Monday morning, after the schoolchildren had left, Mary Ellen carefully bathed and dressed her girls for the last time at home. Eldon helped her get them situated in the car, then he placed a bag containing the girls' clothes in the trunk. They drove to Mary Ellen's parents and dropped off Phyllis. Since they couldn't bear the thought of explaining to the children what they were planning to do, they had simply told them nothing. *They'll find out soon enough,* Eldon thought grimly.

Guiding the car onto the highway, they began the two-hour ride to

Winfield. The car was quiet as the sober parents thought about what they were doing. Behind them, the girls lay on the back seats, which had been reclined to make them comfortable.

Mary Ellen turned her head to watch the girls, memorizing their faces with the chronically vacant eyes and their small bodies—so twisted and imperfect, yet so familiar and dear. *Our little babies. How can I do this to them?* "Are you sure this is the right thing to do?" she asked Eldon again. In her anguish, she kept questioning their decision.

Eldon's voice held a quiver, but his face was set. "I can't go on like we have been the last while. It's them or me."

Mary Ellen said no more—but her heart squeezed with the agony of what they were about to do.

Once again they carried the girls up the sidewalk to the entrance. In silence they made their way to the office, where a kind nurse was expecting them. Pulling out a file, she laid it on the desk in front of her. "Let's see," she said, her finger scanning the report. "Lynette is ten years old, and Faith is four. Is that correct?"

The parents nodded dumbly.

"What lovely names!" She smiled at the two girls, then turned her gaze to the parents. "It looks like everything is in order. You are welcome to come back and help them get settled, but feel free to go home any time you want to. You both look tired and in need of rest."

The nurse buckled Faith and Lynette into wheelchairs, then Eldon pushed Lynette while Mary Ellen pushed Faith as they headed up the ramp to the ward on the second floor. They were sure the girls did not understand what was going on. Not wanting to leave, Eldon and Mary Ellen stayed for an hour. They saw the beds the girls would be sleeping in and marveled at all the equipment that would greatly aid in the comfort and care they would receive. But finally they both knew it was time to start for home.

The nurses stepped out of the room so they could say their farewells. "Goodbye, Kaye-Kaye." Mary Ellen stroked her oldest daughter's arm, her mother face contorted with pain. "And goodbye, Faithy." Her voice broke as she turned away.

"Goodbye, girls!" Eldon's voice was cheerful, but tears glistened in his eyes as he rested his hand on Faith's knee. "We'll come back to see you as often as we can."

As they turned toward the door, they knew that for better or for worse, things would never be the same.

The trip home was another silent one. Both parents sat brooding about what they had just done, hoping they had made the right choice. They knew they now had to tell the other children where their babies were.

It was late afternoon when they got back to Grandpa Yoder's place to pick up the children. "Where are Kaye-Kaye and Faith?" Carolyn asked as soon as she climbed into the car, clutching her lunch box and backpack.

Mary Ellen held back the tears that threatened to spill down her cheeks. "We took your sisters to a hospital that is made especially for children like them. There they will get therapy and care we can't give them at home. I know it's hard to understand, but we just couldn't take care of them anymore." She turned away from the shock she saw on Carolyn's face.

Phyllis craned her neck at her mother, looking puzzled. "Why can't we keep our babies? Other families get to."

Eldon looked pained. "Your sisters aren't like other babies. As much as we love them, we know they can get better care where they are now."

But Carolyn still could not believe her sisters were gone. "We didn't even get to say goodbye," she said bitterly.

"I know." Eldon's face was sad. "As soon as we can, we'll take you to visit them."

The next few days were filled with haunting echoes of the girls' voices. Over and over, Mary Ellen's ears perked to the sound of a cry, a cough, or a grunt, only to be reminded that the girls were no longer there.

"I want Kaye-Kaye and Faith to come home again," Phyllis wept one night at bedtime.

"I know, Phyllis," Mary Ellen sympathized, rubbing her daughter's back.

"So do I. But the nurses can take better care of them at a place that has lots of babies like them."

Carolyn frowned. "I could feed them just fine. I helped you all I could. Besides, they were *our* babies."

"Oh, Carolyn! You were such a good help to me," Mary Ellen reassured her. "I could never have done it without you." Inwardly she hoped Carolyn could have a more carefree childhood now. It sometimes seemed the heavy responsibilities that had been thrust on her young shoulders had made her serious beyond her years.

The next few mornings, Eldon found himself tiptoeing around as he got ready for work. "I didn't realize how conscious we were of the babies all the time," he told Mary Ellen. "Each morning when I come out of the bedroom, I walk softly and close the door quietly so I won't disturb them. Then I suddenly remember they aren't here."

A knife turned in Mary Ellen's heart. And yet she had to admit that she felt more rested than she had in years. She could see Eldon felt refreshed too.

On Wednesday evening, it seemed strange for the whole family to be heading out to the car for prayer meeting at church.

"Who is taking care of the babies?" Myron asked, then he stopped. "Oh."

And everyone remembered. This was the way it would be from now on. The car was quiet as they all kept their thoughts to themselves. How they missed the girls and mourned the huge hole they left! Yet how free they felt to be able to do things a normal family would do. How could such pain and such relief be in their hearts at the same time?

Slowly Eldon's nerves began to heal, and Mary Ellen enjoyed the lovely gift of rest as her stress level dropped. Both parents were starting to comprehend just how much tension they had been under. How had they ever done it?

The family was beginning to adjust to the new normal, but Eldon and

Mary Ellen knew it was important to take the other children to Winfield soon to see the girls in their new home and find closure and acceptance. Although money for fuel was tight, they made the trip on a Sunday afternoon three weeks after the girls were admitted.

The children's eyes were huge as they walked through the long, gray wards. Rows of white iron beds lined the walls. In each bed lay a disabled child. A sharp odor reminded the Bontragers of the familiar difficulty of keeping so many incontinent children dry and clean.

Together they walked up the ramp to the ward on the second floor where the girls lived with twenty other children with disabilities. What a joyful reunion they had when they found their beloved babies! Although it was difficult to tell how intentional Lynette and Faith's responses were, they seemed pleased to see their family. They were in a good mood, laughing and flapping their arms. Happily Carolyn, Phyllis, LaVon, and Myron cooed to the girls and patted their hands. It was a delight for the whole family to see their babies so happy and comfortable in their new home.

"Oh, Mom!" Phyllis coaxed. "Let's take them home with us. See? They aren't crying now!"

Mary Ellen smiled through the lump in her throat, but Eldon shook his head. "They'll be better off here." He could see the girls were getting excellent care. Their small bodies had already gained weight, and both girls seemed more relaxed. However, the good results still did not take away the responsibility and guilt he felt as a father.

A nurse came in as the Bontragers were preparing to leave. "Do the girls spend most of their days in these seats?" Eldon asked her.

"They spend most mornings in them," she replied. "In the afternoon, we put them on tumbling mats. They love to roll around on those, and then they sleep better at night."

Eldon nodded. "They never did sleep very well. How would you say they're doing here?"

"They're doing great!" The nurse cheerfully smoothed Lynette's curls. "They both eat so well. Lynette eats like a little pig." She chuckled affectionately.

Mary Ellen smiled. The hospital seemed to have an excellent therapy program, and she felt both girls would continue to respond positively as time went on. The caregivers did well to keep the hyperactive tension down and therefore got more interaction from the children. How could the Bontragers take back their girls when they were doing so well here?

Suddenly Lynette started crying and getting restless. Mary Ellen reached down and stroked her arm. "We love you, Kaye-Kaye, and we will be back," she said lovingly. Did Lynette sense they were getting ready to leave? She turned and hugged little Faith. "I love you, Faith," she whispered in her ear. Then, with one last glance at their babies, the family headed down the ramp, through the long hall, and out the door.

"What a relief to see them doing so well!" Mary Ellen said as they walked to the car. "I just hope they don't forget us."

"I'm glad they don't seem homesick, though," Eldon said. "That would be even worse."

The children got into the car with conflict in their hearts. On one hand, they were glad to see their sisters so happy. But on the other hand, they wanted them at home, not in that huge, cold building.

The decision Eldon and Mary Ellen had agonized over was received with varying opinions in the community. While everyone wanted to be supportive, few people could really understand the deep repercussions the Bontragers were reeling through. Eldon and Mary Ellen tried to forgive the friends who thought it was awful they had placed their daughters in a mental hospital. Those people did not understand the heavy toll that caring for multiple disabled children could take on a marriage and family. The Bontragers also tried to be gracious to those who thought they must be delighted to be free of the stress of caring for their daughters. How could those people know the pain of leaving one's children with strangers?

As they slowly adjusted to life without the girls, the family found themselves as busy as ever. "I wonder how I cared for the girls as long as I did," Mary Ellen confided to her sister Clara Mae one day. "I miss them as you would miss anyone who is absent from the family, but at the same time,

I have so much to do! How did we ever have time for them?"

"God gave you an added strength while they were in your home." Clara Mae's wise words were confident. "You cared for them well. You took seriously what God had handed you."

"I feel guilty about feeling so free. But I also feel rested, like a new person."

"I believe God led you to put them in the state hospital," Clara Mae encouraged. "Don't second-guess yourself."

It took time for the children at home to adjust. They often talked about their babies being so far away, although every other month they made the two-hour trip to visit them. Together Eldon, Mary Ellen, and their four remaining children began to form a new normal in their home without Lynette and Faith.

A Dream Come True

Guilt... The initial benefit of rest from the incessant care of the girls was quickly compromised as guilt set in. It dogged Eldon's heels and gnawed at his heart. He had always strived to live an honorable life and faithfully do his duty. But now, leaving his helpless daughters in the care of people he did not know haunted him with shame. How could a man hold his head high when he had abandoned those who needed him most?

The blissful tranquility of uninterrupted nights soon saw him tossing and turning until the wee hours. Sleeping pills brought only minimal relief. His naturally optimistic outlook dimmed, and even the rare pleasure of a day of cleanup with his Prairie Construction work crew in Topeka after a tornado failed to put a spring in his step.

Still, time moved on. On August 23, 1966, three months after Lynette and Faith had been moved to Winfield, another little girl was born to Eldon and Mary Ellen. Tiny Marilyn Elizabeth, named after her grandmother Lizzie Yoder, was a ray of sunshine in that dark, grieving time. Her bright eyes sparkled with joy, and her happy smiles and giggles brought both healing to the wounded hearts around her and an assurance of normal development. The family doted on the new baby, and she spent her days being passed from one set of eager arms to the next.

"I'm afraid we're spoiling her," Eldon remarked sheepishly as he lay on the floor one evening, making faces for his tiny appreciative audience.

"Yes, I think so too," agreed Mary Ellen, smiling from the rocking chair. "But it's such a joy to watch her learn and do things that Lynette and Faith couldn't."

As time went on and the Bontragers had more time to focus on things outside their home, they began to experience increasing dissatisfaction with their location among so many neighbors who, while friendly, did not display Christian character.

"We need to get our children away from all this ungodly influence," Eldon told Mary Ellen one evening.

"They love to play with the neighbor children," Mary Ellen agreed. "And they aren't all a good influence."

"It feels like our children live like city kids," Eldon said. "They run and play and don't have enough responsibility."

Mary Ellen sighed. "Yes, I should make them work harder. But it's hard to make them stay home when there are so many neighbors playing right outside our house."

In the spring of 1968, an old church house came up for sale close to the nearby town of Arlington, Kansas. Eldon decided to go to the auction and see what it sold for, thinking he could move it into town for a cabinet shop. He bought the building for $150.

Unfortunately, the structure ended up being too tall and too hard to move. So instead of having a shop, Eldon was now the owner of a cute little country church house. In the meantime, their church, Center Amish Mennonite, was overflowing and considering an outreach, so the little church house became a perfect fit for the need. As Center Church continued to figure out the details, its leaders began asking for volunteers to attend the fledgling church.

Although Eldon owned the church building, he struggled to summon up interest to attend services there. One evening after a service at their home church, he expressed his feelings to Mary Ellen. "I suppose I could have offered to attend the church in Arlington tonight, but I just didn't want to."

"I understand," Mary Ellen said. "Change is hard, and we've had plenty of it. I think God knows your heart."

Later that evening Eldon picked up the ringing phone. "Hello, Eldon speaking." On the other end was an enthusiastic realtor, informing him there was a farm for sale close to the church he had just purchased. Eldon's eyes widened as he discussed details and price. He was grinning when he hung up the phone.

"It's incredible," he exulted to Mary Ellen. "There's a farm for sale just a few miles west of the church I bought. And it's within a price range we can afford!"

Eagerly the Bontrager couple debated this new development. The farm was located around fifteen miles from most of the other church people, which felt like a long way out of the community. But this did not bother Eldon. "I like the idea of moving away from the center of everything," he told Mary Ellen. "I think it would be a better environment to raise our children."

Mary Ellen agreed, feeling a pang at the thought of leaving her parents and sister. "It would be so nice to be on a farm. I know you would enjoy it, and I think the children would too."

After they had discussed the farm for a few days, they decided to present the idea to the children. "Children," Eldon began at the supper table one evening, "you know my dream has always been to live on a farm. My heart is in farming more than factory working or carpentry."

"What are you trying to say?" eleven-year-old Carolyn asked, eyeing him suspiciously.

"Well, there's a farm for sale for a good price. But it is far away. It would mean moving out of the community and even going to a new school."

Phyllis's eyes grew large. "I don't want to leave my friends!"

"Oh, come on," LaVon butted in. At almost ten years old, he was always ready for an adventure. "Let's go! I've always wanted to live on a farm!"

"It is far away," Eldon repeated. "And I hear it's a junk heap. But we can work together and make this a family project." His eyes shone with anticipation. Bringing order to chaos, working together, cleaning up messes—these were all things that were high on his list of enjoyment. Who needed a vacation when you could have a fulfilling work project? Eldon loved the thought of teaching his children the rewards of diligent labor.

The family was eager to see the place. The following day, they climbed into the car and headed toward the farm. It seemed they drove forever until they finally turned right and followed the long, straight lane as it bumped across train tracks on its way to the large, abandoned farmstead.

As they pulled up, their wide eyes scanned the disarray spread before them. Trash was scattered around, and an old railcar sat nestled in tall weeds by the barn. Eldon couldn't even drive close to the barn for all the neglected machinery in the way. Cars were strewn randomly over the property. Forlorn outbuildings sat here and there, with grass growing through the rotting slatted walls. The place looked hopeless and forlorn.

Eldon parked the car, and the family climbed out. Gingerly they picked their way up to the ramshackle house and peered inside. Chunks of plaster from the ceiling were scattered all over the floor. Wallpaper hung in shreds. The house looked like it had been uninhabited for years.

Eldon whistled through his teeth. "This is a mess." His comment was quite the understatement.

As they tiptoed through the house, a mouse scurried out from under the rubble. Myron forgot his caution and took off after it, yelling and trying to stomp it to death. The mouse shot down a hole in the bathroom where the plumbing came through the floor beside the clawfoot bathtub. "Lost him," Myron said regretfully, rejoining the others.

"It must be years since someone cleaned up here!" Mary Ellen exclaimed as they descended into the cellar. "Phew!" The basement was full of dog feces that reeked up the entire house. She pinched her nose shut with one hand while holding almost-two-year-old Marilyn in the other arm.

Eldon's optimism was in full swing. "At least it has a good foundation," he said as they went back upstairs and toured the rest of the house. "And no windows are broken." The mess did not change his opinion. To him, the farm felt like both a challenge and a dream come true.

Riding the wave of Eldon's enthusiasm, the family decided the farm was the place for them. The title was signed off, and they became the new owners. Then the summer's work began. With Eldon at the helm, the family spent days at their future home, picking up trash, starting bonfires, and getting rid of load after load of junk.

The neighbors were glad to see the farm being cleaned up. Joe Steele, the farmer to the south, drawled, "If I saw any other farm with that much smoke, I'd call the fire trucks. But I know it's just the Bontragers doing some more cleanup."

One of the first things they did was plant trees. This job was placed squarely on the shoulders of LaVon and Myron, who would have much preferred exploring their new stomping grounds over planting baby trees and watering them endlessly. "We need to get them growing," Eldon encouraged. "It will take years till they give any kind of windbreak." The farm was on a slight rise, and the wide, flat prairie surrounding them was home to winds ranging from playfully boisterous to viciously brutal.

"It seems a few more weeks wouldn't make that much difference," LaVon whispered to Myron.

"Yeah, I agree," Myron replied as they dug another hole, put in a small tree, and covered it with dirt. They stomped down the ground around it to make sure the tree was secure before dousing it with a bucket of water to give it a good start. Then they moved on to the next marked spot and started planting another tree. Even though they didn't understand the urgency of planting right away, they did the best they could and still found some time for play.

With that project taken care of, Eldon began building a fence along the driveway. Day after day the work went on. Eldon's heart soared at the improvements he saw happening, and he enlisted his children to help paint the new fence white.

The sun beat down on them as they painted. "I hope this is worth all the sweat," Phyllis said. She pushed some strands of hair out of her face as she dipped her brush and stroked it on the next board.

"Oh, I think it looks nice!" Carolyn was catching her father's vision. "There's nothing like a white fence to line a driveway."

Inside the house, Mary Ellen worked hard as well, cleaning the filthy house from top to bottom. Even bleach didn't eliminate the smell right away, but at least the rooms felt cleaner. Next came a coat of fresh paint, and it was amazing how much better things looked. A makeshift kitchen was set up in an extra room until Eldon had time to remodel the original one. By the time August and moving day arrived, the house was in fine, livable condition.

Thankfully, there were already multiple large trees around the house, providing much-needed shade from the broiling sun. In the pasture, the cows enjoyed a pleasant oasis as well. An underground spring kept the lower part of the pasture green even in tinder-dry weather, and the cows grazed there luxuriantly.

The Bontragers settled down to life on the farm. LaVon was old enough to help with the work, and with time he learned to love his new responsibilities. The pony had moved with him. Every afternoon he saddled her and

The Arlington farmhouse that the Bontragers cleaned up and renovated.

went out to check the cattle for drooping ears and general animal health.

At first Eldon still worked for Prairie Construction. Often it was late by the time he came home. With the added work of running a farm, it became harder and harder for him to keep up while still working on the construction crew. Finally he made the decision to leave Prairie Construction. He purchased his own building in Arlington to do trim work and make cabinets. As his sons grew, they both worked in the family business. The strengths and weaknesses of the three menfolk complemented each other, and the business prospered.

Mary Ellen had known it would be different to live twelve miles away from her parents and twenty miles from Hutchinson where they did all their shopping. The little white country church house they attended now with several other families from Center Amish Mennonite was a change as well. But thankfully, some things hadn't changed. Highway 61 still passed by on the south side of the farm, and their familiar railroad track, the main freight line from Chicago to Los Angeles, ran right across the lane. The trains still blew their whistles through the fabric of the new life the Bontragers were weaving.

The longer they lived on the farm, the more they found healing for their frazzled, stressed minds and bodies. They continued to visit Lynette and Faith every other month, but besides that life settled into yet another normal—the most normal, happy life the children had known.

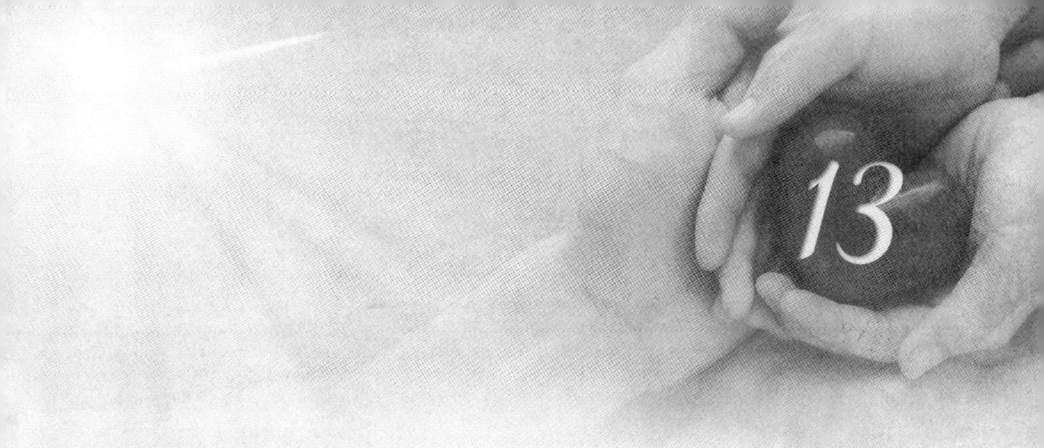

13

Making New Friends

When school started that fall, the Bontrager children had another change to face. Their old school had been filled with many Amish and Mennonite children, but at Arlington Public School, they were the only ones. Each grade in this new school was in a different classroom. Carolyn was in grade six, and LaVon and Myron were together in grade four, since LaVon had to repeat second grade. Little Phyllis was in grade two.

The first day of school arrived with the expected amount of trepidation. The Bontrager children tried not to attract more attention than they already were generating. Their eyes were wide as they tried to figure out this new setting.

Their eyes weren't the only wide ones. The other children watched them cautiously. They didn't know what to think of these strange new students.

"Are you Amish?" one boy finally asked.

"No, we're Mennonite," Carolyn corrected, but it made no difference. From the very beginning, they were dubbed "the Amish," and the Bontrager children could not explain otherwise.

Despite their differences, they began making new friends and learned to love school. "I like that no one here in Arlington knows our family," Carolyn said one evening.

"Why don't you want people to know our family?" Mary Ellen asked.

"So we can just be normal." Carolyn dropped her head. "They don't know we have babies at Winfield."

Mary Ellen winced. "I understand how hard it must be for you sometimes," she said. "But your sisters aren't a shame unless you allow them to be. Even if the children did know, they would still love you for who you are."

"I'm still glad we can have a new start here," Carolyn declared.

The first month, the children ate their lunches in the school cafeteria every day just like they had done at their old school. But when the bill for $35 arrived, Mary Ellen's eyebrows rose. "That's a lot of money for lunches! I am sure I could make your lunches for half that price."

"Do whatever is the least work for you," Eldon encouraged. He knew Mary Ellen cringed at spending unnecessary money and trusted her to make the best decision.

"Making our own lunches would be kind of a hassle, but the girls could help me, and it would go fast. It would be nice to save the money we pay for lunches in the cafeteria. It wouldn't hurt if Carolyn would eat less anyway."

Eldon smiled. "She's a growing girl. I wouldn't worry about how much she eats. The children need good meals at school. And as you know, the boys' stomachs are bottomless, so there would be a lot of lunch to pack!"

"That's true, but..." Mary Ellen wavered. Then her thriftiness won out. "Let's try packing lunches and see what we can save next month."

It became Carolyn's job to prepare the four lunches while her mother went out to feed the twenty-five calves. Mary Ellen loved going outdoors as the sun was rising. The birds sang, and the world seemed at peace.

One school morning two-year-old Marilyn was up early, so Mary Ellen took her along to feed the calves so she wouldn't disturb the routine. "I like the cows," Marilyn declared, holding her mother's hand and taking big steps to keep up. "Can I feed them?"

Mary Ellen gave her a bucket with feed. "Here, I'll help you pour it in the manger." Marilyn lifted the bucket as high over her head as she could. The calves crowded around her, pushing her until she plopped down on the dirty floor. Wails pierced the barn as Mary Ellen picked up the indignant child and wiped her off as well as she could.

"Mean old cows!" Marilyn glared at the frisky calves, kicking at the closest one.

Mary Ellen hid a snicker. "They're not mean, they're just hungry. Here, let me finish. You run to the house and ask Carolyn to clean you up. I'll be there in a bit." Mary Ellen watched Marilyn walk gingerly to the house, her dress plastered with muck. "She sure goes through life wide open," she murmured. Smiling, she finished the feeding and headed to the house, where she found the children almost ready for school.

One day just before Christmas, the children burst excitedly through the door. Phyllis was waving a yellow paper that was carefully folded and sealed with a sticker. "Mom! We're having a program on Friday for all the parents. You'll come, won't you?" She handed the paper to her mother.

Mary Ellen read the invitation, then laid it on the table. "I'll see if I have time."

Phyllis's face fell. "Please?"

Mary Ellen felt she hardly had time for something extra, but how could she resist her daughter? "I'll see if I can make it."

Phyllis twirled excitedly. "The whole school is going to do something about Kansas."

"Phyllis!" Myron was shocked. "We're supposed to keep it a secret."

Phyllis froze and clapped her hands over her mouth.

Mary Ellen chuckled. "That's okay," she encouraged the stricken girl. "It's hard to keep secrets. I'll pretend a mouse coughed just then and I wasn't able to hear you." She winked at Phyllis, who grinned sheepishly and headed off to change out of her school clothes.

Mary Ellen placed the program invitation on the counter so she wouldn't forget about it. Little by little, the Bontragers were making new friends. This community was beginning to feel like home.

Eldon faced his own challenges in building friendships in Arlington. Farmland was cheap in the area, and Eldon's operation grew quickly. He bought or rented several fields, and nothing brought him more joy than spending his days on a tractor working the land.

Arlington was a small, close-knit community, and the arrival of the Bontragers and the new Mennonite church had not gone unnoticed. As the Bontrager footprint expanded, they made more and more friends. Most of the neighbors loved the energy and enthusiasm the Bontrager family put into their projects. A few farmers, however, were suspicious of newcomers and kept Eldon at arm's length.

One spring day Eldon was about six miles from home, driving a load of cattle past one of his fields and admiring the lush green carpet of wheat seedlings. The last few days had brought some beautiful rains, and the wheat was growing by leaps and bounds. He turned onto the pasture lane that twisted through the field along the top of a steep terrace. But the mud was much deeper than he had realized, and soon the heavy trailer bogged down and came to a stop.

Now what do I do? Although he had often waved to Arnold Chase, who owned the nearby farm, he had yet to sense a reciprocating friendship. Eldon hated the thought of asking him to use his phone to call for help. "I guess I'll have to walk to Arlington to call home," he said, resolutely getting out of his pickup and starting on the two-mile trek.

When he returned an hour later, Eldon was surprised to see that Arnold had just arrived with a tractor to pull him out. Working together, they were able to pull the truck and trailer back onto the road.

"Thank you, Arnold." Eldon's gratitude was sincere. "I really appreciate your help! I walked to town to call home for a tractor, but now I see that wouldn't have been necessary."

"No problem," Arnold said. "If you ever need help again, don't walk to town. My shop door is always unlocked. There's a phone in there and a fridge full of pop. Treat your boys someday."

Eldon shook hands with his neighbor. "And I always want to be there for you too. Thanks again for your help."

From that moment on, Eldon felt accepted and welcomed into the farming community. He was always grateful for the help and support the local farmers gave each other.

14

The Blizzard

The Kansas climate was rough and rugged. During the summer, blistering winds came screaming up from Texas and Oklahoma, whipping fields into dust storms, ripping laundry off wash lines, and turning every carefully coifed hairdo into a tousle. Winter brought its own winds, this time from the north, whistling through the tightest walls and waltzing in through tiny cracks around windows. Even in the freshly remodeled Bontrager house, the winter winds sometimes froze liquids in the upstairs bedrooms during the night.

One winter storm in particular surpassed the norm. On Sunday, February 21, 1971, the worst blizzard of the twentieth century hit Kansas. For three days the heavy snow came down, with ferocious winds whipping it around and packing it into massive drifts, shutting down businesses, roads, and railroads. When the snow finally stopped, the winds did not. The situation quickly became an emergency for both people and animals. Aid programs used military cargo planes to airdrop hay to cattle stranded in far-flung pastures.

Despite the screaming wind and deep snow, the chores had to continue on the Bontrager farm. The cows kept producing milk even though the world was frozen stiff. "It sure is cold out there," Eldon puffed as he set down his pail on the fourth morning. "It wouldn't be so bad if the wind would stop blowing."

But the wind didn't stop. It howled through the cracks in the windows, rustling the curtains. It whipped around the barnyard, deepening some drifts and flattening others. At the end of the driveway, the drifts completely engulfed the railroad tracks.

"Those drifts must be eight feet deep," Myron said, looking out across the front field. "I wonder how long it will take before the trains come through?"

"It'll probably take them awhile since the snow is packed so hard and deep," Eldon said. "They'll need to clear the tracks somehow. The trains need to get supplies and mail to people all across the state."

When they thought about their basement full of food, the Bontragers paused to thank God. "Father, bless those who are less fortunate," Eldon prayed. "And may we be truly thankful for our blessings."

The days passed quietly in their isolated world. The boys helped Eldon feed the animals, and the girls had hot food and drinks ready for them when they came inside. Not until Friday morning did the tempest die down, with the sun shining brightly. Around midmorning, the Bontragers heard a train whistle in the distance. Everyone ran to the windows and saw a very unusual train coming down the tracks! Four engines, puffing out great clouds of smoke, pushed a huge snowplow through the drifts. The snow spewed out on each side, creating even taller piles. But now the track was clear.

The next day the freight trains started running. The children watched the trains pass, one after another. It seemed they would never stop. They had been backed up for miles, just waiting for the tracks to open.

On the Bontrager farm, the blizzard was seen as an adventure. The children spent the first days of the storm with their noses pressed against the icy windowpanes, exclaiming over the ever-growing drifts. By Saturday, Eldon had dug paths around the yard and the worst of the cold had abated. When the boys came downstairs, they pulled on their boots and outer garments and rushed outside.

"Look at that!" LaVon yelled. "We can walk right up to the haymow!" Snow had blown against the barn, forming a slope all the way up to the haymow door. The boys ran up and down the hard-packed hill, their cloudy breath puffing into the clear stillness.

After a bit, the girls ventured outside too. They made tracks out to the pond, where the wind had swept the ice clean. Cautiously they stomped around the edge until they agreed the ice was thick enough to hold them.

"Whee!" four-year-old Marilyn cried as she slid out onto the pond. "This is so much fun!"

Carolyn and Phyllis joined her. Their shrieks of laughter filled the air as they slipped and slid. Kansas was not often blessed with skating weather, so there was plenty of opportunity for a good chortle at someone's clumsy collapse. Finally a fresh gale picked up speed, chasing the girls back to the house.

Snow days were vacation days at the Bontrager home, and when the girls got back to the house, their mother had steaming cups of hot cocoa waiting. They sipped the sweet chocolate with relish as they regaled Mary Ellen with descriptions of the wintry world outside.

"Let's play a game," Carolyn suggested as they drained their mugs.

"Yay!" shouted Marilyn, who was always in the mood for a party.

"What shall we play?" Phyllis asked.

"Why don't we play Probe?" Mary Ellen suggested. She loved playing games with her girls, and Probe was a favorite. Marilyn was too young to help, but she enjoyed watching. They played all afternoon, guessing each other's words, then choosing new ones and guessing again.

Suddenly Mary Ellen gasped. "The sun is going down! I guess I was having too much fun. I need to quit playing and get some supper started." She hurried to the pantry for potatoes, then took them to the sink to wash and peel. Then she put them on the stove for supper. The girls put the game away and set the table for the whole family. It was so different now without Faith and Lynette to feed. They could enjoy a normal meal together.

Eldon attached his plow to the old tractor and scraped the lane until they could get a vehicle out. That weekend, the road grader finally came through, and by Monday morning school resumed. Some of the back roads, however, had drifted shut so deeply that six weeks passed before they finally were opened. It had been quite a storm.

Despite the storm, spring eventually came, and the leaves started budding on the Osage orange trees growing in rows along the back roads and pastures. After the Dust Bowl had swept the plains in the 1930s, the government's Works Progress Administration had planted these fast-growing trees for windbreaks, along with cottonwoods and elms, hoping to prevent more dust from blowing across the plains. The thorny, hard Osage orange wood was especially useful for sturdy fenceposts and good firewood. When cut down, they grew back quickly.

When summer came, the trees dropped their grapefruit-sized fruits, often called hedge balls. These rough green balls were not worth anything except to the squirrels, who shredded the fruit and buried the seeds found in the center. As a result, more trees sprouted, and the hedges became thicker and more impenetrable.

Eldon asked the children to pick up the hedge balls in the pasture so the cattle would not choke on them. To make the job fun, the girls stockpiled the bumpy green fruit close to the henhouse. They waited until Eldon and Mary Ellen were not watching, then they hurled the balls against the side of the small building. The tremendous thuds caused the chickens to become completely unglued. This brought much entertainment to a boring afternoon.

"Our chickens just aren't laying like they used to," Mary Ellen commented one evening at the supper table.

Marilyn's ears grew red, but she said nothing. She knew she was guilty of pestering Mary Ellen's prized fowl.

Marilyn looked sideways at Phyllis. Her partner in crime was innocently spooning green beans into her mouth. Mom would never know what went on in the chicken pen, but in the future the girls tried to lob the hedge balls more gently to tone down the reaction of the hardworking hens inside.

During late summer, the fields of corn were cut to be put up as silage for the winter. Farmers worked together to fill their tall concrete silos with feed for the animals. When one farmer's fields had been stripped, they moved to the next farm and did the same thing.

Today was the day to help Eldon's uncle. Twelve-year-old Myron woke up early so he could drive their tractor the fifteen miles to Henry's farm. As the men gathered, Eldon called to Myron, "Since you're already on the tractor, I'm thinking you're old enough to haul a wagon today."

Myron straightened his shoulders to look as tall as he could on the tractor seat. He was glad he was allowed to drive a rig in the field. That was a prized job, and he took it very seriously. All morning, he pulled his wagon alongside the chopper to fill it with silage. When the wagon was full, he headed to the silo where a blower at the end of a conveyor blew the silage inside. He did this repeatedly as the morning sped by.

At lunchtime, the hungry men washed at the outdoor pump and dried off with towels. The women had prepared a feast; the tables were loaded with food.

The farmers removed their hats as Uncle Henry led them in prayer. Then they ate quickly so they could get back to work.

For three days, they worked on Uncle Henry's farm. Myron spent the nights there so he could start early with the rest. When the job was done, he felt he had done a man's work. Feeling satisfied, he drove the tractor home. Even though he was quiet and didn't always enter into the conversations, he loved being part of the crew and experiencing the connection of a community working together.

15 Small Pleasures

As the children grew older, the bi-monthly trip to Winfield State Hospital became like a family outing. The Bontragers were always eager to see their babies, and the institute had become a familiar place.

Everyone was excited as they drove up the hill to the large, sprawling complex. As they entered the hospital, a lady at the desk handed them their pass, then they headed over to a large brick building. Stepping through the doorway, they were hit with the familiar unpleasant smells.

The family stopped at the nurse's station in Lynette and Faith's ward to show their pass, then they headed to the visiting room. Because of a new privacy act, they couldn't visit the girls in their rooms anymore, so the nurses had to wheel them out to the visiting room.

Physically, the girls hadn't changed much in the past five years. They were still very small and skinny for their age. And the problem with visiting them was always the same. How do you visit with someone who can't talk? At least Lynette showed occasional excitement, which made Eldon and Mary Ellen feel sure she recognized them. But not Faith. She had been only four when she left home and showed no sign of remembering her family.

Sometimes the girls would sleep through the whole visit. At other times they seemed to enjoy the interaction. Today they were awake.

Eldon took Faith on his lap, hugging her closely. "Faithy," he crooned, stroking her arm.

Mary Ellen ran her hands through Lynette's curly hair. "Oh, Kaye-Kaye," she said. "It looks like they cut your hair again."

Carolyn touched the hair falling over Lynette's forehead. "Look at her bangs!"

The other children stroked the girls and talked to them in soothing tones, even though there was no obvious response to their interactive attempts.

"Look at this dress," Phyllis said, fingering the skirt of Faith's dress. "It's . . . interesting."

"It's downright ugly," Marilyn declared, stating the obvious truth. The hospital supplied all the clothing for the children in the institute, so the Bontragers never knew what their babies would be wearing. Sometimes it was something cute and flattering, and other times it was something distasteful.

They strapped the girls back into their wheelchairs, then Carolyn and Phyllis wheeled them down the ramp opposite the nurse's station. Eldon had given them a quarter to buy a bottle of pop, so they wheeled the two girls all the way to the end of the hall where the pop machine sat with its cooler humming. "What kind shall we get?" Carolyn asked her sisters, inserting the quarter.

"Grape," Phyllis said. Carolyn punched the button and the ice-cold bottle clattered down to the bottom, where she picked it up. From the counter beside the pop machine, the girls gathered some flimsy, pointy-bottomed paper cups and headed back to the visiting room.

Eldon divided the drink between them all. "Kaye-Kaye, do you want some pop?" he asked, putting a cup to her mouth. Lynette drank eagerly.

"Faithy? Do you want a sip?" He put the cup to her lips. As soon as the soda was in her mouth, she spit it out. "I guess her taste for pop hasn't changed," Eldon chuckled, wiping the sticky liquid from his pants.

The other children swooped in to drink the rest of the cup. Everyone wanted their fair share. "Children!" Eldon was embarrassed by the commotion. "This is no time to be greedy!"

Lynette and Faith were starting to look sleepy, so the family wheeled them down the hall for the nurses to take them back to their room. After disposing of their trash, the Bontragers headed home.

Excitement ran high as they pulled into the city of Derby. Eldon filled the car with gas and bought ice cream cones for the whole family. This was a special treat and made the remainder of the trip home seem shorter.

Spreading below Winfield State Hospital was a wide green lawn with a pavilion. Dozens of large trees added their restful shade. Every summer, the families of the hospital residents were invited for a picnic on the lawn. The families and residents gathered in the park-like area.

Whenever Eldon mentioned the picnic, the whole family responded with fervent enthusiasm. There was something comforting about being with others who understood the joys and challenges of having disabled children in the family.

On the day of the picnic, the family piled into the car, all wanting seats by a window. Carefully Eldon guided the car over the railroad tracks and down the road. The clear summer sun shone brightly—perfect weather for the picnic.

The familiar Winfield grounds were bursting with activity. The nurses had wheeled out the residents to join their families. Across the lawn, the Bontragers spotted some friends: Lucille Yoder sat with her parents, Albert and Fannie. Phyllis smiled when she saw that their daughter her own age had come along.

Eldon and Mary Ellen walked over to Faith and Lynette's wheelchairs, leaning down and patting their faces lovingly. "Are you excited to be outside with us on the picnic?" Eldon asked. As usual, the girls acknowledged nothing.

The institute provided a lovely picnic with a wide variety of food, then gave out gifts and prizes. The younger children grew restless as the picnic dragged on. Carolyn sat beside Lynette, holding her hand. Phyllis sat close to her friend, talking with her in low tones. Marilyn flitted here and there, playing with other little girls, while LaVon and Myron fidgeted on their bench. Myron sat gazing at the roof of the pavilion, the surrounding activity fading away as he eyed the stout beams holding the structure in place. Quietly he got up from the bench while Eldon was talking to Lucille's father.

"Watch this," he said to LaVon. Climbing up a post, he grabbed a beam. Swinging from it, he grinned at his older brother. "Bet you can't do this."

"You should get down," LaVon said nervously, but his eyes twinkled with mischief.

Out of the corner of his eye, Myron saw a resident shuffling closer to watch the excitement. "You better stop that," the resident mumbled, waving a warning finger. "You might break it. Somebody did that last summer." He looked up at the swinging boy, shaking his head, his face worried.

Myron saw other heads begin to turn in his direction, and suddenly he felt embarrassed. Never one for the stage, he quickly dropped down and slid back into his seat. Relieved, the resident shuffled off now that the danger was over.

Beside Myron, LaVon snickered. This would make a good tale for the rest of the family on the way home.

They finished the picnic with watermelon, then said their goodbyes. It had been another good outing.

The Bontrager farm was a busy one, and restful Sundays were days to look forward to. The newly formed church in Arlington, where Center Amish Mennonite had started having services, was not far away. Even though Eldon and Mary Ellen hadn't originally joined the outreach, they knew that the locality made it the best option for them. They had come to enjoy meeting with the smaller group in the little white country church house.

Sunday school was a highlight for all the children, especially Marilyn. This year was particularly exciting, since the superintendent had announced there would be a box of small gifts they could choose from on their birthday. But Marilyn's heart fell when she realized that the term began in September and ended in August. Her prize for turning six would have to wait until near the end of the term.

Each time another friend picked out a prize, Marilyn would see the same sheet of beautiful stickers. *Oh, how I want those stickers,* she thought. *I hope they will still be there on my birthday!* She watched closely, and each Sunday she noticed that the sheet remained in the box. But what were the chances it would still be there next August?

At last the big day arrived! After Sunday school class, the preschoolers went out to join the rest of the children in a big class assembly, where the superintendent joined them. He beamed down at them. "Welcome to children's class! It looks like we have one birthday left for the year." Marilyn held her breath.

"Marilyn?" the superintendent called.

She hurried to the front of the room to receive her gift. Was the coveted sheet of stickers still there?

It was! Marilyn happily hugged the stickers to her chest, her eyes glowing as she took her seat with her friends. Later that day she took the stickers home and put them away in a special place in her bedroom. "I'm not sure I can ever make myself use them," she told Phyllis. "It will sure have to be something special."

16

Crushed

After five happy, busy years of life on the farm, the family had the surprise of their lives. They were going to have another baby.

Seven-year-old Marilyn was ecstatic. She was so excited upon receiving the news that she bent down and kissed her mother's feet.

"Oh, Marilyn," Phyllis giggled. "Get control of yourself. You are so dramatic."

Marilyn was beyond caring about her sister's opinion. "I'm just so excited! I've never wanted anything so much as I want this baby." She danced a giddy circle around the living room.

Phyllis and Carolyn were older and able to express their happiness more normally. The boys tried hard to be stoic and not show any excitement. But they all looked forward to the baby.

Sixteen-year-old Carolyn had been doing housework for a local family ever since she quit school after eighth grade. Mary Ellen called the lady she was working for and informed her that Carolyn would be needed at home toward the end of the year.

On November 27, 1973, excitement pervaded the house when the children woke up to discover their parents had gone to the hospital. "Do I have to go to school?" Phyllis asked. "I want to be here when the call comes."

"Yes, you need to go to school," Clara Mae said, who had come to get the children out the door. "Maybe we'll have news when you get home!"

Sure enough, the baby was born during school hours. That afternoon, the eager children hurried home, brimming with anticipation. Eldon greeted them with a big smile. "We have a little girl! Her name is Regina Anne."

Regina was a bundle of cuteness, winning the hearts of all her family. But it wasn't long before Mary Ellen felt the sharp pang of worry that she knew all too well.

"O Lord, not again," Mary Ellen groaned in private as she bathed her little one. No recognition or emotion registered on the tiny face. Mary Ellen's heart sank within her. *What will Eldon say about another handicapped child? And what about the children?* The family had now had a taste of normal life on the farm, and Mary Ellen knew this would be devastating to all of them. The children were old enough to be deeply affected by this new development.

Over the next several days, her fears continued to be confirmed. Finally she voiced her fears to Eldon. "Is it possible that God has sent us another handicapped child?" She hoped against hope that he would laugh away her concerns.

Eldon sighed heavily. "I've been watching her anxiously myself," he admitted. "But I was hoping my fears were groundless."

They took a moment to pray and cry together. They had just entered their forties. Their youthful days were behind them. How could they manage another disabled daughter?

Eldon opened his Bible to Isaiah 43. Finding the second verse, he read,

"'When thou passest through the waters, I will be with thee; and through the rivers, they shall not overflow thee: when thou walkest through the fire, thou shalt not be burned; neither shall the flame kindle upon thee.'" They both clung to that promise as they headed to bed.

The next morning was a Saturday, which signaled a more leisurely schedule. As Mary Ellen stood at the counter making pancakes, the children chattered and laughed while setting the table and preparing their traditional breakfast. Phyllis had managed to snag tiny baby Gina and was crooning happily to her.

"Oh, you are just the cutest, sweetest baby ever!" she cooed, stroking her baby sister's face. "Isn't she just perfect, Mom?" She beamed at the little baby.

Mary Ellen stood wordlessly at the counter.

Marilyn piped up, "When I'm in eighth grade, Regina should be in first grade."

Mary Ellen stared out the window as she struggled to control her rush of emotions and find words to reply to her daughter. "Marilyn," she said gently, "I don't think Regina will be able to go to school with you. We think she has some problems."

The kitchen grew quiet as the words started to soak in. Mary Ellen felt Eldon's gaze and answered it with a helpless look. Finally Eldon cleared his throat. "God, in His goodness, has sent us Gina. We would not have chosen another child like Lynette and Faith, but it seems Gina may have the same problems." He pulled out a handkerchief and blew his nose.

If the kitchen had been quiet before his announcement, it was now deathly still. Mary Ellen's shoulders shook with sobs as she watched her children absorb this blow. One by one, their faces crumpled and they left the room, fleeing to a private spot to sob out their grief and ask God, "Why?"

Eldon and Mary Ellen were left in the kitchen with baby Gina. They cried as they looked down at her. Although the entire family adored her cute little self, she might never be able to return their love.

That evening the family sat in the living room and discussed the future. The trauma of leaving Faith and Lynette at Winfield was still all too vivid. Eldon looked around at all the sober faces. "It takes more work than you ever dreamed of taking care of a handicapped child. But you children are a lot older now. How much do you think you can help with taking care of Gina?"

Carolyn was vehement. "I don't think I could stand it if she had to leave. Surely if we all help, we can keep her at home. I'll work my fingers to the bone before I send her away!"

"Yes," Phyllis chimed in. "We can all pitch in."

The other children nodded. They would band together and help take care of Gina. None of them could imagine their baby sister being admitted to a mental hospital.

"Well—" Eldon's voice broke. "Thanks for your support, children. Let's give it a try. I think we can do it if everyone does their part."

Experience had taught Eldon and Mary Ellen that early intervention was the best hope they had, so they took Gina to Dr. Slocum in Des Moines, Iowa. Once again, they had a doctor who had high hopes. The Bontragers made thirteen trips to his clinic before Gina was a year old, but nothing really changed. They finally received a diagnosis of cerebral palsy, but naming it made no practical difference. Like her older sisters, Gina would need lots of care.

During the year of those many trips to Iowa, the boys became overwhelmed with all the work on the farm. In addition to caring for their herds of beef cows and dairy cows, they did crop farming and custom cutting and baling. Ambitious Eldon sold balers and did various other jobs, and the work on the farm was too much for the boys to do alone. One evening LaVon and Myron had a discussion in the barn while they were milking. When their parents returned home, they took their plans to Eldon.

"Dad," LaVon said, "we boys hate milking. And we are too busy for it anyway. We're behind on the field work and there are several neighbors needing us to bale their hay. We have way too much going on, and Myron and I think we should sell the cows. With Gina taking all of Mom's time, she can't do the milking like she planned. So now no one has time!"

"Yes, we have enough other things to do," Myron agreed.

"Milking isn't your favorite job, is it?" Eldon asked understandingly.

"No, I dislike that job more than any other," Myron admitted.

Eldon nodded. His sons were right. Although they would miss this portion of their income, saving the time for other things was more important than losing the money. He knew he was too busy with cabinetry and other farm work, and that brought in better money anyway. "I think you have a good point," he agreed. "Your Uncle Melvin has been wanting to buy the cows. I'll talk to him."

Mary Ellen was sad to see the cows go, but she knew it was the right thing to do. No one would miss the extra work.

It soon became obvious that Regina had sensory issues. She cried inconsolably when she was held too much. "Oh, Gina," Mary Ellen crooned to her daughter, "I'd love to just hold you. But it seems you don't even want to be touched!" She wiped a tear in disappointment.

The family cleared out the small room beside the dining room and put in a waterbed for Gina. She spent hours on the bed. When it was kept less than full, any gentle motion created small waves that seemed to calm her somewhat. The fluffy family cat also moved onto the bed and kept Gina company day and night.

Regina's disability was a blow that shook the family to its core. Having gone through the monumental stress of caring for Lynette and Faith and then getting a glimpse of what normal life was like, facing another high-needs child looked like an unscalable mountain.

Eldon processed his grief by becoming detached and burying himself in work. He loved the farm, so it was easy to ward off the pain by doing what he loved. He worked at carpentry in the winter and tilling the soil in the summer. He stayed busy with hay baling, baler sales, and caring for the beef cattle. He was his own repairman and could fix anything around the farm with things he had on hand, repairing equipment to sell.

Mary Ellen became protective, investing her life in baby Regina. She loved her little "chickadee" so much and was determined to keep her at home. But being unable to hold her as much as she had Lynette and Faith, Mary Ellen would feed her and lay her down immediately on the bed. She spent much of her spare time reading, trying to block out the disappointment in her heart.

The children also had various ways to process their pain. When the bliss of the normality they had learned to love was hopelessly crushed again, Myron began a journey of acceptance that lasted for years. One day he stepped into Gina's room and watched her roll back and forth on the waterbed, staring into space and moaning to herself. His thoughts became words as he observed his helpless sister. "What could possibly be the purpose of this, God? Why did this have to happen again? What enjoyment can she possibly get out of life?"

In his head, a voice seemed to say, *Maybe she can't get enjoyment out of life as you see it, but her destination is sure. Satan can never touch her.*

As Myron thought of his own youthful temptations, he felt this revelation lift the cloud of frustration and anger from his heart. *Thank you, God, for showing me that.* He bowed his head. *Regina is blessed to be safe in your hand.* From that time on, he felt at peace. Instead of fighting what God had dealt to their family, he felt a resignation to His will.

Like a typical fifteen-year-old, LaVon tried not to show his emotions. Yet he too struggled. *Why, God?* he asked. Perched on the edge of Gina's bed, he looked at her lying there, helpless. *What are you trying to prove, God?* he cried inwardly. *Wouldn't there have been a better way?* Having disabled siblings seemed to be the worst thing that could have happened to him. Then a new thought struck him. *Gina has a free ticket to heaven.* As he began to reconcile why his family was different, he realized something: *There are worse things than being handicapped.*

It was especially hard for Carolyn to accept another sister who was severely disabled. She remembered all too well the hard, endless days of caring for Lynette and Faith. *What are you thinking, God? How can you bring another child like this into our home? Especially at Mom's age? How will she ever be able to meet the demands of caring for her?* It was a grief Carolyn carried every day. Heavy responsibilities were once again on her shoulders, and though she rose to the challenges, she longed for the carefree days that her friends had.

Thirteen-year-old Phyllis's heart ached as if pierced by a dagger. "Again, Lord?" she prayed, struggling to accept the reality of another disabled sister. But it seemed as if God was saying to her, "Yes, Phyllis, again." She did her best to resign her will to God's on this difficult path.

At seven, Marilyn's former routine vanished. Bedtime, homework, and mealtimes became random since Mary Ellen was often overwhelmed and sapped of strength.

On one occasion, Mary Ellen had invited company, and Gina was very fussy. Since her room was right off the dining room, it was easy to hear her crying. Marilyn sat at the table listening to Gina, feeling more and more embarrassed. Finally she couldn't stand it anymore and fled to her room. Throwing herself facedown on the bed, she sobbed out her heart at the unfairness of it all.

Suddenly she felt a hand on her shoulder. Looking up, she saw Carolyn. "Come down and be sociable," Carolyn coaxed.

"Why can't we just be a normal family?" Marilyn sobbed.

"We can't change the fact that God sent us Gina. Would you really want to trade her even if you could?" Carolyn's sensible voice brought her younger sister back to reality.

Marilyn shook her head. Wiping her eyes, she followed Carolyn back down to the dining room to enjoy the rest of the evening.

Marilyn was eight when Eldon got a Honda ATC90 three-wheeler. Even though the Bontragers pinched their pennies for living expenses, it seemed there was usually enough to buy gas for this little machine. Originally intended to be a farm tool, the three-wheeler quickly became Marilyn's playmate, and she spent hours cruising back and forth on the driveway.

Wrapped up in caring for Regina, Mary Ellen gave Marilyn a lot of leeway. One day the young girl was roaring out the back lane on the three-wheeler. The wind was blowing fiercely, and dust got in her eyes. Taking a quick look ahead, Marilyn put down her head and squeezed her eyes shut. After a bit she reopened them, and there, right in her path, was the large Case tractor.

A wide-eyed Myron didn't know how he could avoid this collision. He turned the tractor sharply, driving right through the fence. Marilyn shot past, narrowly missing a disaster. The mercy of God had kept her from being killed that day.

The following year, the family had another near disaster. Phyllis was helping Marilyn clean the upstairs. Mary Ellen was out running errands, and Gina was on the floor downstairs in the living room. Phyllis went down to get some rags and found the main floor filled with blue smoke. Gina had yanked on a lamp cord, and there was a bulb-sized burn spot on the carpet—and a burned live cord lying there! The lightbulb had also left a deep burn about the size of an egg on Gina's skinny little leg. With a little salve, she soon seemed as good as new, and the family thanked the Lord for His protecting hand.

That winter, God once again showed His protection. One snowy morning, Carolyn, who had her driver's license by this time, headed off to her babysitting job nearby. Trying to avoid the icy main road, she went out their back lane and got stuck in a drift. *Now what do I do?* she wondered, allowing the car to idle. *It's too cold and icy to get out of the car. Ed will call Dad when I don't arrive at their house, so I'll just wait here in the warm car.*

Eldon's little country church house near Arlington, Kansas.
Greg and Trish later turned this into their home.

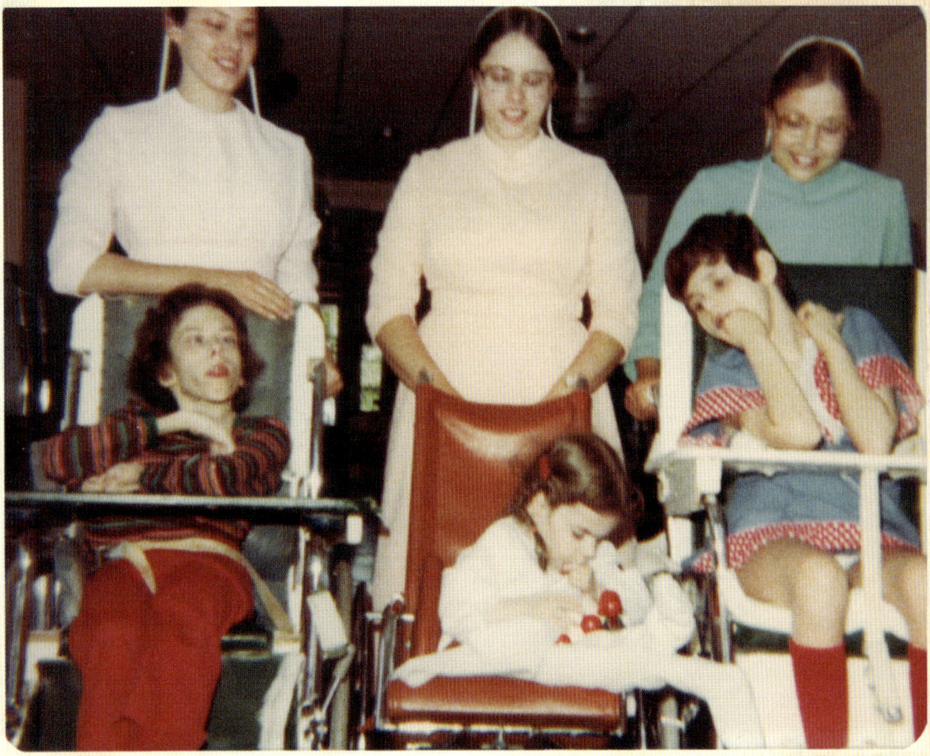

A sisters' gathering just before Carolyn left for Mountain View Nursing Home in 1978. Back row, left to right: Phyllis, Carolyn, and Marilyn. Front row, left to right: Lynette, Regina, and Faith.

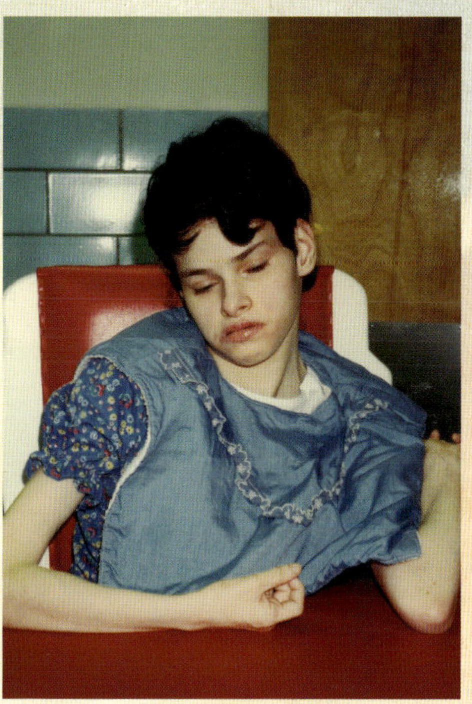

Faith in the early 1980s.

Regina celebrating a birthday.

Eldon, Mary Ellen, and all their children in October 1992. This photo was taken the only time the entire family was together. Since travel with Regina was difficult, she was usually left with relatives when the others visited Lynette and Faith. Back row, left to right: Carolyn, Phyllis, Marilyn, Mary Ellen, Eldon, LaVon, and Myron. Front row, left to right: Faith, Lynette, and Regina.

Regina and her waterbed. Note the water spot hinting at the problem that eventually caused the ceiling to collapse on the day of her funeral.

Grant at four years old.

A family portrait in 1997: LaVon and Mamie, with Greg, Angie, and Grant, in front.

Grant and Jen's wedding on June 21, 2021. Left to right: Levi and Angie and family, Grant and Jen, Mamie, and Greg and Trish and family.

Grant sharing his story at the Haiti hostage reunion on February 27, 2022.

Grant and Jen Bontrager with their children, Spencer and Zayla. Spring 2025.

The snow was packed under the car, causing exhaust fumes to filter up into the interior. Carolyn began to get sleepy, not realizing the odorless fumes were the cause. She lay back in her seat and closed her eyes.

The next thing she knew, Eldon was pounding on the window. "Carolyn!" he yelled. "Carolyn! Can you hear me?"

She woke up slowly. "Unlock the door! Quick!" Eldon said, panic in his voice.

Still in a daze, Carolyn unlocked the door. Eldon opened it and helped his daughter get out. "I got stuck and couldn't go anymore," she said groggily.

"Yes, Ed called and said you hadn't shown up," Eldon said. "You scared me when you didn't answer my knocks. I wasn't sure if you were alive or dead!"

Slowly her brain cleared as she breathed in the fresh air. "I'm sure glad you showed up," she said, finally realizing what had nearly happened. "If you hadn't, I might never have awakened."

"I never would have forgiven myself," Eldon said.

Using Eldon's pickup and a chain, they got the car out of the snowdrift. Carolyn continued on to her job, just a bit late. She never forgot that scary experience.

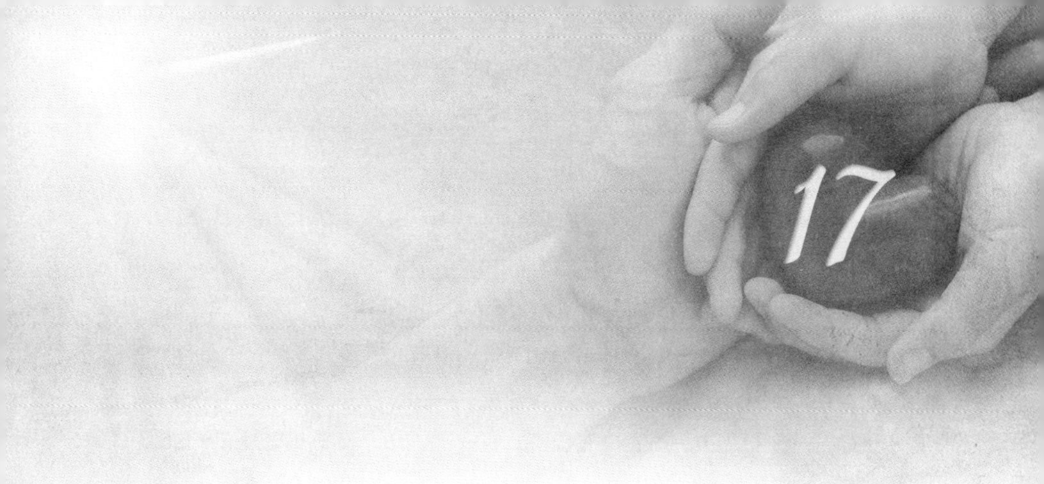

Change for the Better

When Gina was three years old, physical therapists began to come regularly to the house to help give her exercises. They also gave the family tips on how they could better help her. The first therapist, a petite Asian lady named Gay, brought along a barrel. She laid Gina on top and quickly rolled her forward, trying to get her to throw out her hands and catch herself. "Now we're going to sit her up and lean her forward," she said, helping Gina do what she couldn't do herself.

After the session was over, Gay pulled beautiful colored paper out of her bag as the intrigued girls gathered around. She carefully folded her origami, making fun shapes for them to admire.

Another therapist named Margie switched a squeaky toy from one hand to the other. "Over here, Gina," she coaxed, trying to get her to follow the toy with her eyes.

One day Margie brought along a bottle of pop, stuck a straw in it, and put it in Gina's mouth. Squeezing the straw to draw up the liquid, Margie helped Gina learn to suck. All eyes were on the little girl. "She's sucking it up," Phyllis said incredulously. Everyone cheered for Gina. She caught on quickly, which was unusual. After Gina had her fill, the other girls finished off the pop.

As Gina got older, she grew in length but weighed only about thirty-five pounds. She was fussy day and night. Seeing her parents' exhaustion, Carolyn often carried Gina upstairs with her at night so they could get some much-needed sleep. On those nights the children were the ones who struggled to sleep. But between them all, they managed.

Back when they were in the thick of caring for Lynette and Faith, Eldon and Mary Ellen had been forced to expend all their energy into their own home. With Regina being a calmer child, and with the blessing of older children to share the load, they were able to regularly attend a new church when it opened.

The little country church in Arlington had closed its doors, as it was just too small and too far for most of the church people. With Center Amish Mennonite overflowing, a new church house was built on the other side of the main highway. It was named Cedar Crest. The community divided itself geographically between the two churches, and the Bontragers became members of Cedar Crest.

The opportunity to bless others was also added back to their life. They eagerly helped with community projects, such as canning meat for a worldwide relief aid program, rebuilding homes struck by natural disasters, and sewing and knotting comforters for needy people around the world. Knowing so keenly the feeling of desperation, the Bontragers relished the opportunities to give to those less fortunate.

In 1975, Congress passed the Education for All Handicapped Children Act to mandate equal access to public education for children with disabilities. This legislation asserted that all children had a right to be included in mainstream education classes. For one little family on the plains of Kansas, this made all the difference in the options available for Gina that had not been there for her older sisters.

When Gina turned five years old, she started kindergarten. Every weekday, a wheelchair-accessible bus from the public school arrived to pick her up. Gina was wheeled onto the bus and taken to her school to participate in the early childhood intervention program. Those six hours gave the Bontrager family the break they needed to continue as caretakers. The program, in turn, gave Gina the stimulation and therapy she needed to function the best she could.

There were three other disabled children in Gina's class: Nicky, Lisa, and Jay-Jay. Their teacher, Mary Lou, was an enthusiastic woman who loved her job and threw all her energy into giving her four students the best life possible.

Society had changed in the years since Lynette was born. There was no longer shame and embarrassment in how people viewed disabled children. Rather, the children were validated in their unique traits, and there was a push to meet them at their level and help them rise to their highest potential.

This view also filtered into the church. The church members' love and care for Gina and her family did much to soothe the frayed nerves of the Bontrager family. The community was involved in Gina's care and accepted her in a way that was healing to the family's souls. Since the Bontragers were able to attend church more regularly than they had when Lynette and Faith were babies, these growing-up years with Gina were a blessed, redeeming time.

Another godsend was the love and acceptance Gina enjoyed from other children. Since she attended the Severely Mentally Handicapped (SMH) class at Elreka School where many other church families attended, the children were used to seeing her and her wheelchair. Often they came up to talk to her or push her around in her chair. It warmed Mary Ellen's heart to watch their kindness. How she wished things could have been like this with her other two special-needs daughters! But she knew this was a different era, so she did her best to accept the change as a gift and not look back with regrets.

The Arlington community was remarkably supportive as well. One evening neighbor Don and his wife stopped by to visit and ask a question: "Could we bring our pastor to pray over Gina?" These neighbors were from a nearby Apostolic church. Although their doctrinal views were not the same as that of the Mennonites, they showed a tremendous amount of love and care to the Bontrager family.

"Well, I don't think it would hurt anything," Eldon cautiously replied. "We want to accept whatever God brings into our lives, but of course we all wish Gina could be healed."

The next evening, the neighbors brought their pastor as they had promised. "Let's gather around little Gina," the pastor instructed. He, his wife, and the neighbor couple gathered around Regina and placed their hands on her. The Bontrager children stood watching with wide eyes. From their more stoic Amish Mennonite experience, the scene was dramatic.

The pastor lifted his eyes toward heaven and prayed fervently. "Dear heavenly Father, we entreat you to heal this dear girl. You tell us to ask in faith, and we claim that promise this evening. We renounce any doubt in this room. Thank you for victory in Christ. In Jesus' name! Amen!" There wasn't a dry eye in the room when the prayer was finished.

"Thank you," Eldon said simply. "Now we leave the healing in the hands of God." He knew God would touch Gina if it was His will, but if not, Eldon wanted to accept this path before them.

The visitors soon left. After they were gone, Eldon looked at his family. "Children, we don't believe it's right to demand for God to do something for us. But we do believe that He can heal Gina if it is His will. I just want you to know that even if Gina isn't healed miraculously, it doesn't mean

God didn't hear our prayer tonight."

The Bontrager children still felt a keen disappointment when God didn't heal Gina, but the care and concern they felt from their neighbors and the pastor stayed with them for the rest of their lives. And although nothing changed for Gina physically, it did seem that from then on she could handle the stimulation of crowds without becoming overwhelmed and frustrated.

Gradually life began to take on a new normal. The children broke the usual number of bones and buried the typical number of farm pets. They went on fewer trips but perhaps bonded more than the average family as they worked shoulder to shoulder to farm the land and take care of Gina. Eldon continued to bury himself in too many tasks, but he learned to whistle as he worked. Mary Ellen found great fulfillment in caring for Gina, and gradually, with the help of her capable daughters, she was able to bring the Bontrager home back into a functional routine—although she continued her avid reading as an escape. There were still scars from the difficult journey they had gone through, but they all saw the gracious hand of God on their home.

With time, they learned to see blessings they would have missed if they had been free to run hither and yon. They had become a close-knit family, playing lots of games, reading together, and having bonfires.

When Carolyn was twenty-two years old, she left for a term of service at Mountain View Nursing Home in Virginia, and nineteen-year-old Phyllis took charge of taking care of Gina. Phyllis was a patient sister and thrived in her care of the girl. Crying babies bothered Mary Ellen more than they used to, so the rest of the family did all they could to lighten her load.

The 1980s brought many more changes to the Bontrager family as the children found partners, married, and moved out. LaVon spent a year working at Hillcrest Nursing Home in Arkansas, where he met Mamie

Stoltzfus. They were married in 1982. That same year, Phyllis also left to serve at Hillcrest, and the care of Regina fell to Marilyn and Mary Ellen. Two years later, LaVon and Mamie presented Eldon and Mary Ellen with their first grandchild, a little boy named Gregory. Three years later, the first granddaughter, Angie, was born. That birth brought complications, and LaVon and Mamie were unable to have more children.

Phyllis also met her life partner at Hillcrest, and she and Gareth Yoder were married in 1983. After several moves, Gareth and Phyllis found themselves a home in Texas.

Myron formed a friendship with Ilene Miller from the local youth group, and the two got married in 1987. As the weddings rolled around, the grandchildren continued to arrive. One year followed the next, and the Lord faithfully gave increase to the Bontrager family.

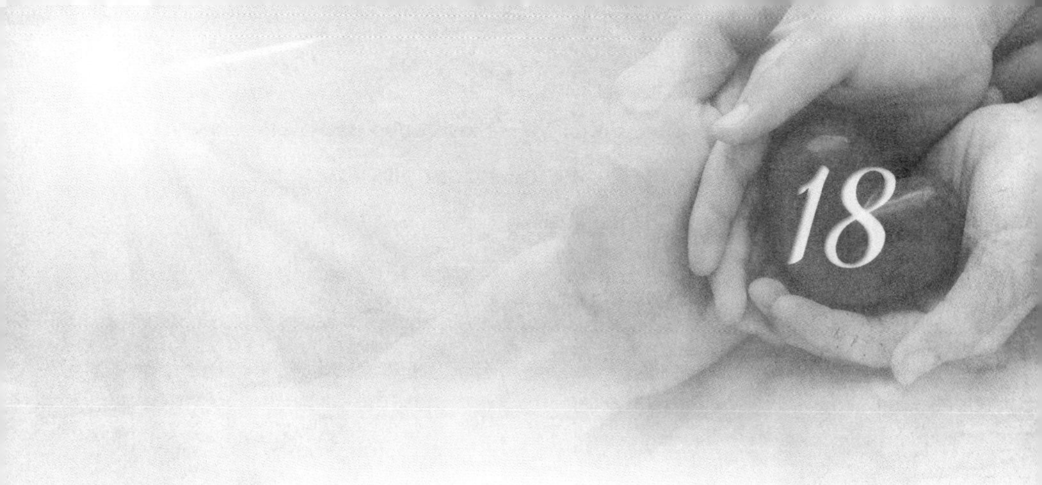

18

Carolyn's Essenhaus

In a small town like Arlington, with a population of only four hundred, everyone knew everyone else. When the Bontragers did their banking, their business was taken care of by personal friends. Errands such as a stop at the post office or filling up at a gas station could become lengthy as the townspeople discussed the weather and other local news. In the small, slightly musty library, the regal Marguerite Fountain—the librarian who presided over the small domain—welcomed them by name.

Carolyn worked at a local Mennonite retirement facility, where she got to serve some of her former friends from Arlington. Often visitors at the facility were people she knew as well, and she enjoyed chatting with them as she worked at the front desk. One subject kept coming up occasionally.

"We need a decent restaurant in Arlington," Glen Snell said pointedly one day.

Carolyn gave him a polite smile. "What am I supposed to do about that?"

"Well, your family made the most delicious pies and cinnamon rolls at the Arlington Centennial," Glen said.

His wife Greta nodded in agreement. "You really should consider opening a restaurant."

Carolyn grinned. "Making pies is a lot easier than running a restaurant." She had been gone during the centennial the Snells were referring to, but she had heard stories of how Mary Ellen and Marilyn had hauled pies by the dozen into town during the one-hundredth anniversary of their hometown. The Bontragers had sold the desserts out of their cabinet shop in downtown Arlington. Carolyn was sorry she had missed it—she loved baking.

One day soon after her conversation with the Snells, Carolyn noticed a "For Sale" sign on her way home from work. It was in the window of Branding Iron Bar & Grill, a building in Arlington near the cabinet shop where her dad and brothers spent their winter months.

A spark ignited.

"Well, would you look at that?" Carolyn said out loud. "There's the place for my restaurant." She smiled to herself.

"Guess what I saw in Arlington today?" she announced as the food was passed around the table that evening.

"What was it?" Marilyn asked.

Carolyn's eyes shone as she relayed the news. "The Branding Iron is for sale. We should buy it!"

"What do we need a building like that for?" Eldon asked warily.

"The Snells say they wish we would start a restaurant. I think I would enjoy that."

"Are you sure you'd want to tie yourself down like that?" Mary Ellen asked.

Carolyn nodded thoughtfully. "I've dreamed of doing something like that. It might be time to make the dream a reality."

"It sounds like a big undertaking to me," Eldon said. "But if you do decide to do it, we can all pitch in and help. I'm guessing it would take a lot of work to get that bar in decent shape, but I'm sure it could be done."

Carolyn heard her father's hesitation, but she knew he would be the first to roll up his sleeves and make her dream happen. Since he had recently passed the cabinet shop over to his sons, he would have more time to help her out.

On May 20, 1989—the same day that Myron and Ilene ushered their first baby, Kaylene, into the world—the building was purchased. Carolyn immediately called in the troops to help.

Foam covered the windows, giving the building a dark, foreboding atmosphere. "This foam has to go," Eldon said. "We need light in here."

"And lots of paint," Carolyn said emphatically. The dark brown ceiling, walls, and trim were emanating gloom, and the paneled walls were marked with the local farmers' brands.

The Bontragers rolled up their sleeves, and with a generous application of elbow grease, the dark bar became an airy dining area with tables for customers. Two rooms on either end opened into party rooms for group dining, and in the back was a kitchen and prep area.

Two months later, on July 26, Carolyn's "Essenhaus,"[1] opened to the public. Myron, LaVon, and Eldon had already worked late many evenings before opening day. The night before, the family members hardly went home. Marilyn arrived at 2:00 in the morning to start frying donuts, baking bread, and mixing coffee cakes, and the men were still hammering away feverishly.

Marilyn started on the many tasks that would eventually become routine, but on this first morning they were new and unfamiliar. After a bit, Carolyn arrived too, rushing around to get the last things in order. Finally the time arrived to open the doors for customers.

[1] *Essenhaus* means "eating house" in German.

Carolyn had a knot in her stomach. Would anyone come?

Yes, they would. Richard and Karen, the newspaper delivery service, popped in right after the doors unlocked. They laughed at a sheepish LaVon, who was gathering up his tools.

"Well, well! I can almost still hear the hammers!" Richard said.

"Yeah, you might want to be careful," LaVon retorted. "The dust is still settling." They all chuckled as Carolyn ushered her first customers to their seats.

Richard and Karen ordered hash browns and eggs, and Carolyn hustled back to the kitchen. In the meantime, Marilyn finished up her donut trays and tied an apron around her waist to begin waitressing. And not a minute too soon!

More and more customers poured through the doors. Everyone in town had been watching the recent activity at the restaurant, and they all wanted to see what the new and improved place would be like. For the little restaurant on its very first morning, it seemed like a mad rush.

Carolyn was a whirlwind of activity in the kitchen, flipping plate-sized pancakes, frying eggs, and buttering toast. Marilyn waitressed at a rapid pace, and several cousins helped her. Around 9:00 a bouquet of flowers arrived, compliments of the bank ladies. The kind gesture overwhelmed her already taut nerves, and Carolyn promptly burst into tears. But that bouquet was far from the last. Six more followed before the day was over!

When the doors finally closed and cleanup was done, the exhausted Bontragers went home and collapsed. The first day had brought 149 people to their tables. Surely such a rush of customers couldn't last!

But Arlington had waited quite a while for a good restaurant, and the people were more than pleased with the new local business. By its first weekend, the restaurant began to run out of food, resulting in some disgruntled customers.

"You can't be out of chicken-fried steaks!" One lady was shocked at the news.

Carolyn felt appalled herself. "I'm very sorry! We had no idea we would be so busy our first week. Please come back next week and we'll have plenty."

By the end of Saturday, a frazzled Carolyn reported to Marilyn, "We served 213 people today. I hope I haven't overcommitted myself."

"I think it's just amazing!" Marilyn, with her boundless energy, was thrilled with the success of her sister's enterprise.

Carolyn grinned wearily. "Yes, it truly is!"

Arlington clasped the little business to its heart. It soon became a popular meeting place for the locals. Area businesses took turns donating the morning coffee each week, so for a lot of farmers Carolyn's Essenhaus became the first stop of their day. They read the paper and caught up on the local gossip as they sipped their free cup-o-joe and ate one of Carolyn's delicious fresh donuts.

After the lunch crowd was past, the locals came back, catching an afternoon break at the round table and quenching their thirst with iced tea. Carolyn's homemade pies, carefully crafted from the best recipes in Mary Ellen's stash, became favorites of many customers and would eventually win awards for her. The big mixer in the back cranked out beautiful loaves of homemade bread, just like the ones she had grown up with. Her entrees were made the old-fashioned, homemade way, and their superb flavors reflected that. At the end of the first year, Carolyn had tallied up 13,463 meals, served from July 26 through December 31.

Carolyn loved her new role in the heart of the community and found great fulfillment in serving her friends and neighbors in this way. She had many opportunities to show the love of Jesus to her customers, both in the food she prepared and in the listening ear she became to many people. The Bontrager family rallied around her to help in any way possible. Eldon dropped his duties and came running to fix anything that was broken, and Marilyn and Mary Ellen helped with waitressing and baking as much as they were able.

Eventually Marilyn quit at the restaurant and took her turn volunteering at Hillcrest. She came home a year later with a fine young man in tow. She and Dan Korver got married in 1990 and settled in Kansas for the first few years of their marriage.

Now all the children were gone from home except for Carolyn and Regina. Carolyn helped with Regina's care as much as she could while juggling her restaurant responsibilities.

The Bontragers had no idea their world was about to be blown apart.

19

The Hardest Blow

November 21, 1991, dawned just like any other late fall day in Kansas. Though the sun lacked the heat of summer, it still shone brightly in the deep blue sky. A quiet breeze stirred the countryside, whisking leaves through the clear air.

Around noon, the phone rang in the Bontrager home.

"Hello, Mr. Bontrager. This is Dr. Lybarger from Winfield State Hospital."

"Well, hello, Dr. Lybarger." Eldon was surprised to hear from the presiding doctor at the institute. "I hope everything is fine with the girls."

The line was quiet for a moment. When the doctor spoke again, his voice was grave. "Mr. Bontrager, I need to come to your home to talk in person. It's very urgent. May I come this evening?"

Eldon felt himself go cold with dread. "Of course, Doctor. That should work." He put back the receiver with a trembling hand, without even saying goodbye.

"Who was that?" Mary Ellen asked sharply from the sink, seeing his expression.

"Something must be wrong with the girls," Eldon said. "Dr. Lybarger wants to come see us this evening."

"Why, what could be wrong?" A hard rock of anxiety settled on her heart.

"I don't know. He didn't give any clue. Maybe it's... Maybe it's nothing to worry about..." Eldon's voice trailed off doubtfully. Twenty-five years had passed since the girls had been admitted to the institute, and so far there had been no major problems. What could be going on?

Carolyn caught wind of the upcoming visit and arranged her schedule so she could be at home to support her parents through whatever news might be coming. Around midafternoon, LaVon's wife Mamie called to ask if she and the children could come over for the evening as well, since LaVon was out hunting. Mary Ellen welcomed her but warned her of the visit.

That evening Eldon finished the chores early and hurried in. Seven-year-old Greg and five-year-old Angie were playing upstairs with Grandpa's fun toys, and the adults were clustered around the table in the kitchen, making feeble attempts at small talk. They were all deep in their own thoughts, waiting for the doctor to come. Eldon sat at the head of the table, brooding. *What could be so wrong that the doctor needs to come to our house? Why didn't he just tell me over the phone?*

Finally a sleek gray car turned in at the drive and carefully bumped over the railroad tracks. The knots in the stomachs around the table leaped into throats. The family was about to find out the reason for this puzzling visit.

Slowly the car drove up the lane and parked in front of the house. A man and a woman walked up the sidewalk, and Eldon greeted them at the door. "Hello, Dr. Lybarger," he said, shaking the doctor's hand. Turning to the lady, he said, "And you must be a nurse?"

"Yes, I am," she replied, returning his handshake. "I help care for your lovely daughters."

"Well, come on in. You can join us here at the kitchen table." Eldon couldn't disguise his anxiety as he ushered them to their seats.

Soberly and silently, the doctor and his nurse sat down. Looking around the circle, Dr. Lybarger rested his arms on the table. His face seemed troubled as he cleared his throat. "What I have to tell you this evening isn't easy." He glanced at Eldon and then at Mary Ellen.

Silently they met his gaze, waiting for him to go on. He cleared his throat again. "Recently one of our nurses noticed Faith's abdomen was swollen. The nurse told me about it, so I ordered an X-ray, thinking your daughter might have a tumor in her stomach."

The nurse spoke up. "And what we found wasn't at all what we expected."

Dr. Lybarger shook his head. "No, it was not. The X-ray didn't show any abnormal growth. Instead, it showed—" his voice wavered. "It showed a fetus."

The Bontragers' collective gasp filled the deathly quiet room. The doctor's eyes brimmed with tears as he looked at their faces. "I am so sorry. She is about six months pregnant."

Carolyn clutched at the table. "No, not Faith! Oh, the poor child." Anger and helplessness racked her face. Eldon's mouth hung open in shock, and Mary Ellen's face was white. Only Mamie kept a calm composure, but her troubled eyes revealed the magnitude of the blow.

Dr. Lybarger's mouth trembled, but he pressed on resolutely. "We are looking into the situation, trying to figure out how this could have happened. Obviously, this is a tremendous stain on our hospital as well. We are already working on better policies about male attendants having unattended access to our disabled girls." He ran his unsteady hands over the tabletop.

Eldon's jaw quivered as he tried to control his emotions. "That doesn't really help this situation."

"No, it doesn't," the doctor agreed, his voice filled with regret. "I feel totally responsible for what has happened." He paused, then went on. "Since Faith weighs only sixty-five pounds, and since the baby was exposed to radiation and other medications that could harm it, I doubt this child will ever live to see the light of day. And even if it does, what kind of future would it have? I recommend that Faith have an abortion."

Mary Ellen gasped.

Dr. Lybarger looked at Eldon. "We will, of course, cover all costs that might come with the procedure."

"And it will need to be done soon." The nurse's voice was brisk. "She's pretty far along already."

Eldon did not hesitate. "We will not abort this baby," he said firmly. "Will we, Mary Ellen?"

Mary Ellen was already shaking her head. "No! Of course not. We could never knowingly take the life of an unborn child."

Dr. Lybarger seemed surprised, but he maintained his professional composure. "It is, of course, your decision. And I won't attempt to change your mind." He paused, thinking. "If you feel sure about your decision, we will assign a private nurse to Faith. Your daughter will be well taken care of. This nurse will stay by her side, giving Faith her undivided attention. We will do all we can to deliver a normal, healthy baby." He paused again, uncertainty flickering through his eyes. Then his gaze rested on Mary Ellen. "The results of the ultrasound show that your daughter will be having a boy."

With that, the meeting was over. Having nothing more to say, the subdued doctor and his nurse headed out the door.

Eldon and Mary Ellen sat woodenly. They watched in numb silence as the gray car drove out the lane and disappeared down the road.

Mamie and Carolyn sat motionless as well, stunned and shocked, both lost in their own thoughts. Their minds spun as they processed the implications of this dilemma. What a disaster! How could this nightmare be happening?

"Poor Faith," Mamie murmured. "How could anyone do such a horrible thing?"

Eldon's heart broke for his daughter. "How can she even carry a baby in her small body?"

"I was wondering about that too." Mary Ellen felt sick to the core. She covered her eyes with her hands. "Faith, pregnant? I can hardly wrap my mind around it. The poor girl!"

"What did the doctor mean about a normal, healthy baby?" Carolyn asked. "How in the world could this poor little boy ever be normal?"

Eldon shrugged. "I can't imagine he has much chance of that. But even if he isn't normal, that changes nothing. We will love him and care for him as if he were our own."

Mary Ellen's sense of reason was returning. "But Eldon, we can't. We're too old to take care of another child. Who will raise this boy?" Suddenly a thought dawned on her. Turning to Mamie, Mary Ellen asked with pleading eyes, "Would you consider taking the baby?"

Although LaVon and Mamie had thought Angie would be their last child, the longing for motherhood had not faded from Mamie. Now, as she thought of this tiny life needing love and nurture, everything inside her leaped for joy.

"Yes!" she said without hesitation. "Yes, we would!" She knew with all her heart that she wanted another child. Although she was sorry LaVon wasn't with her, Mamie felt sure he would say the same thing.

As they all continued processing the shock, Mamie gathered her children to head home before the evening grew late. As they headed out the door, she heard Eldon talking on the phone with Paul Miller, the bishop of their church.

"Good evening, Paul. Are you free this evening? We're having a family emergency and could really use some counsel. Would it suit for you to come over right away?"

Later that evening, after the children were in bed, Mamie settled in the living room with LaVon to discuss the day. After a bit of small talk, she looked up at her husband and took a deep breath. "Dr. Lybarger came out to see your folks tonight."

"Who's Dr. Lybarger?" LaVon asked, yawning as he leaned back in his recliner.

"He's the supervising doctor at Winfield, where the girls are."

LaVon frowned. "Why did he come out to visit?"

"He told them that Faith is . . . that she is—she's going to have a baby!" As the terrible words came out of her mouth, Mamie could hardly believe they were true.

LaVon jerked upright, his mouth dropping open in shock. "What in the world? What do you mean?" A surge of anger nearly choked him. "How on earth is that possible!"

"I know." Mamie's face was grim. "It's just awful. You would think she has suffered enough in her lifetime."

"But how could anyone do such a terrible thing? You would think a place like that could be trusted!" LaVon was horrified at the suffering of his innocent sister.

"But listen, LaVon—there's more! The baby is going to be a boy. They don't know if he will survive or not, but if he lives, someone needs to take care of him." Mamie eyed her husband meaningfully.

"Let Winfield take care of him. It's their mess; they can deal with it."

"LaVon! This is Faith's baby! And besides, your folks asked me if we would take him, and I said yes."

"What? Now wait a minute." LaVon snapped shut the footrest of his recliner and leaned forward. "We need to think about this. We don't know what kind of man did this, and we can't be expected to take responsibility for his child. You have no idea how much work a handicapped child is!"

As he spoke, LaVon's mind flashed back over all the years his family had cared for the girls, reflecting on all the sacrifices they had made. Yet the rage he felt at the sinful act inflicted on his sister consumed his thoughts most of all.

"Yes, let's think about it and pray about it," Mamie agreed. "Maybe God will show us what we should do." She could tell LaVon was in no frame of mind to discuss it further at the moment, so she got up and began tidying the living room.

His face drawn, LaVon headed for the shower. As the water continued to run on and on, Mamie finished her evening tasks and went to bed. Finally LaVon crawled in beside her. Mamie was still awake, mulling over the shattering news of the evening.

"Mamie..." LaVon stared at the ceiling. "I've been doing some thinking. I guess...I guess if there was ever anything I could do for Faith, I would do it in a heartbeat. If she needs someone to take care of her baby, I would consider it an honor." He turned his face toward his wife. "If this baby is handicapped, that's just the way it is. And if he's not handicapped, it sure would be nice to have another son tearing around our place. If you're sure you're all right with it, we'll tell the folks we can take him."

"Yes, I'm sure. I want that little baby more than anything else."

They lay there in silence, contemplating the bizarre turn of events. Suddenly Mamie gasped. "LaVon! I just remembered something! Remember how I told you that Angie has been wishing for a baby and I told her we can't have any more? Well, maybe about a half year ago, she was playing outside one day when she suddenly came inside. She looked me straight in the eyes, just as solemn as could be. 'Mom!' she said. 'We are going to have a baby!' I was so surprised, I just said, 'We are?' She said, 'Yes!' and then ran back outside. I just stood there and wondered what that was all about." Mamie rolled over to face him. "But LaVon, listen. Faith is six months along! Think about that!"

LaVon grinned. "Well, it sounds like God gave Angie a little heads up, didn't He?"

Their laughter was tinged with hysteria as they struggled to come to grips with the crazy spin their life was taking. Late into the night they lay awake, discussing the many aspects of this unbelievable news and how it might change their lives.

Shock waves reverberated through the Bontrager family as Eldon and Mary Ellen broke the news to the other children and their spouses. Although they all knew they must forgive, each member of the family had times of fierce anger toward the unknown man who had so appallingly wronged someone they held dear. The days seemed dark as they struggled to accept the situation that had been thrust upon them.

On one thing they all agreed: LaVon and Mamie seemed a perfect fit to care for Faith's child. And having already wrestled through the decision, LaVon and Mamie willingly consented.

The next Sunday at Cedar Crest Amish Mennonite Church, the children were all sent out at the end of the service. It was obvious there was a very solemn matter at hand as the congregation sat waiting. After the last child's footsteps faded away, Bishop Paul Miller gravely got to his feet and read a letter:

> Dear friends,
>
> You have all probably heard the news about a severely handicapped girl at Winfield State Hospital being violated by a male nurse. This involves one of our church families—the Eldon Bontrager family. The victim is 29-year-old Faith.
>
> We face the following uncertainties:
>
> - Because of the mother, this pregnancy may not go full term.
> - The child may not survive early birth.
> - The mother's condition is delicate.
> - The child has the potential of not being normal.
>
> The Bontrager family is experiencing God's grace. They

invite you to pray for them and to respect their privacy.

We acknowledge that God may take or give life to the unborn child. If life is granted, the family's wishes are as follows:

- To bring this child up in the ways of God.
- To ask that our young children be spared the details.
- To ask the church for acceptance.

Let us pray for God's will and that we can respond as Christ would. The hospital is protecting the family's identity, so let us be confidential as well.

Thank you,

The ministry at Cedar Crest

The congregation sat in stunned silence except for the sobbing of Mary Ellen, Carolyn, and Marilyn, who were sitting together in the back. Paul folded the paper and put it in his Bible. "Let us rise for a word of prayer," he said, leading them in a benediction.

Not an eye was dry as the church mourned with the Bontragers and gathered around them to offer comfort and support. The usual after-church conversation was hushed. Everyone quietly dispersed and went home to digest the awful news.

What would the future hold for Faith and her unborn child?

Part TWO

20

The Birth

Newspapers exploded with the unbelievable story. Headlines across the nation proclaimed the horrible news:

> **"Retarded Patient Pregnant after Rape!"**
>
> **"Hospital Rape Victim's Family Will Not Abort Fetus!"**
>
> **"Male Nurse Charged with Rape of Retarded Patient!"**

Thankfully, the staff at Winfield State Hospital refused to divulge names, sparing the Bontrager family any unwelcome publicity. The hospital recommended a social worker and a lawyer to work with Eldon and Mary Ellen and the prospective adoptive parents, LaVon and Mamie. Eldon and Mary Ellen had legal guardianship of the baby until all rights were severed from Jeremy Williams,[1] the man who had confessed to being the biological father—and was on his way to prison.

Despite the negligence that had caused the situation, Winfield State Hospital provided excellent support for Faith and the unique needs she was facing. As promised, they assigned a personal nurse to help her through her pregnancy and delivery. Kay Carmody took the responsibility seriously, guarding Faith like a watchdog. Every morning she took Faith's vitals and prepared protein-rich foods to help her feed the baby growing within her. Winfield also arranged for an obstetrician to take care of the delivery. Dr. Randall Morgan was competent in his field, specializing in trauma pregnancies.

Mary Ellen, Carolyn, Marilyn, and Mamie traveled to the hospital in Wichita for Faith's first checkup. When Dr. Morgan finished the examination, he sat down with the troubled women in the waiting room. "If you want to have an abortion done, there is still time," he said. "I know you have already decided not to, but I do need to mention that option."

The receptionist was watching like a hawk from behind the counter. Mary Ellen wasn't sure what she was thinking, but it didn't matter. "Abortion is not an option," she said. "We feel it would be wrong to take a life, and two wrongs don't make a right."

The doctor nodded. "I assumed you wouldn't change your minds. If saving the baby is your wish, we will do everything we can to help."

"It is," Mary Ellen affirmed. The others sitting with her nodded their assent.

The receptionist ducked behind the counter. She appeared busy with her work, but Mary Ellen knew she was still listening.

Dr. Morgan leaned forward and lowered his voice. "I do want you to understand that although the mother's medications might affect the baby negatively, there is also a good chance that they won't."

"Dare we hope he might be a normal child?" Mamie asked.

---

[1] This is not his real name. It has been changed for security purposes.

"Of course. He might be perfectly fine."

Dr. Morgan couldn't answer every question, but his quiet, confident explanations helped quell some of the Bontragers' fears. They went home willing to rest in the Lord.

But the waiting was not easy. The heavy publicity from the media, as well as potential criticism for allowing the pregnancy to continue, made them work hard to keep quiet about their involvement in the situation. Aside from the church, few people knew the backstory of the little boy LaVon and Mamie were preparing to adopt.

Not only was the threat of negative publicity always present in their minds, but there were also other uncertainties and unanswered questions that kept the Bontragers awake at night. But there would be no answers until Faith delivered the child.

Eldon and Mary Ellen, along with their church and family, constantly prayed for God's will to be done. Even so, there were moments of doubt. "How will beauty ever come out of these ashes?" Mary Ellen asked Eldon one night. "I always found comfort that my three handicapped girls were innocent and blameless before God. But now we are facing such a dreadfully horrible thing. How can God make this a blessing?"

Eldon looked thoughtful. "One thing that comforts me is that Faith is still innocent before God. And so is her child. Despite all our questions, these things are sure." Eldon's calm voice dispelled his wife's fears. "I found a comforting verse this morning," he added, opening his well-worn Bible to Psalm 27:13. " 'I had fainted, unless I had believed to see the goodness of the Lord in the land of the living.' I can't help but remember when I had that beautiful dream about Faith, way back when she was so sick as a baby. I saw her perfect and whole, wearing a white angel robe. She was so beautiful. Remember?"

Mary Ellen nodded. The dream had painted a lovely picture in her mind as well.

"At the time," Eldon went on, "I had a clear sense of God having a specific purpose for Faith. I never dreamed it would be something like this, but I trust Him to work out His goodness in a special way."

By the time the birth was near, LaVon and Mamie had obtained all the necessary papers to adopt the child. There had been no legal obstacles. It seemed clear God was preparing a way for Faith's child.

When LaVon and Mamie told their children they were adopting a baby, Greg and Angie cheered. Many times over the next weeks, they talked about the new baby whose mom and dad were unable to care for him. Daily they prayed as a family for the baby's protection and well-being.

After two months of vigilance, one morning Kay Carmody noticed her patient was becoming restless. She took Faith's vitals and discovered signs of labor. Kay knew the baby was early, but she also realized they had never expected Faith to carry this pregnancy full term. Working quickly, Kay notified the proper people and soon an ambulance pulled up to the entrance of Winfield State Hospital.

The media had been camped outside for days, awaiting this event. Seeing the ambulance, they deduced the time had come. "Which hospital are you taking her to?" the reporters hollered from across the barrier holding them back. "Tell us where you're going!"

As the emergency personnel tucked in her patient, Kay jumped aboard, yelling, "St. Francis Hospital has a good NICU!" Then she slammed the door and told the driver, "Take us to Wesley Medical Center."

As the media rushed to their vehicles and headed off to St. Francis, the ambulance drove in the opposite direction. Kay chuckled as they unloaded Faith at Wesley Medical—no reporters were around to disturb them!

The Bontrager family had been notified as soon as Faith showed signs of labor. This was the second time they received a call like this, but the first time it had been a false alarm. After that sleepless night, they had agreed that the next time Eldon and Mary Ellen would go to the hospital alone and let LaVon and Mamie know if it was indeed time for the baby to be born.

But this time, things moved faster than any of them could have anticipated. On January 23, 1992, there was no false alarm. Eldon and Mary Ellen got to the hospital only slightly before the wee little boy emerged into the world. The delivery was much smoother and quicker than anyone could have imagined. Mary Ellen just missed witnessing the birth because she was still putting on her protective gown, and LaVon and Mamie were still at home, sleeping.

The staff immediately whisked the child away for monitoring and testing. The examination took about three hours. To Eldon, it seemed the doctors were determined to find some disability. Although Dr. Morgan had been respectful and supportive of the Bontragers' decision to save the child, the criticism they had sensed from other staff was difficult for Eldon to swallow. He found it hard to believe they really wanted the child to live.

"Are they giving him oxygen for sure while they're examining him?" he stewed. "He's so tiny. Will he survive? Maybe they're thinking if they can deprive him of oxygen for the first few hours, he'll die and they'll feel like they've won."

But finally a nurse returned to escort them to the baby. He was nestled in a clear plastic-enclosed crib that would reduce sound and keep him warm until he grew big enough to go home. Eldon and Mary Ellen peered in at the tiny, swaddled bit of humanity. Weighing only three pounds and six ounces, the baby had a long fight ahead of him. But a wide grin split Eldon's face as he studied the little boy. "He looks just perfect. I can't see a single thing wrong with him."

Mary Ellen let out a long breath, a beautiful smile settling on her face. "I was so afraid," she admitted. "I'm not sure how I could have handled it if there was something obviously wrong with him."

After admiring their new grandson, they went back to sit with their daughter. "Faith, your baby is beautiful," Mary Ellen told her weary child, stroking her arm. "We love him already."

Faith's small, twisted body lay curled up as usual, her dark hair spread out on the pillow. Mary Ellen studied her face. How much did Faith understand what was happening? Did she sense the evil that had been committed against her? Mary Ellen longed to know what Faith was feeling behind her vacant stare.

Never one to sit around, Eldon soon headed back to Arlington to herald the news while Mary Ellen stayed with Faith. In all the hurry and stress of the birth, Eldon had forgotten to notify LaVon and Mamie.

The first stop on the way home was the Essenhaus. It was only four in the morning, but Eldon knew Carolyn would be there, preparing for the day. He decided to stop in and call LaVon and Mamie from there, rather than stopping in so early in the morning.

Eldon pounded on the restaurant door until Carolyn let him in. "Faith's little boy was born this morning," he told her, grinning from ear to ear.

Carolyn sucked in her breath. "Is everything okay?"

Eldon chuckled. "He's awfully tiny, but he looks like a fighter. He seems like a perfectly normal boy—he just needs to grow a little before they let him go home. Can I use your phone to call LaVon and Mamie?"

"Of course!" Beaming, Carolyn waved him over to the phone.

"Hello," a groggy LaVon answered.

"LaVon!" Eldon's voice betrayed his excitement. "Your son has arrived!"

"He has?" LaVon was instantly wide awake. "How's he doing?"

"He's doing well! He's small, but I can already tell he's a fighter."

"All right!" LaVon exulted. "We'll be out as soon as we can!"

LaVon ran to tell Mamie the news. Despite the momentary disappointment of missing the birth, the adoptive parents were overjoyed. They began to prepare to go to the hospital. The entire family couldn't wait to see the tiny baby who had consumed so many of their thoughts and prayers in the past two months. The attorney called as soon as he was notified of the birth and asked them to sign papers for legal custody, so on the way to the hospital, they stopped in and made the adoption official.

Awe filled their hearts as they peered in at the tiny bundle. As they watched the baby squirm and stretch, they praised God with joy and gratitude for his safe arrival.

"Does the baby have a name?" asked the nurse as she worked on the paperwork.

"His name is Joseph Grant," Mamie replied, pronouncing the syllables carefully. "But we plan to just call him Grant."

"I'm afraid he's stolen my heart already," a thoroughly smitten LaVon confessed to Mamie.

"He looks like my doll," four-year-old Angie declared. "He's so teeny."

"Yeah," seven-year-old Greg agreed. "I sure hope he grows big someday. He's awfully tiny." But the smile on his face let everyone know he was thrilled to the core with his new baby brother.

As the news sped around among the Cedar Crest Amish Mennonite families, the phone rang at Greg's young friend Levi Schmucker's house. Although Levi didn't usually have much use for babies, he knew this one belonged to Greg, so he prayed for the little baby he hoped to meet soon. Little did he realize how his prayer might be intertwined with his own future.

21

Miracle Child

Despite Nurse Kay's outstanding care, it seemed Faith's thin, bent body was unable to supply her baby with adequate nourishment. Grant hit the world hungry—but he never lost an ounce. Slowly but surely he matured enough to survive outside his incubator bed. Gradually his little lungs strengthened, and when he was five weeks old, the hospital released him to go to his new home.

LaVon and Mamie were jubilant as they left the hospital with their squirming little miracle. He weighed four pounds and ten ounces, and the car seat just swallowed him up.

"It's amazing how God has given us this child after we had given up on having more," LaVon said as he guided the car toward home. "Think of the miracle it would be if he actually turns out to be normal." Although the doctors had assured the adoptive parents that Grant was perfectly fine, LaVon's boyhood experience of growing up in a family with disabled children made him cautious.

"Oh, I'm not worried a bit," Mamie said. "Just look at those bright eyes. I think he'll be just fine. I wonder what God has in mind for him?" Her calm confidence helped quell her husband's fears.

LaVon stared unseeingly out the window. "It's such a strange mix of feelings," he mused. "I still think it's terrible and sad what Faith had to endure, yet I love this little fellow. And really, if we want him to grow up as a well-adjusted child, we need to keep a positive attitude."

Mamie nodded. "What happened to Faith was so wrong, but we can't continue being upset about it. The way we think and talk about this will affect how other people view our son."

The white two-story house with the expansive yard seemed to welcome them home after their time in the hospital the past few weeks. LaVon and Mamie had bought this place several years before, remodeling the old house and making it beautiful. They loved their home and were so glad to bring home another baby to live there.

As they drove in the lane, they pondered the big responsibility that stretched before them. In the back seat, baby Grant grunted and stretched his tiny arms over his head. Whatever this new world held, he was ready to be part of it.

That evening Eldon and Mary Ellen brought Angie and Greg back home. The children bounded in the door, then saw that the baby was asleep and tiptoed quietly over to see him.

"It's all right," Mamie smiled. "He isn't easily disturbed." She looked at Angie's expectant face. "Would you like to hold him?"

Angie's face was beaming as she took the tiny bundle into her arms. LaVon chuckled at her excitement. "Well, what do you think of your little brother?"

"I think he's the cutest baby in the world," she told him emphatically.

Greg also took a turn at holding his little brother. His wide grin spoke volumes.

The first days of welcoming Grant to his new home were overshadowed with the care he required. They had to feed him every couple of hours around the clock. LaVon and Mamie watched his every movement closely. The children popped in now and then to make sure he was still there and hadn't disappeared while they were out playing. All the love and care he was receiving made Grant gain quickly.

The two siblings discussed their new brother. "He must be an orphan," Angie said knowledgeably.

"Yeah, he probably is," Greg agreed. "Why else would he be living with us instead of with his parents?"

Angie shrugged. "Well, I don't care what kind of baby he is. He's all ours."

Greg nodded. "I don't care either. He's the best baby anyone ever had."

Having satisfactorily settled the origin of their new sibling, Greg and Angie returned to their new pastime of fighting over who had the longest turn at holding him.

As LaVon and Mamie adjusted to the new baby, Eldon and Mary Ellen were facing their own struggle. Although there had been no evidence of previous abuse at Winfield, it tore at them to keep their girls in that facility after what had happened. But there were few other options for disabled people in Kansas, and with only Carolyn still at home and their own age increasing, it seemed impossible to move the girls back home.

The Bontragers requested only female caretakers for their girls, but the rest they could only trust to God's hands.

When Grant was ten months old, the whole Bontrager family headed to Winfield to see Faith and Lynette. Very rarely did Gina go along, but this outing included her. It was a lovely day for a picnic on the grounds. That day the whole family posed for a picture—three disabled and five normal siblings, plus the parents.[1] It was the only time all the siblings were together in one place, and later they talked about that day with fond memories.

As they chatted and laughed that afternoon, they also watched Grant. It seemed his big, alert eyes were watching Faith with extra interest. What was it that drew his attention? Did he recognize the sounds she made? There was no way to know, but it seemed he was drawn to her.

When Faith became restless, a nurse wheeled her back to her room. Marilyn wanted to visit her privately to tell her about her son, so the nurses pulled the curtain around them.

Gently Marilyn took her hand. Faith seemed calmer now, but unresponsive. "Faith," Marilyn said softly. "Your son is healthy and well. He's beautiful. He was so tiny when he was born, but he's a fighter. I don't know if you can understand what I'm saying, but I just wanted you to know."

As Marilyn stroked her sister's arm, a tear slipped down Faith's cheek.

Marilyn was shocked. Had Faith understood what she was hearing? She continued talking quietly. "You don't have to worry, Faithy. No one outside the family is going to take him away. LaVon and Mamie have adopted him as their own and are taking good care of him."

Faith became restless again. She cried and became inconsolable. Marilyn kept stroking her arm and patting her shoulder, but she could not comfort her.

A nurse poked her head around the curtain. "Is something wrong?"

"I must have upset her," Marilyn said. "I'm sorry. I'll leave now." She leaned down and kissed Faith's cheek before heading back outside.

Marilyn was glad she had taken the time to tell Faith about her child. Any woman would want to know, and she was sure by Faith's reaction that she did comprehend something. It was just impossible to know how much.

---

[1] See color photo section for this picture.

As Grant developed, his grandparents found themselves observing him closely. Could it be true that he was as normal as he seemed? LaVon and Mamie, on the other hand, were soon satisfied with his healthy development and cheered as he progressed through each stage right on schedule. At three months, he gave them his first smile. At six months, he rolled over. At eight months, he was sitting by himself. He crawled at eleven months and started walking at sixteen months.

LaVon holding six-month-old Grant.

Although on the small side, Grant was strong and wiry. When Grandma Mary Ellen came to visit, he liked to show off by hanging on the edge of the table and pulling up his feet until they touched the underside. There he hung like a monkey.

Mary Ellen was alarmed the first time he performed this trick. "Grant! What if you fall?"

Grant grinned mischievously as he hung on tightly. Greg and his friend Levi, who was visiting that day, whooped and laughed at the antics of the toddler. Pretty soon Grant swung his feet back down to the floor and ran upstairs to play.

"He's such a tease," Mamie said apologetically. "I'm sorry if he scared you."

"Oh, I don't mind," Mary Ellen replied, chuckling. "I'm just so glad to see him doing normal things."

22

Gone Without Warning

"Since Gina is turning twenty-one, we should have a birthday party for her," Carolyn said to Marilyn and Mary Ellen one day.

"Would she enjoy it?" Mary Ellen asked. "She's such a hermit, you know. She doesn't really like being around people."

"We should still try it," Carolyn insisted. "It would be as much for us as for her."

"Okay, that sounds like a good plan," Mary Ellen said. "Lots of people in the community enjoy Gina." They began inviting people until they knew the house would be bursting at the seams. Mary Ellen sewed a purple velour dress for Gina to wear for the celebration.

November 27, 1994, finally came. Gareth and Phyllis arrived from Texas in the late afternoon. When they walked in, Gina laughed and giggled, which was very uncharacteristic for her. "Gina, it's so good to see you!" Phyllis exclaimed. "Happy birthday!" Gina giggled even more. Her legs flew out and her arms waved. She seemed excited about her party.

Phyllis helped her sisters get everything ready before the rest of the guests arrived. After the final preparations, she came back into the living room where Gina was sitting in her wheelchair. "Oh, Gina!" Phyllis took her hand so she wouldn't get hit in the face as Gina excitedly waved her arms. "You look so pretty in your new purple dress. We're going to have people coming tonight for your party." Gina kicked out her foot approvingly.

Little Grant came with his family to celebrate Gina. The almost-three-year-old grinned at his aunt, hugging her enthusiastically. Already the active, curly-headed toddler was friendly and uninhibited.

The family made it a very special day for Gina. They gave her many lovely presents, including a stuffed bunny. During the party, she was happy and responsive to everyone. God blessed the family with this one last celebration, for in two months everything would change.

One evening a month later, Carolyn, who was now living in her own house in Arlington, went over to her parents' house to retrieve a book she had left there by mistake. She found Gina upset and crying as Mary Ellen tried to feed her.

"Here, Gina, open your mouth," Mary Ellen coaxed. Gina flapped her hands and hit her mom's hand. Food flew all over the floor, and Mary Ellen sighed. "You must be full," she said, grunting as she bent to clean up the mess.

Then she noticed Carolyn at the door. "Well, hello," she said, smiling. "I was just trying to get Gina fed early tonight."

Carolyn walked to the table and picked up her book. "I just came to grab this." She paused. "You look tired, Mom."

Mary Ellen sighed and nodded. "I am," she admitted.

When Carolyn arrived home a few minutes later, she was met by her ecstatic little Schnauzer, Baxter, who shared her home with her. She was so deep in thought she didn't even notice the dog trying to get her attention.

"Lord, how long can Mom do this?" Carolyn prayed aloud. "She looked so tired tonight. She's already sixty-one, and she isn't getting any younger." Carolyn knew some decisions had to be made about Gina's care, and questions ran through her mind as she took a shower and headed to bed. *Will I need to sell the restaurant and help take care of Gina? Or will we need to put her in a home like we did Faith and Lynette?* She knew what the answer would be to that, but she also knew her parents were getting too old to handle this level of care much longer.

The decision never needed to be made. A month later, on the morning of January 24, 1995, the day started as usual. The school bus picked up Gina for her special ed classes. As Mary Ellen watched her go, she told Eldon, "I can't begin to imagine what I would do without these few hours of respite. I am a bit worried about her though. I'm not sure she was quite well when she left."

"Don't worry," Eldon said. "They always care for her every bit as well as we do."

A while later the telephone rang. Eldon answered. "Hello?"

It was the school principal. "Mr. Bontrager, I'm sorry to tell you this, but your daughter is on her way to the hospital. When the bus arrived this morning, she wasn't breathing."

"Oh, no!" Eldon cried. "We'll head right on over." He slammed down the phone. "Something's wrong with Gina! We need to get to the hospital."

Mary Ellen gasped. "Oh, I should have kept her home." She followed her husband out the door. Dust billowed out from behind their car as they roared toward town.

When they got to the hospital, they could see Gina was in bad shape. She was breathing again, but in a coma. The doctors couldn't find any medical reason for the incident, but it was clear that unless there was a miracle, death was near.

Eldon and Mary Ellen quickly notified the children, and soon those who could come were crammed into the tiny space beside Gina's bed. Tears flowed as they sang and prayed, taking turns holding Gina's hand and talking to her even though she wasn't responsive.

By afternoon, her breathing was becoming shallow. And before evening, Gina passed away.

"I can't believe she's gone," Mary Ellen grieved as they drove home.

"She went so fast," Eldon mourned. "But we wouldn't ask to have her back. Just think of it—she has a new body now, perfect and whole."

The pain in their hearts intensified when they walked into the silent house. Gina had been the only child left at home—now it was just the two of them. In the stillness, they felt drawn to Gina's bedroom. They wanted to see the place where she had spent so many hours of her day.

But when they opened the door, they were greeted by a nightmare. The suspended ceiling, which had been weakened by an unknown water leak, had collapsed. A mound of debris was piled on the waterbed where Gina always slept. Not only was she gone, but the bed that had rocked and soothed her lay in ruins.

Mary Ellen was both shocked and awed. "It's just like God is saying she doesn't need this bed anymore."

Quietly they cleaned up the mess and went to bed. They both lay awake long into the night. Their hearts ached for their baby girl, but they knew she was finally whole in heaven.

The next few days were a blur of preparing for the funeral. Food and flowers appeared as if by magic. Family and friends from various states began trickling in.

A chilly January dawn greeted them on the day of the funeral. There was a hushed bustle of activity in the old farmhouse as Eldon, Mary Ellen, and Phyllis's family dressed and prepared to head to the church. As they headed for their vehicles, the wild winter wind caught at their hair and coats, chilling them to the bone.

Inside the warm church house, the family followed the wooden casket down the aisle, then filed into the front rows of the auditorium. They settled down to hear the message.

The bishop of Center Church, David Yoder, who was also Mary Ellen's cousin, preached the main message, and his kind words were comforting to the family. "It is appropriate that we gather here this morning," he began. "We are here to glorify the God who made Regina. We are here to exalt the God who strengthens and comforts us in times like this. We are here to ponder the works God wanted to accomplish in having brought Regina into this life. In times like this, we mortals often pause and wonder why God plans these things. Why does He do certain things the way He does them? We can't expect to find all the answers on this side of glory. But this morning we have full confidence that Regina has been given a new body. She was unaware that she needed one, but I can only glorify God that He has made provision for such a little one like Regina."

Tears of joy and sorrow were present as the family pondered how short a time they had loved Gina and how much she must be enjoying the glories of paradise.

Phyllis's thoughts had spilled out onto paper and were read at the funeral:

> Dear Gina,
>
> Your teachers were planning a graduation for you in May. But God in His wisdom gave you the most glorious graduation there could be. Your little soul is spotless! How you must be shining in those mansions above. When you look down from those realms of glory, do you wonder why our hearts are torn and we can't seem to stop crying?
>
> Yes, on that Saturday morning when we learned you were handicapped, we cried because we thought God had robbed us of a blessing. But now we know blessings come

in different ways.

Blessings come when a family binds together because each one knows the mountain is too great for any of us to climb alone. Blessings come from knowing that the soul is spotless; really, it is the soul away from God who is handicapped. Blessing is the opportunity for the church and community to show they care in many deeds of kindness to those in need. Blessing is knowing God is carrying us through.

We want to say thank you, Regina, for being part of our family and for the blessings you brought. You deserve your reward!

Lovingly,
Your sister Phyllis

After David Yoder read the obituary, Paul Miller, the bishop of Cedar Crest, stood and addressed the congregation. "It hurt me to see in the obituary that Regina only 'attended' Cedar Crest Church. Although she wasn't a member, I feel she was one of us. And maybe that's the best we can do because membership denotes that there has been a baptism, and that would not have seemed quite appropriate for her. Still, I feel that I owe her an apology that she couldn't be listed as a member."

He looked over the congregation before going on. "Let's turn to 1 Corinthians 12:12-27. 'For as the body is one, and hath many members, and all the members of that one body, being many, are one body: so also is Christ...'" As he read the beautiful words of unity in the body, he gave special emphasis to verses 22 and 23: "'Much more those members of the body, which seem to be more feeble, are necessary: and those members of the body, which we think to be less honourable, upon these we bestow more abundant honour...'"

He finished the passage and closed his Bible. "Jesus welcomed the children. Although Regina was one of the 'more feeble' members, this passage says that she was also more necessary. Just because my blood vessels and nerves are not on public display does not mean they are not part of my body. No, they are a vital part of it. Today we have lost a vital member. She was one of us. When Regina suffered, we rightly suffered with her. When Regina's family suffered, we rightly suffered with them."

Tears flowed throughout the congregation as Paul spoke. The Bontragers keenly felt the solid wall of support they had been blessed with for so many years.

"We cannot change Regina's obituary," Paul continued. "But from now on, I would like to designate Lynette and Faith as honorary members. They are innocent and have no need of baptism, but I think it is good for both us and them to know that they are a part of our church and a part of us."

Eldon had tears in his eyes when Paul shook his hand in the cemetery after the graveside service was over. "It means a lot to me that you accept my girls into our church family. Thank you."

"It's the least we can do," Paul said. "Not because they are sinners who need salvation, but because they are safe in the arms of Jesus here and through all eternity. And because they have much to teach us."

As spring came to the farm, something else arrived as well.

"Eldon," Mary Ellen said one evening as they sat on their porch swing. "We got an unusual letter today." Her face showed concern as she handed the envelope to him.

Eldon held the envelope close so he could read the postmark. "Who would be writing to us from Wichita Prison?" he mused, pushing the swing back and forth with his feet. Suddenly his eyes grew wide. "Oh! Do you think it's from Grant's father?" They knew receiving a letter from him was a possibility since the Victims Offender Reconciliation Program had reached out and asked them if they had any desire to communicate with the father. Eldon and Mary Ellen had agreed to allow him to write.

Mary Ellen nodded. "It could be." Then she added gloomily, "I dreaded the day this letter might come."

The swing rocked slowly back and forth as they looked at the envelope together. Finally Eldon turned it over in his hand, tore it open, and pulled out a single page. Clearing his throat, he read aloud:

May 30, 1995

Dear Mr. and Mrs. Bontrager,

I was excited and nervous when I got Mr. Regier's letter stating you would accept a letter from me. Nervous because I'm not sure what to write. Excited because I can finally tell you how sorry I am for causing Faith, yourselves, and everyone so much pain. I'm sorry! If there was any way I could take back what happened and take the hurt away, know that I would do it in an instant. You can't know how many times I have regretted my actions.

I'm glad you found it in your heart to forgive me. Thank you. It was important that I personally ask you for your forgiveness because it says in the Bible to ask forgiveness from those we have wronged. Even though I don't read my Bible often, I still try to live by it. I get along with people, I don't cause trouble, and I try to help people who ask me for help. I know there is a lot more to do and I'm trying.

Mr. Regier has told me you are nice people, and the child is growing up in a good home. That's great. I have always hoped for the best for him. As I have told Mr. Regier, if at any time you wish to stop your involvement in the VOR program and have no further contact, I will not go against your wishes. Doing so would cause pain and everyone has gone through more than enough. Thank you for the opportunity to communicate.

Sincerely,

Jeremy Williams

Eldon folded the letter and carefully slid it back into the envelope. "Should we write back? Maybe we shouldn't have given him permission to contact us."

Mary Ellen's eyes shimmered with tears. "I don't want to lose Grant to this... this predator." Her voice was sharp.

Eldon patted her hand. "I know. It's hard to know what is best. What if he tried to connect with Grant? The boy is doing so well; I would hate to rock the boat. Why don't we just lay this letter aside for a while and think and pray about it?"

"We should probably talk to LaVon and Mamie before we give an answer anyway," Mary Ellen agreed. They put the letter away but could never quite forget it was there, still unanswered.

Grant, now three years old, was an intense, expressive, and affectionate little boy. Late that summer, LaVon and Mamie took him along to the Haiti Benefit Auction in Ohio. The grounds swarmed with people, so they watched him closely, knowing they could lose him in an instant. But as an auctioneer sold a beautiful quilt, they were distracted for a few minutes. "Six hundred, six hundred, who'll make it fifty?"

As the chant continued, suddenly LaVon looked around. "Where's Grant?"

"Don't you have him?" Mamie asked, alarmed.

"He must have slipped away!" LaVon spun around and they hurried through the crowd, searching frantically. "We're looking for a little boy with a purple shirt and curly blond hair," they told curious onlookers. Word spread as others joined the search.

All the searching was to no avail. The police checked all the cars leaving the premises. No Grant could be found anywhere.

Finally a little head poked out of a loft window in the sale barn. "Can you please help me?" Grant called when he saw his father searching outside.

LaVon rushed upstairs to retrieve the little scamp. “You scared us,” he told his son, trying to be stern amid his overwhelming relief.

“I was just playing,” Grant said seriously. “I wanted to see what was upstairs. Then I couldn’t get down.”

LaVon hugged him tightly. “Well, I’m just glad we found you.”

Grant clung to his daddy’s neck and grinned his charming smile. “Yeah, me too. I was afraid I would have to stay up there forever.”

LaVon’s heart melted. He felt he should punish his son, but he couldn’t bring himself to do it.

Grant’s huge eyes and halo of blond curls were a striking combination. His outgoing, friendly personality made him a gift to his family and the whole Arlington community.

One day Grant was wandering around the Essenhaus restaurant, hoping Aunt Carolyn had some of those big, puffy pastel mints by her cash register. Sure enough, the bowl was full. As he helped himself, he struck up a conversation with the lady paying her bill. “Hi! I’m Grant. What’s your name?”

“My name is Jill,” she answered, grinning. She paid the cashier, then bent down to Grant’s level. They chatted about various subjects until Grant asked, “So, where do you live?”

Jill smiled. “Well, you see, I just moved to Arlington, and you are the first person in this town to really talk to me.”

Grant grinned. “I like talking to you and to everyone in the whole world.” He gestured a big circle to include everyone.

Jill laughed. “You’ll go far with that attitude. The world should have more people like you.”

The following years were a time of change. Since both Cedar Crest and Center Church were bursting at the seams, a joint outreach was started in 1997. Several families from the two churches formed a small congregation, so Eldon's country church house was put into use once more, opening its doors for worship as Arlington Church.

If there was something this new church had in abundance, it was children. When the children's Sunday school classes were dismissed, three quarters of the church walked out. For such a small group, there were many strong and varied personalities, but with plenty of communication, things hummed along amazingly well. Eldon and Mary Ellen, Carolyn, LaVon and Mamie, Myron and Ilene, and Dan and Marilyn were all a part of the new little church.

As the church sorted through its adjustments, things at Winfield State Hospital were changing too. The hospital had a long history of turmoil, and finally, after being open for 116 years, it closed its doors. Many of its clients were placed in community programs in the area. Creative Community Living, the largest of these programs, had built seven duplexes in residential areas of Winfield, nearby El Dorado, and Arkansas City.

Lynette and Faith were moved to a group home in El Dorado. It was homey, with only six residents and the staff who cared for them. The atmosphere was welcoming and friendly for visitors. The staff celebrated birthdays and sent out cards every year with pictures of the girls.

With Gina gone and El Dorado being closer than Winfield, Eldon and Mary Ellen tried to visit the girls at least once a month. On their visits, the staff made sure either Lynette or Faith met Eldon and Mary Ellen at the door. The atmosphere couldn't have been more different from the sterile, impersonal setting of Winfield State Hospital.

Lindy, a dear Down syndrome girl whom Eldon and Mary Ellen came to love, often met them at the door with "Facie," as she called Faith. "Want some coffee?" she would ask before the visitors had a chance to sit down.

"Sure, I'll take some," Eldon would say with a smile. As they settled into the comfortable couches, Lindy headed off to get the coffee. She always wanted to make sure they felt welcome.

"I wasn't sure how this change would be, but it feels almost like coming home," Eldon told Mary Ellen after one visit. "We just knock on the door and we can go in. I'm so grateful the girls have the opportunity to live in a place like this."

"It makes me miss Gina all the more," Mary Ellen said. "But I will never regret keeping her at home with us. Looking back, the time we spent together seems so short—so precious."

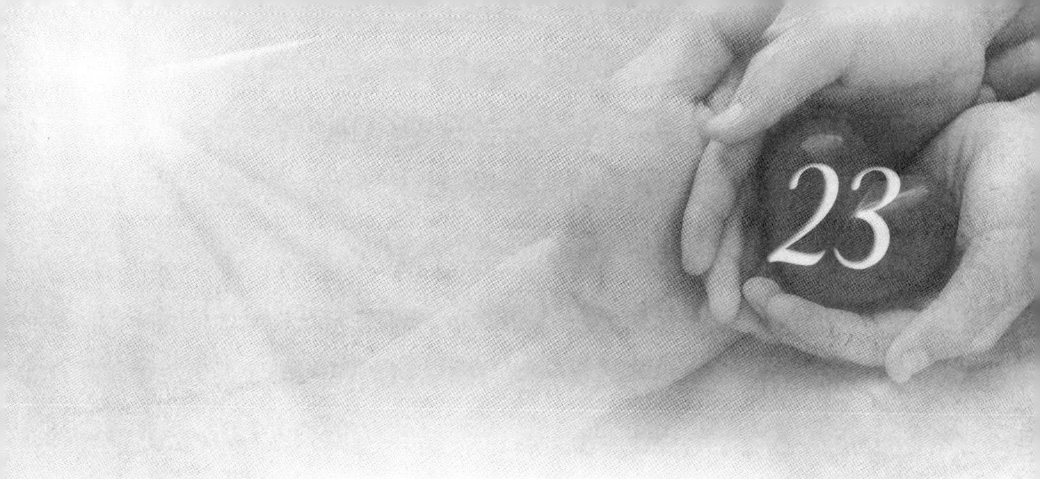

23 Adventures at School

Grant knew early on that he was adopted. He knew that somewhere out in the great big world were a mom and dad who were unable to care for him, and that was why he was growing up with this fine family. At first this information satisfied him. But one day when he was six years old, Grant's mind was whirling as he rode beside Mamie on their way to town. Suddenly he voiced the question Mamie had known would come someday: "Who is my mom?"

Mamie jerked her thoughts away from the upcoming shopping trip. *He must be ready to hear the truth.* Their case worker had said Grant would ask when he was ready to hear. In a way, she was glad the moment had finally come.

"Well, Grant, this might be hard for you to understand, but your birth mom is Faith," Mamie replied simply.

"Faith?" Grant gasped in surprise, his eyes growing wide. "But she's in the El Dorado care home with all those... other children." His face registered shock and disbelief. "She's really my mom?" he asked in an awed voice.

"Yes, Grant, she is. She couldn't care for you when you were born, so we took you in. We chose to adopt you so you could be our child, just like Greg and Angie. We love you just as if you had been born to us."

Grant listened intently but did not utter another word. Mamie wished she knew what was going through his curly blond head. Reaching over, she squeezed his little hand. Grant smiled up at her but remained silent. His mind was still straining to grasp this new realization.

Questions began to plague Grant after he found out about his biological mother. *Why is my mom so different? What does that mean about me? And who is my dad? Where is he?* Despite his happy-go-lucky ways, the questions kept burning within him. But for the time being, he kept these thoughts private.

Grant never doubted his adoptive parents' love, but he sometimes wondered if they could possibly love him as much as they loved their own children. He often thought about his handicapped mom. *Why is she like she is? I can't even talk with her.*

"Mom," he asked Mamie one day, "am I left-handed because I'm adopted?" His normally happy face was clouded with concern.

"Why do you think that?" Mamie asked.

"Well, there's another girl at school who's adopted, and she's left-handed too."

Mamie held back a smile. "So you're wondering if all adopted children are left-handed?"

Grant nodded solemnly.

She pulled him into her arms, hugging him tightly. "No, Grant, God made you just the way you are. Some people are left-handed and some are right-handed, and it has no connection to being adopted. Every person is special just the way God made them."

Grant's face cleared, and he hurried out to ride his bicycle. Mamie watched as he vigorously rode back and forth on the lane. "He sure does everything with all his might," she said aloud. "Poor boy. It must be hard to sort this all out in his mind."

Despite the questions that nagged at him, school was a great social party for Grant. He thrived on the stimulation of being with people all day. In fact, there were often so many fun things to watch that it was difficult to keep his mind on his work. But as always, his enthusiasm for life spilled over into the classroom, and soon all his classmates were his friends.

Not long into Grant's first year, the school had a fire drill. Miss Yoder helped her wide-eyed students recall what they had learned about emergencies. "Remember, walk to the playground and wait there for the rest of the students."

Keyed up and unable to hold still, Grant went bounding out the door ahead of the pack. "Where's the fire? Where's the fire?" he yelled. Finding the older students already outside, he went to his sister Angie and squeezed her hand. "I'm so scared," he whispered.

"You goose," Angie replied with fifth-grade condescension. "It's just a fire drill."

"But it seems so real," he whispered back.

Miss Yoder came over and took Grant's hand. "Let's go back in," she said to her students. "We're all safe and accounted for."

As they marched back inside, Grant hollered back to the rest of his class, "I was so scared, I could almost smell smoke!" Everyone laughed and agreed.

"It did seem real, didn't it?" Miss Yoder smiled. "But that is the reason we do fire drills. So if it would be the real thing, you will respond just like you did today."

They walked into the schoolroom and sat down at their desks. "Children," Miss Yoder said, "you all did marvelously. Let's take a moment and thank God it was just a drill."

With sober respect, the children bowed their heads.

Miss Yoder used character sketches to teach the students various traits. One morning they were studying the trait of responsibility.

"When we stop to help a child who got hurt, that's part of being responsible," Miss Yoder told the class.

Grant waved his hand wildly to attract her attention. "Once I went biking and fell down. I got right up and kept riding."

Puzzled, Miss Yoder asked, "And how does that show responsibility?"

Without hesitation, Grant replied, "I picked myself up without anyone helping me."

The twinkle in Miss Yoder's eyes betrayed the chuckle she hid inside. "Well, Grant, that is part of it. You keep doing your best."

After the character sketch, it was time for math class. This morning Miss Yoder dramatically introduced the number zero. "Poor zero," she said, drawing a zero on the blackboard. "He just cries and cries because he thinks he's not important. And by himself, he is nothing. If he compares himself to all the other numbers, he sees that all of them have pointy things except the eight, and he has two circles. But the zero has only one."

The children listened carefully. Then Grant raised his hand.

"Yes, Grant, what is it?" Miss Yoder asked.

"We should pray for poor zero," he said in all seriousness, his soft heart hurting for the desolate number.

Miss Yoder paused. "Yes, poor zero. But he really is very important." Again the smile lurking at the corners of her mouth threatened to spill over.

"Now," she said, quickly moving on before a chuckle could burst out, "I want you all to copy a row of zeros onto your paper."

Grant's hand waved again. "I can't find my pencil," he complained.

Miss Yoder went to his desk and peeked inside. The desk was a chaotic mess. "If you kept your desk neater, you would be able to find a pencil," she advised, helping him stack his books and papers in an orderly way.

"Hey! Here's one," he exclaimed. "And another and another! One, two, three," he counted. "And here's another one!"

After everything was neatly arranged in his desk, Miss Yoder helped him count the pencils they had found. "Twelve whole pencils," Grant said, grinning. His curly head bent over his paper as he painstakingly drew his zeros.

The days sped by, and Christmas was fast approaching. For the annual Christmas program, the school was preparing to act out the Christmas story. The students carefully memorized Bible passages and tried to learn their various acting assignments.

One day things weren't going very well in practice, and Mary and Joseph were delayed in making their appearance. Grant was waiting with the shepherds behind the door and feeling restless and impatient. After what seemed like an eternity, he heard the shepherds' cue: "And they rejoiced with exceeding great joy." The shepherds burst out onto the stage, with Grant prancing around, playing his part perfectly. When the practice was over, it was high time for recess. "I'm sorry practice took so long this morning," Miss Yoder apologized. "We will keep working on your parts."

As she dismissed the class, they heard whooping and hollering from the other children who were already playing. "Miss Yoder," Grant said, still in the Christmas story mode, "I wonder if they see the star?"

Miss Yoder smiled. "Maybe that's what all the noise is about, do you think?"

Grant grinned and bounded off to join the others. Despite the many questions he kept bottled up inside, his perpetual enthusiasm always put people at ease. No one suspected the inner struggles this outgoing little boy faced.

One day Miss Yoder led her students in a discussion on adoption. "Some parents can't care for their own children, so they have to put them up for adoption. These children are adopted into families who want children to love and care for. We have two children in our room who were adopted when they were little."

The children looked around with big eyes. Who in their room was so special? They all wanted to have that privilege.

Grant eagerly raised his hand. "We are both adopted," he volunteered, pointing to himself and a girl in the class.

Their classmates looked at them in admiration. "It must be special to be adopted," remarked one little boy longingly.

"Yes, it is," Miss Yoder said.

Grant straightened his shoulders and pushed out his chest as far as he could. He was glad to know he was special.

One day the fifth- and sixth-grade teacher, Miss Schmucker, decided to start a "Run-Across-Kansas" project for her girls' physical education class. Six laps around the school grounds equaled one mile. The state of Kansas has 220 miles from its southern border to its northern border, so "running across Kansas" would take many laps around the property.

Peer pressure soon spread through the school, and the older boys began the same project. The running fever finally filtered all the way down to the youngest students.

"Miss Yoder, can we help run across Kansas too?" Grant asked. He had an abundance of energy, and recess was his favorite time of the day.

The next recess found his class trotting around the school grounds. "I ran five laps," Grant panted as he came back inside. And the next day he reported, "I ran six laps."

The students were tenacious, keeping it up until all 220 miles had been run.

Although Grant loved the social aspect of school, focusing on his studies was hard work and took a toll. Although fun projects made school exciting, his favorite time was still the dismissal bell when he could head home to his dog, his creek, and his home.

A New Minister, Indians, and Exploding Eggs

In 1998, Myron, Ilene, and their five children moved from their little house in town to the big old farmhouse. Eldon and Mary Ellen were now living in a trailer house beside the white-fenced lane.

As Mary Ellen was cleaning out their desk one day, she found the unanswered letter that had been waiting for three years. After discussing it with LaVon and Mamie, Eldon and Mary Ellen were encouraged to answer the letter.

Still a bit reluctant, Mary Ellen took out a pen and began to write:

> March 8, 1998
>
> Dear Mr. Williams,
>
> We received your letter several years ago and appreciate the spirit in which it was written.

We felt unsure how to respond—so we procrastinated in answering.

We do want you to know we have fully forgiven you and appreciate your care about the pain you inflicted on Faith and our whole family. We are also glad that God heals pain and helps us move on in a positive way.

If it were not for the nature of the situation, we would be glad to meet you face to face. But the child's adoptive family and we as his grandparents feel it best for the child if we refrain from further communication until he chooses to do so. He seems well adjusted now, and we hesitate to make any moves that would disrupt this.

We encourage you to read your Bible and apply it to your life. Our prayer is that you can find complete victory and peace in Christ Jesus.

We wish you God's best and hope you can have a good life.

Sincerely,

Mr. and Mrs. Bontrager

Mary Ellen carried the letter to the mailbox, hoping it would satisfy Grant's biological father and that he would not try to contact them again. They had wrestled through many layers of forgiveness, and although Jeremy Williams seemed to be sorry, it was still too hard to think of meeting this man.

In 1999, Dan and Marilyn moved their family to Wisconsin. In September of that same year, Arlington Church prepared to ordain a minister to assist the current minister, Willis Nisly. They gathered on a Friday evening to cast lots. It was a sober affair, as ordinations usually are. Becoming a minister was a life-changing event.

After giving their votes to the ministry, LaVon and Mamie's family returned home to await the news of who had been chosen for the lot. The children had lots of questions, since this was the first time they had been involved in an ordination.

As they rummaged through the kitchen for snacks, the phone rang. Everyone froze, and the knot in LaVon's stomach jumped into his throat. He and Mamie exchanged glances as he swallowed hard and walked over to answer the call that could mean only one thing. Sure enough, LaVon was one of the three men who had been chosen for the lot. He hung up the phone and shared the news, answering the question in the anxious eyes around him.

Seven-year-old Grant's fist shot into the air. "Yes! I think you'll get it!" His grin reached from ear to ear.

After a startled silence, the rest of the family laughed hysterically, evaporating some of the tension in the air.

"You make it sound like I'm campaigning for the job," LaVon said, grinning wryly. "That's not exactly how this works."

Grant could not be subdued. "Oh, Dad, you would do great!"

"This is a serious calling, son," LaVon told him. "I'm willing if I'm chosen to fill that role, but in all seriousness, I wouldn't think of campaigning for it."

That Sunday evening, the church sanctuary was quiet and tense. Three identical black hymnbooks lay on a small table at the front of the room. Everyone knew that one of the men sitting on the front bench would draw the book containing a slip of paper, but only God knew who it would be. The other two men's lives would go on as they had before, but one man would be a new leader of the congregation.

LaVon and Mamie didn't hear much of the devotional that evening. They were seeking the face of God and trying to surrender their lives to whatever plan He had for them.

As the devotional ended, David Yoder stepped forward. As the bishop of Center Amish Mennonite, he also had oversight over Arlington. The moment had come. Now was the time the congregation would find out who was being called to fill this need. David spoke calmly to the nervous congregation, then he sent a trusted man to a side room with the hymnbooks to insert the paper and shuffle the books. When he returned, a separate man was sent to bring back the books and arrange them once more on the small table.

Each man in the lot chose a hymnbook as he felt led and returned to his seat beside his wife. Then David stepped off the platform and began to open the books. LaVon was the second in line, and when his book was opened, the slip of paper was clearly visible. LaVon's head dropped, and Mamie gulped. David removed the paper and stepped back. "The lot is cast into the lap, but the whole disposing thereof is of the Lord," he read solemnly.

The rest of the service was a blur for LaVon and his family as they struggled to process the change this would make in their lives. After the benediction, the members filed forward to give the new minister their support and blessing. Grant's bright eyes and soft heart took in the emotion around him, but it was difficult for him to grasp the seriousness of the occasion.

It was late when the Bontragers finally climbed into the van to head home. LaVon and Mamie were weary with the intensity of the evening, but there was peace in their hearts as they accepted the work set before them.

As they quietly pulled onto the road, fifteen-year-old Greg shared his thoughts. "Well, Dad, I think it's kind of neat that you're a preacher. It sure isn't anything to be sad about."

LaVon cleared his throat. "Thanks, Greg. It means a lot to hear you children accept this."

Grant's voice rang with triumph. "Dad! I just knew you were going to win it!" Everyone laughed, and the solemn mood was broken.

Despite Grant's carefree exterior, the questions that burdened his heart got harder and harder. *Why is my mom so different? Who is my dad? What does this mean about me?* Several times he had sensed the anguish in his extended family in the rare instances when Faith's pregnancy and his birth were referred to. He could read from their faces that the subject was too painful to discuss. He didn't understand that for the rest of the Bontragers, the agony they felt for Faith had nothing to do with her son. But for Grant, there was no such distinction, and he absorbed that sense of pain—even shame—as part of his identity. Despite the love surrounding him, Grant felt alone in his questions. He felt different from everyone else—an oddball. He became increasingly lonely.

Because of his desire to avoid the painful subject, and because it was difficult for him to have serious conversations about the things bothering him, Grant's struggle remained an inward one—only occasionally bursting out in unexpected ways. One evening, after a hard day at school, he stormed into the house and threw his lunch box on the table. Without saying a word, he tore out across the yard and took a well-worn path through the belt of trees. Anger seethed in his heart.

On the way home from school, Greg had asked him, "Grant, why are you so mad?" Grant knew his answering explosion had been ridiculous, but sometimes he himself didn't know why he lost his temper. The frustration just burst out without warning.

As the path reached the river into which he typically would have plunged, Grant slowed, breathing hard after his furious sprint. He felt something cool against his hand. Turning, he discovered that his loyal dog, Hansi, had followed him and was nosing him affectionately. Still out of breath, Grant rubbed Hansi's head, grateful for his companionship. His fury eased a bit, but he wasn't ready to go back. The heavy thoughts in his mind were more than an eight-year-old boy should have to bear. He just wanted to walk and think.

With Hansi slipping through the tall grass at his side, Grant tromped along beside the river, hurling sticks and rocks far out into the lazy water.

After a time, the seething turmoil in his mind formed into a prayer. *Lord, I can't do this by myself. I feel so sinful. I get so angry at my friends and my brother. I need you. I need you.* Grant stopped abruptly, startled at the realization of what he was thinking.

Dropping to his knees, he knelt there on the riverbank and prayed. "Lord, sometimes I don't know who I am. I feel angry and sinful. I need you to come into my heart and help me." Tears streamed down his cheeks. A warm peace flooded his heart, and he looked up at the calm blue sky. "Thank you, Jesus, for saving me." He knew without a doubt that his sins were forgiven. For the first time he could remember, he felt a sense of blessing and freedom.

For a long time, Grant remained sitting on the riverbank, reveling in the tranquility in his soul. Then, as the shadows began to lengthen, he slowly picked his way home. Although his questions remained, he knew he had met God.

Grant's newfound peace didn't change his circumstances, but it did help him deal with the questions tormenting him. One day he was draped over the hood of a tractor with his chin propped in his hand, watching Angie feed her chickens. "Well, Angie?" His voice broke the stillness of the afternoon. "I guess it's a miracle that I'm normal."

Angie looked up, startled. "Why do you say that?"

"Well, my mom is handicapped, so I could have been too." His nonchalant manner belied the seriousness of the topic. "Mom told me who my mom is, you know."

Angie was quiet for a long time. She scattered food in the pen so the chickens could scratch it, then slowly filled the water containers. Finally she closed the gate and came over to the tractor. "Yes, Grant, it is a miracle. But you sure don't have anything to worry about. Does it bother you sometimes?" She watched his face intently.

Grant shrugged. "I dunno. I was just thinking about it." In one easy motion, he leaped off the tractor. Grabbing his bike, he careened down the drive with Angie's goat kids in hot pursuit.

As Grant grew older, he liked to tag along with his brother and his friends. Greg's friend Levi often came over to spend a lazy Sunday afternoon. Grant much preferred the exciting things teenagers did over taking a nap.

But what he loved most was playing with his cousins. Since Dan and Marilyn had moved far away to Wisconsin, that left only Myron and Ilene's children.

Kaylene, Kevin, Connie, and Andy loved to go to Greg, Angie, and Grant's house. With younger siblings around at Myron and Ilene's home, they weren't allowed to make fires and cook food independently. But at Grant's house, LaVon and Mamie were more lenient, and the cousins soaked up the freedom. Together they spent many hours down by the river.

One summer day they were playing "Crocodile," one of their favorite games. As the others tried to cross the river, the "crocodile" tried to snag them.

Just up the river was a bridge where the highway crossed. As the children played, they suddenly heard a vehicle approaching. Angie yelled the warning signal: "Geronimo!" Instantly everyone dropped underwater and waited with plugged noses until the vehicle had passed. Gasping for breath, they resurfaced.

"Do you think people would actually kidnap us?" Kaylene asked dubiously as she rubbed murky water from her stinging eyes.

"People kidnap children all the time," Greg informed her solemnly. "And they have wild parties under that bridge. We find beer cans there sometimes."

Everyone's eyes got just a bit bigger as they pondered this information.

Grant shivered and moved closer to Angie.

"But they're past now," Angie grinned. "And remember—I'm the crocodile!" She lunged for Grant as he dove away. Forgetting the terrible kidnappers, the children resumed frolicking in the water, but they kept their ears peeled for the sound of another vehicle and the warning signal. They stayed far away from the bridge. In addition to the threat of kidnapping was their dread of the poisonous snakes they were sure infested the cool, deep holes around the pillars of the bridge.

Eventually their tummies were rumbling, so they emerged from the water and tramped through the row of trees looking for scrap wood.

"I think we have enough to start the fire," Greg finally said, arranging a pile of twigs and dead branches in the fire ring. "Angie, did you bring anything to roast?"

"No, but I'll go get something." Angie headed off. By the time she returned with the loot she had scavenged from Mamie, a bonfire was burning cheerily.

The boys had whittled some roasting sticks with their ever-present pocketknives. Eagerly the children threaded marshmallows on some sticks and apples on others. They each took a stick and held them over the hot embers like spokes of a wheel.

"Here goes my hunk of meat," Angie announced, holding her marshmallow stick carefully over the coals. The cousins had switched to Indian mode.

"You'd better calm down that fire," Kaylene cautioned. "That smoke could be seen for miles!" Quickly they kicked dirt over the outer edges. As their fertile imaginations carried them far away, they roasted their "meat" to the eerie sound of howling wolves and the rustle of approaching rival tribes.

"Hey, Grant!" Greg's yell broke the spell. "Your marshmallow is burning!"

Quickly Grant whipped his stick back and forth, narrowly missing the heads of his rapidly retreating cousins.

"I'll blow it out!" yelled Andy. He extinguished the flame with a great puff of air.

Greg gazed ruefully at the blackened marshmallow. "Too bad, Grant."

"Oh, it's still fine!" Grant blew off the ashes and popped the snack into his mouth. "Just a bit crunchy, that's all."

"Well, I don't like them burned," Connie declared. "I like them just lightly browned on the outside and all melted on the inside."

Once the food was gone and their clothes were dry, the cousins straggled back up to the barn to take turns milking Angie's goats and daring each other to drink the goaty-tasting liquid.

As Grant grew older, his bike became his ticket to participating in anything happening in the area. He biked around town, sniffing out action and popping in and out of the restaurant and LaVon's cabinet shop across the street. Occasionally he even showed up at Eldon's house several miles away.

One day he burst through his grandparents' door like a whirlwind. "Hi, Grandma!" he shouted.

"Hi, Grant! What brings you here?" Mary Ellen smiled a welcome as she piled some old eggs into her compost bucket.

"Just coming to see what you and Grandpa are up to." Grant grinned widely as he plopped onto the couch.

"I was just ready to ask Grandpa to take out these eggs. You can help him. They're rotten, so be careful not to break them."

Eldon emerged from the adjoining room. "Did I hear my name?"

Mary Ellen handed him the compost bucket. "Can you toss these rotten eggs on the compost pile for me?"

Eldon's eyes twinkled with mischief. "We sure can, can't we, Grant?"

Grant leaped to his feet. "Let's go!"

They headed out to the compost heap. "Don't you think it's kind of a pity to waste these eggs?" Eldon asked conspiratorially. "I think we should do some target practice."

"Yes, let's!" Grant whooped.

"It would be fun to see if we can hit that tree over there." Eldon stooped to pick up a few of the putrid little bombs. Grant laughed as he helped himself to a handful. Carefully following his grandpa's example, he took aim and flung an egg as hard as he could. *Pop!* The egg resounded as it slammed into the tree. Grant shouted with laughter.

"Isn't it great?" Eldon grinned.

"Oh, yeah!" One by one, grandpa and grandson flung the stinking orbs at the tree, cheering as they splatted against the trunk. When every last egg had been hurled at the target, Eldon looked a bit sheepish. "Now don't do this with fresh eggs," he warned.

The two walked back to the house, partners in mischief. Grant scampered into the kitchen, bursting with excitement. "Guess what Grandpa and I just did!"

Eldon came in and studiously washed his hands at the sink.

"Sounds like trouble to me," Mary Ellen chuckled. "You're the spitting image of your grandpa."

Grant laughed gaily. "You should have heard those rotten old eggs. They just exploded when they hit that tree."

Mary Ellen looked at Eldon. "They did?"

Eldon's eyes twinkled, and a grin was visible behind his beard. "Oh, I thought it would be a shame to just waste them, so we were practicing our aim a bit."

25

Fun on the Farm

Summer brought harvest on the farm. For two or three weeks, life revolved around the fields. As the sun beat down out of clear blue skies, the great golden fields of wheat were cut by a big, dusty combine harvester. Although it was a hectic time for the Bontragers, it was also a much-loved season.

LaVon had stepped out of farming to concentrate on cabinet work, but eleven-year-old Grant and his bike made sure they never missed out on the action at the farm. In fact, every child in the area flocked to the harvest fields. It was a farmer's nightmare to maneuver the bulky combine and the grain trucks past the swarms of children. Thankfully the Lord and His guardian angels protected the youngsters from bodily harm through many years of harvesttime chaos.

Today Grant sat on the coveted ledge beside his uncle Myron in the combine cab. He watched through a film of dust as the header cut the wheat heads and fed them into the threshing cylinder. The rub bars pulled them farther back, where the grains were separated from the straw and collected in a big bin behind the cab. The dusty straw sprayed out behind the combine, falling on the ground in rows.

Grant watched the bin closely. "Uncle Myron, the hopper is almost full!"

"You're right," Myron agreed. Finishing the row, they headed for the dump truck parked at the edge of the field.

"Would you like to pull the lever for the auger?" Myron asked. He knew Grant loved the excitement of unloading the wheat into the truck.

From the end of the long auger, the grains of wheat flowed as a golden stream into the waiting truck. "Oh, just look at it go," Grant said, bouncing with delight.

"Looks like the truck is full," Myron said. "Do you want to ride with Grandpa to the elevator in town?"

"Umm..." Grant contemplated, eyeing the many cousins waiting to hop aboard as soon as he abandoned his post. "Well, yeah, I guess this time I'll go with him." He opened the cab door, swung down the ladder, and hopped onto the ground. His cousin Andy immediately made his way up the ladder.

Grant hurried to the dump truck, his bare feet treading gingerly over the prickly yellow stubble. "May I go with you?" he hollered to his grandpa, who was climbing into the driver's seat.

"Sure!" Eldon grinned at the enthusiastic boy as Grant hopped into the grimy cab. Dust billowed from the seats as they arranged themselves. The air was hot, dry, and smelled of fuel.

The trip to the elevator was almost as exciting as the ride in the combine. Grant watched Eldon guide the truck onto the scales to weigh the wheat. Then the men at the co-op motioned him to the unloading pit. Eldon drove the dump truck slowly onto the grate over the pit and unloaded the grain amid the hollering of the men and the clang of shovels as they scraped out the last of the wheat.

As they headed back to the co-op to weigh the empty truck, Grant held his breath. Would they give out treats to little boys today?

Eldon figured out the technical details as Grant's eager eyes watched. When business was concluded, the man at the desk looked at Grant with a twinkle in his eyes. "Is it warm enough for a can of pop?" he asked.

"Yes, sir!" Grant's hearty reply brought a chuckle. The man disappeared to find a can of grape soda for the boy.

As Eldon puttered out of the co-op to head back to the field, Grant sipped his pop in ecstasy. It had been worth losing his spot on the combine for this.

During harvesttime, everyday routines changed to focus on the all-consuming task of bringing in the wheat before it rained. Ilene and Mary Ellen took turns bringing picnic meals out to the fields, and the men would grab a quick bite as they had time. The picnics provided a way for the family to be together for a tiny bit of time during those chaotic weeks. The combine typically didn't stop until the dew fell, which was often not until midnight.

Mornings, though, tended to be lazy, since nothing could be cut until the dew dried off again. This was hard for Grant to remember. One morning he leaped off his bike at 7:00 and threw open Uncle Myron's front door, expecting to find a flurry of activity. Instead, he found only a sleepy Ilene, who had just gotten up.

"Well, Ilene! Where is everyone? We need to get going!"

Ilene's laugh was a bit weary. "Did you forget they can't start cutting until at least nine? You need to give us a little time. We got to bed late last night."

"Oops!" Grant quickly backpedaled out the door to wait impatiently until the action started. He didn't want to miss anything.

After harvest, the summer stretched out as one long hot day followed the next. For Grant, it was an unceasing battle against boredom.

He was thrilled when Carolyn stopped in one day with an enticing proposal. "Do you want to go with me to Sam's Club in Wichita to stock up on groceries for the restaurant?"

"Oh, yes!" He leaped to his feet. "Let's go!" He delighted in helping Carolyn. Once they were at the wholesale warehouse, he helped push the big flat cart and watched Carolyn fill it with the impressively large boxes of supplies. "Are you getting any puffy mints today?" he asked, licking his lips as he eyed the candy aisle. He knew she always kept a bowl of them by the cash register at the Essenhaus.

"Oh, yes, we can't forget those," Carolyn chuckled. She began piling cases of candy and gum onto the cart. Grant knew she would be selling the packages at the store, but he sure hoped she would slip him a package or two.

Samples abounded throughout the store, and Grant happily tried each one. After they finished getting groceries, they stopped at McDonald's for lunch. Eating out was a special event, and Grant chomped down his lunch with gusto.

During the long summer days, Grant often rode his bike the half mile to Arlington where Carolyn put him to work at the Essenhaus during the busy lunch hour. He watched customers like a hawk, ready to clear their table as soon as they were finished. His energetic friendliness quickly gained him popularity among the customers.

When the lunch crowds dispersed, Grant and his growling stomach headed back to the kitchen.

"Well, Mr. Hard Worker, what do you want for lunch today?" Carolyn asked. "Fajita chicken salad?" Since he was underage, she couldn't legally pay him for his work, but for Grant, a full belly was an ample wage.

Grant thought for a moment. "No, I think today I will have chicken-fried steak with french fries. And give me lots of gravy!"

Carolyn soon had the meal dished up, and Grant sat down to dedicate himself to the task of eating. She sat across from him. "Are you full?" she asked when he had shoveled the last bite into his mouth.

"Almost," Grant said, eyeing the nearby donuts and twists.

Carolyn laughed. "Yep, you can grab a donut or something. And get yourself a candy bar or a pack of gum on your way out."

Grant sighed with contentment. He took his plate to the kitchen, wiped off his table, and headed out. "Bye," he called as he grabbed a donut twist and some gum. As he pedaled the mile home, he thought, *That was way more fun than sitting around at home.*

The fall work of plowing and preparing the fields for winter passed, bringing a slightly slower time to the farm. On the first Tuesday in November, Eldon took Grant on a trip to the sale barn. They sat on the crowded bleachers encircling the big, dusty ring. Grant whooped with delight as the herders ran the animals in one door and out the other.

At lunchtime, Eldon took Grant to the restaurant in the building. "Want a hamburger?" he asked.

"You said it!" Grant grinned. "I'm starved. I've been waiting for a burger all morning."

All too soon they were on their way home. Grandpa seemed pleased at the price his cattle had brought.

Grant turned twelve in January, and Mamie hosted a birthday party. Six of Grant's friends—and Aunt Carolyn, of course—came to celebrate the birthday boy. It was too cold to play outside, so Greg benevolently offered a wrestling match in the living room. Six boys against twenty-year-old Greg. Who would come out on top? Although the determined little boys were unable to overpower Greg, neither was he able to pin them all simultaneously. Once everyone was exhausted, they called it a draw and trooped out to the shed.

Mamie had made a pinata out of paper shopping bags. It hung from the shed ceiling, and they took turns whacking it with a stick until it finally broke apart and the candy spilled across the floor. With a whoop, the boys dove headlong into the mess, grabbing as many pieces as they could. Grant beamed all over. His home was typically much calmer and quieter than this, so he reveled in the noise and excitement.

But there was something most observers never guessed. Deep down, this active twelve-year-old had much confusion, pain, and turmoil hidden in his heart.

26

Family Fun

Grant waited anxiously at the front window. His cousins, Dan and Marilyn's family, were traveling down from Wisconsin for a 2004 reunion and would arrive any minute. The excited boy shut his eyes and imagined the familiar sights the visitors might be driving past as they neared their destination. First the mini-barn shop named Sturdi-Built, then Cedar Crest Church, next Arlington Church, and lastly Carolyn's Essenhaus. *Where can they be? Why aren't they here yet?*

His eyes popped open when he heard a vehicle slow down and turn in at the driveway. "Mom!" he screeched as he barreled out the door. "They're here!"

Dashing down the sidewalk, Grant bubbled with excitement as the big van with Wisconsin license plates rolled up the lane, pulling a travel trailer. His cup of happiness was filled to the brim as his cousins Matthew and Ryan hopped out of the van and enthusiastically greeted him. The two boys planned to spend the nights at Grant's house during their week's visit while the rest of the family stayed at Grandpa's place in the travel trailer. Carolyn had moved into a house beside Grandpa's lane, and with Myron's family living in the big house, the farm would be the center of activities that week.

"Come on, boys," Grant whooped as the visitors unloaded their luggage. "I just about couldn't wait till you got here! You wanna see a skunk?" Marilyn's eyebrows shot up as the boys ran toward the barn.

"Don't worry, Aunt Marilyn!" Grant called back. "It's just a baby!" But this calmed her misgivings only slightly.

The cousins had looked forward to seeing what rescue projects were underway at Uncle LaVon's place. Today it was a skunk and a hedgehog. The creatures were passed around and admired at length.

And, of course, they had to see the baby goats, the cats, Chika the horse, and all the other critters that had accumulated since their last visit.

Gareth and Phyllis arrived from Texas early that evening. The Bontrager family was still more inclined toward work projects than vacation time, so there was lots of action planned for the week.

One evening after painting the fence and pouring concrete at Grandpa's house, everyone trooped into Myron's farmhouse to enjoy Ilene's delicious homemade pizza. Afterward a huddle of cousins told late-night stories on the front porch. Cousin Brian from Texas had just returned from a short mission trip to Ukraine and had a few dramatic tales to spin. As the story "Herman the DeWalt Moth" got wilder and more entertaining, the cousins keeled over in appreciative guffaws. Brian's storytelling ramped up in proportion to his audience's enjoyment. As the night grew later and later, the party got louder and louder as more cousins came out to join the fun.

Dan and Marilyn had made a poor decision when they picked a spot for their travel trailer to reside for the week. As they and their small children lay in their beds at the edge of the yard trying to sleep amid the gales of laughter from the porch, their typical appreciation for stories grew rather dim.

Suddenly a window scraped open on the travel trailer, and a voice hollered out, "Time to go to bed!" In surprise, the storytellers on the porch checked the time and found it was already 11:00. They shushed up quickly, and the huddle dispersed for the night.

The rest of the week found the men working hard at adding a garage and a front porch to Eldon's trailer house. The cousins finished painting the fence and helped Carolyn weed the flower beds.

By afternoon, it became too hot to keep working, so Carolyn's hot tub became the place to be. A schedule was soon worked out for both the boys and the girls to take turns, and trails of water puddled on their benevolent aunt's kitchen floor while they traipsed in and out of the bathroom to change clothes. When Carolyn got home at night, there was always a bunch of little girls draped over her bed, reading stories and eating candy as they prepared to spend the night. Carolyn's patience knew no bounds.

As usual, when the family was visiting, Mary Ellen and her daughters cooked up a storm of waffles for brunch. The waffles were merely a springboard for many different toppings, ranging from peanut butter to sausage gravy. Everyone saved some space for the end, when ice cream and strawberries showed up for the dessert waffles. Eldon's little house was packed as people ate wherever they could find a seat.

While the grownups continued visiting, Grant and the other cousins suddenly remembered that the go-cart had not received a workout yet that week. Eldon, with his adventurous spirit, had bought the cart for the grandchildren, and it got lots of use. Quickly the cousins gulped their last few bites and raced outside. Their mothers caught wind of their intentions and called out cautions as the children shot past. "Now be very, very careful, children. Not too fast!"

The words went in one ear and out the other. The youngsters took turns hurtling down the driveway with the pedal to the metal, the wind whipping through their hair. Once everyone had their fill of that, things got even more adventurous. They built ramps and bounced over them, then they spun donuts in the driveway amid clouds of dust. When one load of children tried to spin a donut on the grass, the go-cart flipped and bodies went flying in every direction. When the dust settled, the boys shot guilty glances toward the house. But seeing no one watching, they continued hot-rodding the go-cart around the farm.

All too soon the week of family fun passed, and the Texas and Wisconsin cousins climbed into their vans to return home. Life settled back into an ordinary routine in Arlington—a routine that seemed mundane compared to the excitement of the reunion.

One morning LaVon headed across the street from the cabinet shop for his morning cup of coffee at the Essenhaus. The usual locals had gathered at the round tables and were discussing current gossip. As they talked, a man who delivered Carolyn's weekly food order joined them and began scanning a newspaper lying on a table. Inspired by a headline, he offered his opinion. "I just think it's crazy how these pro-life people think they can throw their weight around. I mean, seriously, what right does anyone have to force a woman to go through an unwanted pregnancy?"

"Yeah, it all boils down to a control issue," another man put in. "No one cares about the woman's circumstances or what she prefers. It's just, 'You need to have this baby. We don't care where it comes from. We don't care if you want it. We don't care if you can provide for it or not. Just have the baby.' "

"It's pretty crazy if you actually think about it," a third man snorted. "You won't catch me letting someone boss me around like that."

"It's wrong," the delivery man reiterated, shaking his head. "They need to give women a choice."

LaVon listened quietly, sipping his coffee. Finally, after the group had gone on about women's rights for a long time, he was ready to leave. Rising to his feet, he asked the question that had been burning in his heart. "So, I'm curious what you all think we should have done with Grant?" He knew these locals loved his son—Grant was part of the fabric of their community.

No one spoke for what seemed an eternity. One of the men finally swallowed hard and admitted, "I really don't have an answer for that."

With red faces and hasty goodbyes, the men got up and left for their jobs. They had a lot to think about.

27

Lost

Grant's exuberant personality continued to serve as a cover-up for a very troubled boy. He lived life full throttle, his extroverted, boisterous ways hiding his deep turmoil from even those who knew him.

One day while Grant was twelve years old, LaVon called him into his office at the cabinet shop. "Have a seat, Grant," LaVon offered. He leaned forward with his elbows on his desk. "I've been watching for a chance to talk to you." He smiled, but Grant thought he saw sadness in his eyes. "How are you doing? Is everything going all right?" His voice was sincere, and Grant could tell he really wanted to know.

Grant shrugged. Everything felt wrong in his heart, but he didn't know how to verbalize what he was feeling. "I guess I often wonder why God brought me into the world the way He did," he finally admitted.

His dad looked at him compassionately. "I don't know the answer, Grant. I wish I knew." LaVon considered for a moment. "But I know God is always good. I hope someday that will become real to you too." He swallowed, and his eyes filled with tears. "Grant, I have something to tell you."

Grant tensed, wondering what it could be. He could see the emotion his dad was struggling to control. He shifted his feet nervously as he waited.

"You have known for a long time that Faith is your mom," LaVon finally continued, "but do you ever wonder about your dad?"

Grant froze, then quickly nodded. "Yeah, sometimes." Seeing other children with their parents always made him feel different. Alone. He knew his mom was disabled, and none of his other friends had a disabled mom. But maybe his father would be someone normal.

"Well, you know Faith and Lynette lived in a hospital." LaVon struggled for a moment. "Your dad was a nurse at that hospital. He committed a great sin against your mom, which is why she had a baby. But, you know, what Satan meant for evil, God has used for good. We are so thankful to have you in our family, and we know God has a purpose for your life." LaVon observed Grant carefully as he spoke, praying that these answers wouldn't damage his son but would help to bring healing to his heart.

More questions flooded Grant's mind. *Where is my dad now? Why did no one keep him from hurting my mom?* But although the truth was difficult to hear, knowing it brought some relief.

LaVon's voice broke through his thoughts. "Do you have any questions about that?"

"Um . . . not really," Grant replied. How could he put into words the turmoil in his mind?

LaVon watched him for a bit. "If you ever do, you know you can always ask." He smiled encouragingly.

"Okay, Dad," Grant said, getting up and heading back into the shop. LaVon sighed as he watched him go. How he longed to lift the burden that weighed down those bony little shoulders. He prayed that God would help Grant in ways he as an earthly father could not.

Grant hung around the cabinet shop, watching Myron and Greg sanding doors, mulling over his talk with LaVon. Although the new information answered some of his questions, it also brought more. *Why did my dad do what he did? Where is he now? Why can't I see him?*

His young mind went to his mother, so small and defenseless, so severely disabled. *Where was God when this happened? Why didn't He protect my mom?* Grant suddenly felt like his existence was an oversight, the inadvertent result of a cruel deed. *My life is an accident, isn't it? I'm just a mistake.* Overwhelmed by a rush of emotion, Grant finally dragged his mind back to his surroundings.

This place would drive me nuts, he thought as he watched the precise work going on and the limited amount of people and activity. *I can't stand just sitting here and thinking.* Ready for more action, he jumped on his bike and pedaled across the road to Carolyn's Essenhaus. The restaurant was always a good place to be distracted from the unnavigable maze in his heart.

That September, Grant and his family traveled to Colorado Springs for a vacation. They spent the first few days visiting Garden of the Gods, Seven Falls, and a zoo. Although they enjoyed this immensely, the main goal of the trip was to climb Pikes Peak, which at 14,107 feet is one of the highest summits in the Rocky Mountains. Growing up in the flatlands of Kansas had given them no experience climbing mountains, but they were determined to give it a try.

On the morning of the climb, the family started off bright and early, taking along water bottles and snacks. Greg ran ahead, with Grant and Angie trying in vain to keep up.

"I wish my legs were as long as his," Grant said jealously as he watched Greg go.

"Yeah, same here," Angie agreed. "What would it be like to be that strong?"

It wasn't long before Greg was completely out of sight, while the rest of the family hiked on together as fast as they could. After several hours, they reached Barr Camp far up the mountainside, so they sat down to rest. As Grant caught his breath, he saw an older man making his rounds through the camp, puffing away at an oxygen bottle. The man came over to the Bontragers and began filling their ears with horror stories about the dangers of hiking in the thin atmosphere up ahead.

"It's terrible," he warned them. "People die all the time up there. And even if they don't die, they often have mental issues for the rest of their lives because of oxygen deprivation. I always advise people to just forget it. Take some pictures from here and head back down. Going all the way to the top is just not worth the risk."

As he droned on about the potential dangers, Grant and Angie watched their parents' faces and realized their chances of climbing to the top of the mountain were evaporating. Disappointment settled in their hearts.

After the man left, they had a family discussion. "You know, I'm just not interested in trying for the peak," LaVon finally said. "I have no experience with this type of climb, and I don't want to risk the dangers. I think we should head back down."

"Aww, Dad!" Grant pleaded. "We won't ever have another chance like this! Can't we at least keep going till we meet Greg?"

Mamie shook her head. "I agree with Dad. We don't know what we're getting into up there. I think we just didn't do enough research, and we're not really prepared for this type of hike."

Angie was getting desperate and attempted a negotiation. "So, if you two don't want to go on up, what if you hike back down, but Grant and I keep going till we meet Greg coming down?"

LaVon and Mamie looked at each other. Since there was only one trail, Angie's suggestion seemed foolproof. Finally they agreed, and the family parted ways. Grant and Angie headed up while LaVon and Mamie started back down.

"I'm afraid we'll meet Greg before we get to the top," Grant complained.

"Let's walk as fast as we can."

"I know," Angie replied. "I want to get to the top of this mountain." They hurried on, determined to reach the summit.

They walked fast and only stopped to rest when they were gasping for breath. Their snacks ran out long before they reached the timberline, and as they got hungrier, they also grew weaker. Finally they had to concentrate on simply getting to the next big rock where they could rest for a moment.

The two youngsters were disgusted with their inability to hurry. As the trail ascended more steeply and the trees thinned out, they became ravenous. After they had taken another quick walk and a flop to rest, a few other hikers came by. One lady paused, looking them up and down. "Now, listen," she said, her voice concerned. "When did you two last have something to eat? Do you have any food with you?"

"Not anymore," Angie said.

"We ate it all long ago!" Grant explained.

"Well, dear me," she said, reaching into her backpack. "You're going to need more to get up this mountain." She gave them a handful of granola bars.

"Wow, thank you!" said Grant, remembering his manners even in this hour of need.

"Yes, thank you," Angie echoed gratefully.

Grant ripped open his package and downed a bar while Angie did the same. The food gave them a spurt of energy, but it didn't take away the annoying headaches from the thin air. "Maybe that man was partly right after all," Grant panted, wiping his brow. "This is hard."

They pushed on as the sky clouded over. When they got above the timberline, they noticed a small cave in a ledge beside the trail. They sat in the opening for a brief rest, then pressed on. Rain began to fall, and sleet cut at their faces. "Oh, no," Angie shivered as they pulled their thin coats closer. Suddenly the air flashed with blue light. *Boom!* Thunder crashed around them.

One thing Grant and Angie had in common was a dread of loud noises, and the crash of the thunder at that altitude was more than they could handle. Clapping their hands over their ears, they bolted back to the cave.

"Now what are we going to do?" Grant asked, his teeth chattering. "This storm is crazy! It's all around us!"

"We'll just wait until it's over," Angie encouraged him. "We can't go back now; Greg can't be too far ahead." They waited in their little shelter until the shower was mostly over, then hiked on.

Meanwhile, Greg had reached the peak. Seeing the rainstorm coming and feeling more tired than he had expected, he decided to ride the cog train down to the van. He felt sure the others had all turned back anyway.

As Grant and Angie rested, another hiker came toiling up. "Hi, kids," he greeted them. "Are you doing all right?" They nodded and watched in fascination at his peculiarly slow hiking style as he passed. He looked like a person walking underwater.

They hurried on, passing him, then had to pause to rest. The hiker passed them again, giving them a grin. "I think we should try walking like him," Angie noted. So as they continued, they imitated his slow, dreamy walk. This worked much better, and they didn't have to stop as often.

Finally, lifting their bleary eyes, they saw a railing above them, with people leaning over it and nothing but the sky beyond. "I guess we made it," Grant mumbled. They were almost too exhausted to be pleased about the achievement.

They spent a minute at the top looking out over what seemed like all eastern Colorado spread beneath them. Then they looked around for their brother.

"Where is Greg?" Grant asked desperately. "He isn't even up here!"

Angie looked around, her brow furrowed. "And our granola bars are gone. I'm starved."

"Me too," Grant sighed.

The children had no money and no idea where to find their big brother. They stumbled into the nearby coffee shop, hoping to at least warm up a bit. Sinking down at a table, they stared at each other in dismay.

"Oh, those donuts smell so good," Grant moaned, his voice as hollow as his stomach.

"Don't talk about it," Angie groaned. "It just makes it worse."

"But what are we going to do?"

As they thought over their options, which were grim, the friendly climber who could hike without resting came to their table. "Hey, kids. What are your plans now that you made it up here?"

"Um, I guess we don't have any plans," Angie confessed.

"We were going to meet our brother," Grant told him. "But he's not here."

"I have my car here at the top," the hiker said. "I can give you a ride to the parking lot at the bottom of the mountain." Even though the children knew they shouldn't trust strangers, they accepted his offer. "We have to get off this mountain somehow," Angie whispered to Grant.

When they reached the parking lot, the friendly climber dropped them off and drove away. Grant and Angie looked for their van, but it wasn't there.

"Where are Mom and Dad?" Grant exclaimed. "This doesn't look right."

"I don't know," sighed Angie. "I don't think this is the right parking lot."

"Then where are we?"

"I don't know where we are, but at least we're not on top of the mountain anymore!" They erupted into hysterical giggles.

Back at the end of the cog train line, Greg hopped off just as his parents exited the trail. "Greg! Where are Grant and Angie?" Mamie's voice was sharp with worry at the sight of him alone. "They aren't with you?"

Greg shook his head. "I never even saw them." He told his parents how he had decided to ride down on the train instead of walking in the rain.

LaVon was very concerned as he imagined his children lost somewhere on the big mountain. He headed over to the train ticket agent, and the agent contacted personnel at the peak. To LaVon's dismay, they said there were no children fitting the description at the top.

Some rescue runners at Barr Camp were contacted. They ran up to the peak but didn't find Grant and Angie. LaVon, Mamie, and Greg were baffled and on the verge of panic.

Meanwhile, the missing siblings were sitting on a low concrete wall at the edge of a parking lot on the wrong side of Pikes Peak. "What do we do now?" Grant asked his sister.

"I don't know," Angie replied. "I guess we have to start walking."

They hopped off the wall and headed through the parking lot toward the highway to Colorado Springs. As they neared the small guardhouse at the parking lot entrance, two guards popped out. "Hi, kids!" greeted the taller guard. "Are you the children people are looking for on the mountain?"

"I don't know," Grant said. "Maybe."

"We do need to find our parents," Angie said.

The men got on the phone, and fifteen minutes later the relieved family was reunited.

As they drove home that evening, many thoughts whirled through Grant's head. He basked in the relief of being reunited with his parents. But a puzzling thought kept pestering him. *God protected us... But why? Here I am—a mistake. How could it be possible that God cares about me? I should never have happened.* He shook his head and turned his thoughts to better things. "Hey, Dad! Let's stop for ice cream!"

As hard as it was to have questions, finding out answers seemed even scarier.

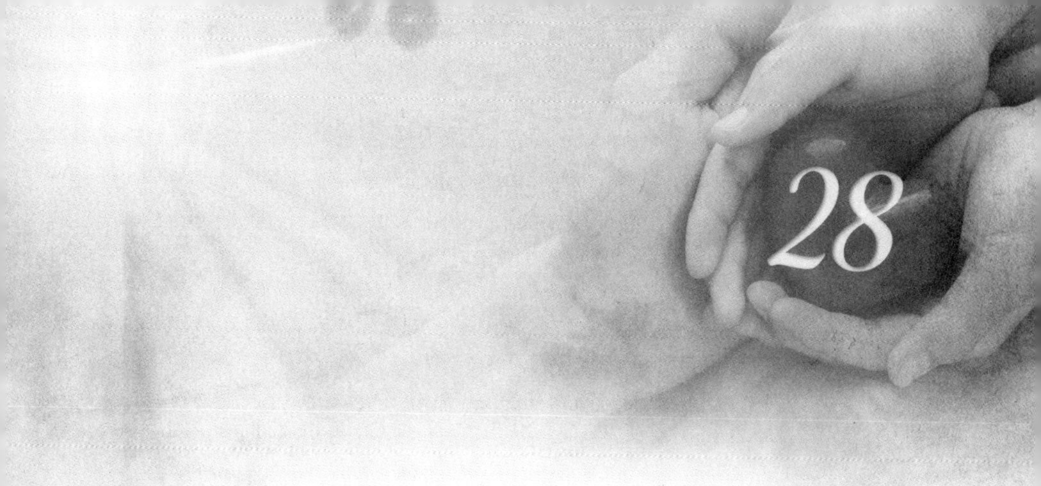

28

A Searing Ache

LaVon had a deep love for deer hunting, which he passed on to his sons. The three of them spent many happy hours in the woods finding good hunting spots, setting up blinds, and searching for shed antlers.

One Sunday afternoon Grant was searching the woods across the road from their house when he spotted a huge shed antler. His eyes wide with excitement, he scooped up his prize and raced back to the house, whooping as he ran.

LaVon was stretched out in his recliner, enjoying a nap, when Grant burst through the door. “Dad, look what I found! It was across the lane in the woods.”

LaVon leaped out of the recliner, his initial annoyance at being disturbed forgotten. “Look at that mass! An antler that big is something most hunters only dream of!"

Greg was also amazed at the enormous antler, and since he was heading out to the traditional Sunday evening singing, he took it along to show to his hunting buddies. Meanwhile LaVon and Grant headed back across the road to scout around. Sure enough, they found the matching antler! The set had been dropped only about 150 yards from their front door.

As they headed back home, Grant was walking on cloud nine, and LaVon was not far below. After Greg returned from the singing with the other antler, they measured the set. Their final calculations put the antlers in the Boone and Crockett Club range, a very high ranking. Grant arranged the antlers on the mantel where they received many admiring comments.

A month later, the family was alarmed when LaVon came home from work doubled over with pain. They rushed him to the emergency room to find he had appendicitis. During surgery, a doctor noticed some abnormalities on the appendix and sent it to a lab for testing. When the results came back, they showed cancer on the appendix.

Grant was shocked—and so was everyone else. How could LaVon, with his vigor and apparent health, be facing a cancer diagnosis? But the doctors were optimistic that the disease had been caught early enough that surgery and a round of chemo should take care of it. Three weeks later, the surgery went well, and Grant was happy to see his dad come through okay.

The whole family was relieved to hear the doctor's report from LaVon's follow-up visit. "None of his lymph glands are affected," the doctor said. "I don't see any need for chemotherapy."

The whole family was grateful they wouldn't need to face the side effects that usually came with chemo. They rejoiced together that the Lord had so miraculously brought the cancer to their attention and that the ordeal was now behind them.

Several months later, during the hot summer days, Greg's friend Levi decided that with Greg having left for a term at Hillcrest Nursing Home, his opportunities to interact with Angie were getting rather scarce. He mustered up his courage and asked Angie if she would be interested in dating. Her answer was a quick and happy yes. They were both young, so with the blessing of their parents, they thought it would be nice to spend the first couple months of dating life without much publicity. They informed their siblings of their plans, stressing the importance of secrecy.

However, the weekend of their first date was also a weekend some cousins came to visit, and Grant found it impossible not to share such a juicy secret. Within a few hours, the whole extended family was excitedly discussing the upcoming event. When Levi came to pick up Angie for the first date, he noticed Grant standing nervously behind the recliner. For Grant's typically bubbly personality, this was quite unusual.

"What's wrong, Grant?" Levi asked. "You act like you're scared of me."

Grant said nothing, but guilt filled his entire face.

"I'm afraid your date isn't a secret anymore," LaVon explained wryly. "I think Grant told all his friends this morning."

Levi and Angie were rather annoyed, but they could see Grant felt terrible about his loose tongue. They soon forgave him and tried to show him there were no hard feelings. Levi knew Grant wasn't hunting deer on his own yet and thought maybe he could patch things up a bit. "Would you like to go hunting with me, Grant?" he asked one day. "I'm going out to the Potter place."

"Yes, sir!" Grant grabbed his bow and followed Levi. With LaVon busy at work and no big brother around, he was glad for a chance to get out in a tree stand.

Levi took him to a big stand he had built in a tree in a rented pasture. The two hunters climbed up and settled down to watch for deer.

"Now, we need to be quiet if we're going to see something," Levi instructed.

"Yeah, I know," Grant said. But although he was alert and tense, he wriggled around anyway. He waited with bated breath for a deer to come into the clearing.

Observing his intensity, Levi was struck with a mischievous thought. *I'll bet he would jump sky high if...* Quietly he pulled out his buck call, held it right behind Grant's head, and blew out a loud grunt.

A startled Grant jumped forward, nearly falling out of the tree. He whipped his head around, trying to find the buck. Suddenly it dawned on him that Levi had been the culprit. They both dissolved into silent laughter. As quiet as they tried to be after that, the deer stayed far away.

Later in the season, Grant wanted to set up in a mulberry tree north of the river on their own land. "Do you think you could help me?" he asked Levi.

"Sure, let's go," Levi said, following Grant to the tree.

Grant shinnied up the tree and pointed at some weeds and branches. "Can you clear those away so I can have a clear shot?"

Levi knocked down a few weeds and broke off the branches to create an open area to shoot through. "Anything else, King Grant?"

High on his perch, Grant gave another command. "Dump that bucket of corn in that bare spot over there."

Levi followed his pointing finger. "Yes, sir," he answered good-naturedly. He dumped the corn, then disappeared into the brush behind Grant's tree. They both waited patiently. This time Grant was as quiet as a mouse. Soon a doe stepped into the pasture. Smelling the corn but not the hunters, she came over and started munching on the bait. Grant let the arrow fly, and the doe ran for only about twenty yards before dropping dead. "Look at that, Levi!" Grant whooped as he hopped out of his stand. "Right in the lungs! And she's a big one."

"You'll get a lot of meat off this one," Levi admired. "And to think you only had to step out your back door to get your deer." Levi chuckled at the mighty hunter and his prize as they dressed out the deer.

One Sunday that fall, the Bontragers left right after church to go to El Dorado Park. There they met Lynette, Faith, and their caregiver for a picnic. After eating, the cousins hiked off to the nearby dam while the adults stayed under the pavilion. Grant opted to stay with the adults, deciding this would be a good chance to get to know his birth mother.

"Hi, Faith," Grant said, sitting down beside her. "I'm Grant. What's up?"

Faith's gaze wandered, flicking heedlessly over Grant's face.

"It's nice to see you!" Grant went on, making an effort to communicate with her. It was hard to talk to someone who didn't answer. "Did you like your lunch? It was good, wasn't it?"

He ducked to avoid being hit in the head as she swung an arm recklessly. Straightening up, he cocked a quizzical eyebrow at her, and his aunts and uncles chuckled. He grinned at them and tried again.

"It would be a lot easier to talk to you if you didn't try to punch me," he informed her drolly.

She rolled her head and stared vacantly in the opposite direction. Grant threw his hands in the air and shrugged his shoulders exaggeratedly, making his audience chuckle again.

"You don't want me to talk to you, do you?" Mock exasperation tinged his voice. When she still gave no response, he ran off to join his cousins. Outwardly he had played the goofy clown, but inwardly he felt a deep ache. He would simply never be able to connect with the woman who had given him life.

That winter Eldon and Mary Ellen received another startling phone call. Though not unexpected, it still felt very sudden. "Lynette was taken to the hospital in El Dorado," the caretaker told Mary Ellen. Lynette, now forty-nine years old, had frequently battled respiratory issues caused by her severe scoliosis. Her health was declining fast.

Mary Ellen hurried to tell Eldon, and they rushed to the hospital. A nurse met them in the waiting room. "Are you Lynette's parents?"

"Yes, we are," Mary Ellen said. "How is she?"

"I'm sorry to tell you, but she quit breathing when she arrived. They resuscitated her, but she passed away just minutes ago. Please accept our condolences."

The shock was huge as Eldon and Mary Ellen processed the death of their firstborn. But just like Gina, they wouldn't have asked to have Lynette back. They knew she was healed in body and spirit, and Jesus had taken her back to Himself.

When Grant finished eighth grade at age fourteen, he asked to quit school. Studying was not his first love, and his active body resisted the thought of spending four additional years in high school. His parents granted his request, and LaVon got him started on sanding and staining projects at the cabinet shop. But it wasn't long before both Grant and LaVon could tell that some things were never meant to be. Grant chafed at the painstakingly dull work that held no outlet for his energy and social nature.

His job of choice was one that involved big machinery, so with LaVon's blessing, he took on a variety of farm jobs: driving a tractor for a local farmer, working on another farmer's dairy farm, and doing field work for his grandpa. Grant thrived on the variety of work, learning valuable skills along the way.

The mental turbulence of his younger years continued to plague him into his teens. So many questions tumbled through his head that at times he became angry and wild. *Why am I here? Am I just a terrible mistake? Where is God? Why didn't He protect my mom?*

As Grant wrestled with his tumultuous thoughts, he became bitter at

God, and his heart boiled with anger and resentment. But the only way he knew how to live was to keep everything inside. He couldn't let anyone know what he was going through.

Although he longed for answers, he had also learned to be afraid of them. Some answers only brought more pain and more questions.

That summer Greg returned from Hillcrest. He had met Trish Schlabach there and they were happily dating.

"Trish has class," he informed his family. "She's not a redneck like some people I could mention. I hope you all can brush up your act when she comes to visit." He eyed his sister, whose dates with Levi had veered far from traditional venues such as restaurants and parks. Instead, their dates were built around activities such as building fence, moving cows, and butchering pigs.

Greg was appalled several days later when he entered the kitchen just in time to see Angie shove open the kitchen window and fling out a pan of dirty dishwater. "What a slop tot! What an absolute Viking! Trish would never do that!" His shocked exhortation was met with a snicker from Angie, who was perfectly content with the low-key relationship and unsophisticated activities she and Levi enjoyed.

As the time for Trish's first visit drew near, Greg worked hard to spruce up any overlooked corners of the property. Grant was roped in to help, and even LaVon was consulted. Together, they did their best to uphold Greg's dignity by getting their place spotless.

Despite the preoccupation Greg had with his fine new friend, he did not miss some of the turmoil Grant was sorting through. He watched his troubled brother with concern.

One day when they were working together outside, Greg asked, "Grant, how are you doing?"

"Oh, I'm fine." Grant's eyes were averted but his answer was casual, giving no hint of his confusion within.

Greg looked at him in silence for a moment. "If you ever want to talk, I'm here for you."

Grant nodded, but it was so difficult for him to verbalize his thoughts that it seemed easier to keep his true feelings hidden. Despite his family's love and concern, it felt impossible to go to them with his heartache.

His older brother let it drop. He didn't want to cause Grant more pain, but it was hard to watch him walking through a darkness that had no words.

When Grant was fifteen, he rededicated his life to Christ. Despite his experience by the river with God and his dog, Grant realized that had been just the beginning. "I'm serious about this," he told his family. He joined instruction class at church and was baptized. Still looking for his identity, he thought joining the church might give him what he needed.

But although he was sincere in his commitment, being baptized and becoming a church member did not bring the peace he longed for. Grant grew restless and sporadic. He observed the people around him, mystified. *It's like I'm onstage in a play where everyone knows their role and their lines except me. I don't know what I'm supposed to say. I don't know how I'm supposed to act. I don't even know who I'm supposed to be.* The frustration he felt constantly dogged his heels.

The painful questions inside drove him to be forever running—first here, then there. His driver's license and pickup truck increased his speed and range, and he flew from one event to the next—from youth volleyball to family gatherings to eating out with friends. His dramatic personality and booming laugh were the life of the party. But suddenly he would disappear, off to the next thrill.

But the thrills were only on the surface. Only a cover-up for the agonizing pain within. *Are there no answers for me? Can nothing heal this searing ache?*

29

A Purpose

For several years, LaVon and Mamie's family enjoyed a happy, normal life. Angie and Levi got married and settled onto a beloved farm of their own in the middle of nowhere, soon adding a baby girl named Alice. Classy Trish turned out to possess a useful set of skills, and after she and Greg were married, she taught the family how to butcher their own deer. Before long they had a baby boy named Joel. LaVon and Mamie celebrated their twenty-fifth anniversary by going to a cabin in Colorado. Grant enjoyed his new in-laws and his niece and nephew, and he was always happy when they came home to visit.

Grant's love of hunting continued to grow. One fall he experimented with sowing corn out behind the barn to see if he could attract any deer.

"Now, Grant." Levi was a bit condescending. "Deer rarely come right up behind the barn."

Grant wasn't easily discouraged. "Yeah, well, I guess I'll try it and see." Sure enough, his patience paid off, and he had the last laugh when he bagged a trophy buck.

LaVon took his regular turn at preaching and viewed his responsibility seriously. One memorable sermon he preached at a neighboring church was titled "Perspectives."

"God has a purpose for each of us here on this earth. He has something in mind that we don't know ourselves. As we go through life, we form perspectives, although not always correctly. But as we grow closer to the Lord, our perspectives change." LaVon looked up and smiled at the congregation, then sobered.

"Cancer is one thing that changes our perspective. It is easy to neglect an eternal perspective when life goes well for us. The Children of Israel so quickly forgot what God wanted to teach them, but He kept reminding them. If I'm faithful, I will keep the perspectives I gained through my cancer journey. Some people seem to float through life while others struggle on. Some have faced much greater hardships than I have. Life isn't fair, but God is always good. He knows what He is doing. He wants to teach us in a language we can understand. It is God's mercy that stops us when we are building our lives on material of little value. He wants to draw us to Himself and prepare us for service. How concerned are we for the lost? How excited are we for the return of Christ?

"I thank God for the healing I have experienced to this point. I don't know what will happen in the future, but I have a peace about it that I can't explain. I have taken a lot for granted in the past, but God is so good. I am surrounded by caring people who have blessed me and provided for my family. I appreciate the church more than ever and what we do for each other."

LaVon's message was simple and came straight from his heart. For those sitting under his words, it was a sermon they wouldn't soon forget. Grant knew his dad lived these words as truly as he spoke them.

A short time later, in February 2008, a routine CAT scan showed LaVon had cancerous fluid in his abdomen around his organs. Cancer had invaded his body again, but this time it was a rare type that was slow but persistent. The news was another blow, but LaVon's optimistic spirit helped Grant and the rest of the family cope.

"You know, I really would like an anointing service," LaVon told Mamie soon after he received this second diagnosis, and she agreed. Following the Biblical command to those facing sickness, the church had an anointing service. It was a meaningful time for the entire congregation.

As LaVon went through a nine-month period of chemotherapy, Grant prayed fervently. Many friends prayed along with the family. After the chemo treatments, LaVon planned to travel to Omaha, Nebraska, where a specialist would perform surgery.

While taking the treatments, LaVon kept himself busy by designing a kitchen for the new church house the Arlington Church was planning to build. This was a good distraction, but it didn't change the fact that he was very sick. The following winter, the local Arlington community held a soup and pie fundraiser to help with his medical expenses. Around 650 people came to support the Bontragers in this way, a testimony to the many lives LaVon had touched over the years. It was humbling and heartwarming to be the recipient of such a united effort.

At the same time, the family started the long process of fixing up the little old church house where Arlington Church used to meet. Since it was empty again, Greg and Trish had purchased it with plans to create a one-of-a-kind home.

Everyone was happy when Grant finally found a job he loved.

Sturdi-Built, a business that constructed mini-barns, was fast-paced and an exciting workplace. Grant loved working with the crew. He demonstrated a good work ethic and gained confidence in his abilities. But at the same time, his restlessness and inner turmoil were becoming more obvious. As his dad was struggling with cancer, Grant was still running from his own pain.

"Come on, everyone!" Grant hollered. "Let's go!" His seventeenth summer was shaping up to be a good one. The annual Youth Fellowship Meetings were being held in Lott, Texas, and Grant was raring to get the weekend started. This would be his first trip without his parents or siblings along. The thought of traveling eight hours with his cousins and the youth group and then spending a weekend with lots of other friends, both old and new, sounded like something right down his alley.

The youth piled into the van, with Grant settling in the back with his cousin Kevin and friend Nate. Spirits were high as Vernon slid into the driver's seat and the van headed out the drive. Before long, the allure of the snack bag proved too much to resist, and they tore into the chips and cookies, tossing them back and forth among jokes and insults.

Two hours into the trip, they stopped in Thomas, Oklahoma, to pick up sixteen-year-old Stephanie Wingard. The youth group she belonged to was small, so she frequently spent weekends with the Kansas youth. They had been happy to oblige when she requested a ride to Texas. Stephanie was excited about the weekend and was especially interested in the scheduled topics. The theme this year was "Being a Missionary Wherever You Are." For Stephanie, who dreamed of being a missionary overseas, it was intriguing to think that she could begin her mission right away.

But right now, she felt foolish. "This is so ridiculous of me," she said, "but I forgot to bring shampoo! Is there any chance we could stop at a Dollar General?"

The carefree group had no problem with incorporating an extra stop, and they were soon on their way again with the shampoo tossed into the back.

The trip went well, with the gaiety and foolishness offset by more serious discussions. It didn't seem long until they were rolling into the parking lot in front of a large shed where a game of volleyball was already in progress.

The evening was hot and sultry, and sweat poured down the young people's faces as they worked off their excess energy. Although they played volleyball with all their might, since there was only one court, everyone had plenty of time to rest, sit, and talk. Again the conversations ranged from deep and rich to lighthearted and silly as everyone reconnected with old friends and made new ones.

Grant was in his element. He bounced from one end of the open shed to the other, clapping friends on the back and whooping encouragement to the volleyball players. The evening ended all too soon for him as he headed to his host's house for the night along with the other fellows staying at that location.

The next morning dawned with the same blistering heat. The boys dressed and ate breakfast before heading to the first service. The speaker was engaging and had prepared his topic well, exhorting the youth to live for Jesus so others could see His power and light. Grant drank in the message like a thirsty plant. In his heart there was a resounding amen to the truth he was hearing. But at the same time, the many questions he still wrestled with kept pushing their way to the top. Could he trust a God who had abandoned his mother at her most vulnerable time? Was there any mission for him, a byproduct of sin?

Grant's mind wearied of the turmoil. He was relieved when the service was over and it was time for another volleyball break. As always, he hid his tormented heart under a storm of energy.

In the evening they all gathered for another message, and again Grant felt torn. On one hand, he wanted to stop running and give himself to God. On the other hand, he was afraid of being yet another person who dropped through the cracks of God's protection. The weekend was becoming more intense than he had imagined, and he was glad when he could get outside and push away his troubled thoughts.

After the last message on Sunday morning, Grant ate lunch with Stephanie, her friend Carmen, and a local boy named Dave.

"Didn't you think that last talk was just the best one yet?" Stephanie asked. She had thoroughly enjoyed the weekend and couldn't wait to get back home to apply what she had learned.

"Oh, I agree," Carmen said. "That part about reaching out to our neighbors—that really convicted me! I want to start doing more of that!"

"Me too," Stephanie agreed. "I can't wait to tell my parents about everything I learned."

The conversation moved on to other subjects. Stephanie and Carmen had interacted with Dave previously and knew he owned a motorcycle. It seemed to them that the hot summer day demanded a long, windy ride. They applied some pressure to Dave, who was happy to oblige. The three made plans to get together later that afternoon.

Most of the youth were heading home after lunch, so there was a flurry of goodbyes as various groups loaded up and left. The Kansas group, however, had decided to wait to leave until Monday. Once most of the others had left, they headed back to their various hosts to rest up after the late nights of the weekend. Stephanie and Carmen, still holding onto their motorcycle ride dreams, headed for Dave's house.

A few hours later, as the oppressive midday heat began to lift, Grant and his friends were lounging around the living room when text messages began to ding into their phones. There had been an accident. Stephanie was hurt. Head injuries. There would be a prayer meeting at church.

The boys stared at each other in disbelief, their lighthearted banter abandoned. Surely it wasn't that bad? Stephanie, with her positive spirit and ready laugh... Surely she would be fine. They didn't dare voice an alternative as they scrambled out the door.

At the church, faces were drawn and sober. More details kept coming in. There had been only one helmet, and although Dave had tried to give it to Stephanie, her youthful invincibility had protested and she gave it back to him. But when the motorcycle left the road and hit a culvert, she was the one who landed squarely on her head. Her injuries were severe.

Voices broke as the youth pleaded for a miracle.

Grant couldn't hold still. As soon as the time of prayer was over, everyone drove to the hospital where Stephanie had been airlifted. There they found Dave and some of Stephanie's friends praying and sobbing in disbelief. Dave's heart had been rubbed as raw as his arms, and he wept uncontrollably, blaming himself for the tragedy. Grant and the other youth gathered around, comforting Dave and pleading with God to spare Stephanie's life.

But God had other plans for the young girl. Soon after her parents arrived via a private plane, a weary doctor emerged to inform the group that Stephanie was gone.

There was nothing for the stunned youth to do but return home. Late into the night, their understanding hosts ministered to the traumatized visitors. Finally, exhausted in every way, they stumbled off to bed.

It was the most difficult night Grant had ever known. *God, how could you take her life? This makes no sense! How can I trust a God who doesn't protect His own people?*

The next morning there were no cheery good mornings as they quietly loaded their van and headed back toward Kansas. It felt utterly wrong to drive off with Stephanie's seat glaringly empty.

Since Gareth and Phyllis lived on their route home, the group had previously arranged to stop there for lunch. Now they all just wanted to go on home. But they decided to stick with their plans since they had to eat lunch somewhere, and no one felt like mingling with people at a restaurant.

It ended up being a therapeutic stop. Gareth and Phyllis had heard the sad news, and they listened sympathetically as the youth poured out their version of the story. Going over all the hard details again brought the first hints of healing. Gareth prayed a blessing over the young people and everyone else who had been involved in the tragedy.

Grant was uncharacteristically quiet as they drove the rest of the way home. He was thinking hard. Stephanie's wish to be a missionary was being fulfilled as he analyzed his own life.

What if it had been you? The insistent voice in his head would not be stilled. *Would you have been ready? Where would you be now?* There was a chill in his heart as he realized he was not sure.

Grant finally arrived home, a shaken, introspective version of the bouncy boy who had left several days before. He and his cousin Kevin walked to the back of the van and opened the doors to retrieve his luggage. A strange floral scent filled the air as a shampoo bottle that had been crushed beneath the heavy suitcases rolled out across the gravel, oozing its contents as it went. Stephanie's shampoo bottle... Crushed... Broken... The two boys stared at it, speechless. It was like being punched in the gut once again.

"I can't deal with this right now," Kevin muttered, gingerly picking up the bottle and tossing it into the dumpster. Grant's stomach heaved as he wiped a smear of shampoo off the van. *What if it had been me?*

As the van drove away, he stood for a minute, staring across the pasture. Suddenly a dove fluttered out of the grass. Grant watched it fly off into the evening sky. *A sign of peace?* He found himself strangely comforted as he turned to walk inside where his concerned family was waiting to hear his story.

Several days later, Grant found himself heading south again, this time to Oklahoma for Stephanie's funeral. Hundreds of people flooded her tiny community to commemorate her life and mourn her death. Many of the same youth who had attended the Youth Fellowship Meetings participated with special singing throughout the funeral.

Donny Swartzentruber, who was Stephanie's uncle from Georgia, pleaded with the hearts of his audience. "The Lord has spoken to us!" Tears coursed down his cheeks. "Stephanie was ready to meet Him. Are we ready as well? Oh, friends, if we are not ready when our time to go comes, it will be forever too late. Don't put it off! Make sure you are right with the Lord today!"

The knot in Grant's heart twisted. He watched as Donny called Dave and then Stephanie's parents to the platform. The audience wept as Olen and Emily Wingard embraced the young man who was so remorseful for his part in the tragedy, reassuring him they held nothing against him.

As Grant rode home with his family that evening, he felt raw from the emotions of the week. How could he begin to find peace amid this terrible event? Both inwardly and outwardly, it seemed sadness and misery reigned. The peace he longed for was always just out of reach.

Maybe I should leave home. Grant knew that wasn't the right thing to do, and he had no idea where he would go. But the thought of continuing as he was seemed nearly unbearable. *Maybe living somewhere else would help. A place where no one knows anything about me. A place where nothing I see will remind me of the mess my life is in.* Everywhere he went, whatever he did—whether it was work or play, hunting or going to church, spending time with his youth group or his family—he dragged along his hurts and confusion.

I can't make it here much longer. I've got to do something. But there seemed to be nowhere to go and nothing he could do with his pain.

That fall marked forty years since Eldon had started the cabinet business, so the Bontragers hosted an open house in conjunction with Carolyn's twentieth-anniversary celebration for the Essenhaus across the street. They served 450 people. The menu was simple—hamburgers, coleslaw, barbecued beans, and sweet tea. The local Lions Club also rose to the occasion, serving cake and ice cream.

For the small town of Arlington, this was a big event. Main Street was blocked off so people could set up lawn chairs and enjoy the evening. Things had come a long way since Eldon and Mary Ellen had first been cautiously welcomed into the community. They had formed deep and lasting relationships with their Arlington friends and neighbors.

Grant thoroughly enjoyed the day, socializing with people who had known and loved him all his life.

The time for LaVon's surgery finally arrived. The doctor felt optimistic that the cancer was gone, but it wasn't long before tests found some aggressive cancer cells. In January 2010, a CT scan found another tumor growing beside LaVon's liver.

LaVon's oncologist could only recommend more chemo, which hadn't seemed to be helping, so LaVon and Mamie decided to go to Oasis of Hope Hospital in Mexico.

After eight months of Oasis's recommended treatment, the tumor had shrunk by 30 percent. The doctors were very pleased, and LaVon resumed his responsibilities in the church and in designing and installing kitchens. The doctors felt sure if he continued the treatment the cancer would remain stable. Grant, his siblings, and in-laws were relieved at this answer to their prayers. During this time, little Cassie was born to Levi and Angie, bringing the grandchild count to three.

Although things were looking up for LaVon, nineteen-year-old Grant was unhappier than ever. Deep down, he knew he badly needed help—and soon. When a spot opened at Partridge Hope Ministries, a local counseling center, LaVon, Mamie, and Grant took the opportunity to seek help. Grant knew his pain was more complex than he could sort through himself. More and more, he longed for peace and freedom.

At the first appointment, Grant almost panicked when he walked through the door and saw three chairs and a box of tissues. *Get me out of here,* he thought, nearly bolting for the door. *What am I doing?* The thought of delving into the difficult, grueling questions he had always tried to force away scared him half to death. But instead of fleeing, he sat down and waited.

In a few minutes, an older man and his wife came into the room and sat down on the other two chairs. They were both sincere and friendly, and as they visited, Grant found himself relaxing and opening his heart. Simply getting his thoughts into the open began to bring a measure of freedom.

During each session, he uncovered another layer until finally he was talking about how he felt about his life. During one session, when they were kneeling for a time of prayer, Grant felt the closeness of God in a very clear way. At last, he was ready to bring his questions back to the One who had made him.

Why am I here? he prayed.

God's answer came back plainly: *You are here for a purpose.*

Grant's shoulders shook with sobs. *There really is a purpose for me. I wasn't an accident.* His mind could hardly fathom this after a lifetime of feeling like a mistake.

Aloud, he asked another question that had tormented him. "Lord, what is that purpose?"

Again God felt close, and the answer was clear: *To tell your story so I can be glorified.*

For the first time in his life, Grant began to believe that God did have a plan for him. God had been right there in the hospital when he was born, holding him, a fragile baby, in His arms. And before that, though God could have stopped that horrible crime against his mother, He didn't.

Why?

Because He wanted Grant to tell his story. Overwhelmed, Grant dropped his head in his hands and wept with joy.

"A purpose! My life has a purpose!" he exclaimed. "I was created for a reason." It was a new thought—a feeling he had never experienced before. He remembered the words of a song he had often sung with the youth group: "Take me, I'm yours."

As he got to his feet, Grant offered a prayer of thanksgiving for the deliverance he felt in his heart. "Thank you, God, for saving me. Thank you for allowing me to be born. If you can use me, take me. I am yours. I am so blessed. If one person can be brought to Christ through my story, it will be worth it."

That night Grant went home as a changed young man. LaVon and Mamie were waiting for him when he walked in, and they saw a peace on his face they had never seen before.

Grant spoke first. “Thanks for staying up till I got home.”

LaVon nodded. “No problem. Is there something you want to share?”

Grant sat down facing his parents. “I never told you this,” he began, “but I’ve struggled a lot with feeling I don’t have a purpose. I felt like an accident—like God brought me onto this earth and then just left me hanging. And that really hurt.” He looked at them sadly. “You might have noticed that sometimes it just about drove me crazy.” They nodded, their eyes filled with tears.

Grant told them about his encounter with God. “I now know I have a purpose. God is calling me to a ministry—to tell my story in churches and prisons.”

He couldn’t hold back the tears. When he looked up, his parents were crying too. “That’s beautiful, Grant,” Mamie said, coming over to lay a hand on his shoulder.

LaVon wiped his eyes and completed the circle of three. “We love you, son. If this is what God has called you to do, we support you wholeheartedly.”

They prayed together, embracing each other, sharing a sacred time of forgiveness and thanksgiving for what God had done in Grant’s life.

30

A Legacy

That same year, in July 2011, the entire Bontrager family traveled to Wisconsin for a much-anticipated reunion on Dan and Marilyn's farm. The family was large by now, with lots of grandchildren and even a few great-grandchildren bringing spice and energy. The Korvers had cleaned out their shop in preparation for the event. Meals and games filled the many tables.

The weekend was fun, with biking, hiking, yard games, and lots of good food. One afternoon included a vigorous canoe trip down the Flambeau River for the more energetic cousins. Ryan and Andy darted ahead and posed as river pirates, capsizing each canoe as it came floating along. Much to the appreciation of their victims, their foolishness was swiftly and authoritatively dealt with when they had the audacity to attack several of their older and more muscular cousins.

That evening the family gathered around the campfire, singing and sharing memories and encouragement. Eldon and Mary Ellen smiled at each other as they viewed the gathering. Though their journey together had turned out vastly different from their expectations, they were so thankful for the family the Lord had blessed them with.

LaVon was filled with gratitude as well. He had just reached the one-year mark of being in remission and was feeling well. His harrowing journey through cancer was a stark reminder that each day was a gift.

The next day a group of cousins, aunts, and uncles wandered out to the pond behind the farm. Grant sat on the bank, absently throwing rocks into the water. Marilyn was seated on one side of him and Dan on the other. Grant was quiet for a long time, deep in thought. His emotions were just under the surface as he watched his family enjoying themselves.

Marilyn's quiet voice broke into his reflections. "A penny for your thoughts."

He met her gaze. "I was just thinking about how in many ways it's been hard to be adopted, yet I still get to be part of this family." Grant swallowed hard. "I'm just so grateful for everyone, for how they accept me for who I am."

Marilyn reached out and squeezed his shoulder. "Well, you're a part of us, Grant—just as much as any of the other nieces and nephews."

Contentment flooded his heart as he looked around at his family—in so many ways his identity. He was grateful again for the healing he had experienced through his counseling, enabling him to fully appreciate his family.

A month after the reunion, LaVon preached a sermon on heaven. Several weeks later, he gave a message on hell. A few days after that he woke up with indigestion, which soon got progressively worse. Within days, his eyes began turning yellow and his skin itched incessantly. Tests showed the tumor had both grown and shifted. Now it was pushing against his liver, obstructing his bile ducts. The doctor inserted a stent and started him on chemotherapy in hopes of shrinking the tumor, but in his weakened condition, he got so sick that each dose landed him back in the emergency room.

After several of these episodes, with LaVon dropping lower each time, Mamie had enough. In his weakness and misery, it was hard for LaVon to think through the decisions needing to be made, but Mamie could clearly see that chemo was not going to help. When the doctor came in to check on LaVon, she was ready.

"Well, LaVon, it looks like we'll soon have you strong enough for another dose of chemo," Dr. Schmidt stated encouragingly.

Mamie's voice was quiet but firm. "There will be no more chemo."

Dr. Schmidt laughed. "Yes, it's been rough. But I think we can tweak it a bit and keep working with it."

"No." Mamie would not budge. "There will be no more chemo." She could see that the battle they were fighting was a losing one. The time had come for her to care for her husband. She could not bear to see him floundering under the effects of chemotherapy anymore.

But caring for LaVon was hard. The miserable itching and nausea nearly drove him crazy at times. Mamie was a vigilant caregiver, administering all his medications promptly, but as the pounds melted off her husband's frame, her faint hopes dwindled. Although she never complained, her children noticed she grew thinner as their dad's health faded.

Full of sadness, Grant began to realize that this time his dad might not recover.

Mamie's mother, Lydia Stoltzfus, had buried a husband herself not so long ago. With an understanding heart, she came to the rescue, flying out to visit every few weeks. Her perceptive eyes and fearless personality helped Mamie endure her unspoken worries.

In September, Mamie's brothers Sam and Ernie came with Lydia to visit. Ernie brought his son Kendrick along to spend time with Grant, who was finding the intensity and stress hard to bear. The visit was a wonderful diversion from the apprehension they were dealing with. Grant and Kendrick ran from one activity to the next, the method of coping Grant understood best.

With a heavy heart, Greg assumed his dad's responsibilities in the cabinet shop, well over ten years sooner than they had planned. Greg had worked alongside his dad in the shop since his teen years. Now he keenly missed LaVon's presence there.

Angie brought over little Alice and Cassie to visit LaVon as often as she could. Another baby was on the way, and the ever-present questions in the back of her mind were, *How much time does Dad have left? Will he get to see the baby?* The due date of February 7 seemed distant.

In November, LaVon was so miserable he could hardly function anymore. He underwent biliary duct bypass surgery so his liver could drain externally. Thankfully, this operation brought a measure of relief.

In December, Lydia arrived in Kansas again, this time declaring she would stay as long as she was needed. As Mamie concentrated on taking care of her husband, Lydia took care of the housework. She served the family cheerfully, preparing food, doing laundry, and cleaning.

Lydia did not avoid talking about the reality: LaVon was dying. She encouraged Mamie and the children to look beyond his suffering to the glory and rest awaiting him.

January 2012 found Grant at Calvary Bible School in Arkansas. Despite his dad's decline, the family had all agreed it would be best for him to have something to do during this arduous time.

While Grant was there, he thought a lot about sharing his story. Now that he had been called to it, he wanted to do it well and in a way that would honor God. One day, alone in his dorm room, he fell to his knees and prayed, "God, please show me a verse or passage I can use when I start sharing my story. Please give me a word from you."

That evening in church, the speaker read from the book of Jeremiah. Verses 5 through 10 in the first chapter seemed to call out to Grant—he felt the force of the words in his heart: "Before I formed thee in the belly I knew thee; and before thou camest forth out of the womb I sanctified thee, and I ordained thee a prophet unto the nations. Then said I, Ah, Lord God! behold, I cannot speak: for I am a child. But the Lord said unto me, Say not, I am a child: for thou shalt go to all that I shall send thee, and whatsoever I command thee thou shalt speak. Be not afraid of their faces: for I am with thee to deliver thee, saith the Lord. Then the Lord put forth his hand, and touched my mouth. And the Lord said unto me, Behold, I have put my words in thy mouth. See, I have this day set thee over the nations and over the kingdoms, to root out, and to pull down, and to destroy, and to throw down, to build, and to plant."

Grant could hardly control his emotions during the rest of the service. *Thank you, God!* he breathed in awe. *Jesus, thank you for this answer to my prayer.* This message from God was a precious confirmation of the call He had given. Whenever Grant read these verses in the following years, they were a rich reminder of God's blessing.

Partway through the term, Grant received a call from Mamie. "Dad is really low. I think you should come home."

Mamie's sister Becky and her husband Jake had just arrived to see LaVon, but when they heard that Grant needed a ride home, they drove to Arkansas to pick him up. When Grant came home he was shocked by how wasted his dad looked.

"I came home, Dad." His voice broke. "I wanted to be with you while I can."

LaVon reached out his frail hand, and Grant took it in his strong one. LaVon seemed relieved to have him home.

As LaVon weakened, it was tiring for him to talk, so he seldom spoke unless spoken to. One day Lydia sat down beside him. She and LaVon had always enjoyed a good relationship. He enjoyed her forthright approach to life, and she liked his pleasant ways.

She took his hand. "LaVon, what do you see as you lie here? Do you ever see angels?"

LaVon gave a slight nod and attempted a smile. "Many," he whispered.

She smiled and gave his hand an encouraging little squeeze.

Grant's twentieth birthday came and went. Day after miserable day passed. Two more weeks crept by.

Angie's due date came on February 7, but there was still no baby. A bad possibility presented itself. "What if Dad dies and I can't go to the funeral?" she asked Trish, wide-eyed.

Greg heard of this latest worry. "No," he said flatly. "We are not having the funeral without Angie. If we have to, we'll postpone it." Angie imagined the logistical headache of such a delay and prayed for deliverance.

By Thursday, February 9, the married children and Eldon and Mary Ellen were stopping in every day to check on LaVon. Angie left her little girls at Uncle Myron's house and came earlier than usual. An unsuspecting Lydia gave her a cheerful greeting, and Angie surprised herself and her grandma by bursting into a flood of tears. After trying in vain to stop herself, she realized she had no lid big enough to shut down the geyser. She went upstairs to her old room and cried herself to sleep.

That evening after the workday was over, the rest of the family trickled in to see how their dad was doing. When Levi and Angie walked into the living room to say goodnight to LaVon, Angie laid her hand on his knee. "Still no baby, Dad. Maybe tonight."

"Maybe tonight," he echoed in a tired whisper.

The next afternoon the baby came. That evening Angie brought little Louis Grant over to meet his grandpa. LaVon laid his hand on the soft little bundle, looking as pleased as possible in his condition.

On Saturday night, Greg and Trish and Levi and Angie came with their children to stay for the weekend. They all took turns cuddling the baby, with Grant being especially proud of his little namesake nephew. They all tried to keep an eye on LaVon without disturbing him.

On Sunday night around midnight, when most of the family was asleep, Lydia peeked into the living room to check on LaVon. His eyes were wide open and shining, gazing at something beyond the ceiling. Quickly she woke Mamie, but already the light in LaVon's eyes was gone and his breathing was slowing down. Half an hour later, in the early hours of February 13, 2012, LaVon died peacefully with his family gathered around him.

Little Louis attended his grandpa's funeral when he was less than a week old. In his life, LaVon Bontrager had a gift for making friends, and his family's hearts were touched by the large crowd of people who came to grieve with them that day. After the service, the family gathered at the cemetery for the burial.

Grant and Mamie sat together on the chairs provided for immediate family as the grave was filled. Mamie was worn out after six months of caring for her husband and dreading his death. She knew there would be lonely times and more grieving ahead, but nothing could be worse than this goodbye. She felt deeply grateful that Grant was still living at home.

Grant watched as the soil filled up the gaping hole in the ground where his dad had been laid to rest. What would he do without the dad who had loved him so much? But there was also a sense of thankfulness for God's timing. How could he have handled this grief without the peace and healing he had found the year before?

Greg sat beside Trish, their wide-eyed little son perched on his knee. He wondered how he was going to make it without his dad. Greg had still depended on his fatherly advice all the way to the end.

The Holy Spirit whispered a simple statement into his heart: *You are not without a Father.* Greg let that truth sink into his heart, a treasure to keep.

Angie sat with Levi and their two little girls, holding her baby snugly in her arms. Although many people offered to hold little Louis Grant for her, she couldn't bear to let go of him.

Underneath the family's sadness was intense relief that LaVon was finally free from the prison his body had become. His legacy of faith and faithfulness was a deep consolation as they grieved.

In the days, weeks, and months after the funeral, the family members began to heal in their own time and according to their individual personalities.

The grandchildren were a great comfort. Alice, Joel, and Cassie, who turned four, three, and two that spring, were too young to grieve deeply over their grandpa, but they loved to talk about him being in heaven with Jesus. Their innocence, mischief, and startling word combinations kept their parents and Grant and Mamie smiling like nothing else could have during this difficult time of missing LaVon's presence and learning how to build a life without him.

31

Right Choices

Despite the healing Grant had found—and the direction and purpose he had received from God—LaVon's death was a deep blow. Why, after everything he had already faced, did he have to lose his adoptive dad?

Grant became restless at Arlington Church where he had always attended. Over the years his group of friends had changed, and he began to feel more at home with some members from Cedar Crest Church. Mamie knew he wasn't happy at Arlington, so she gave her blessing on his decision to start attending Cedar Crest.

An older member named Eli Yoder took a special interest in Grant, taking him along to help with prison ministry. Grant thrived on the purpose and fulfillment he found in the work. At the prisons, he began sharing his story as God had led him to do. Seeing his story impacting other people's lives was a powerful reminder of God's purpose for him.

Being in prison work drew Grant's mind to his biological father. Grant began to feel compassion toward this young man who had been working in a poorly regulated hospital and in a moment of thoughtless selfishness ruined his reputation and spent the next ten years in prison. He wanted to reach out. But how could he find him?

One day at his job at Sturdi-Built, Grant met up with an older man who worked in the maintenance department. Though they had both worked there for several years, their paths seldom crossed.

"You're Grant Bontrager, right?" the man asked.

"Yes, I am," Grant replied, eyeing him curiously.

"My name is Dale. I've wanted to talk to you for a long time, but I've never had a chance."

What does this man want to talk about? Grant wondered, waiting to hear more.

Dale smiled. "You probably don't know me at all, but I spent some time in prison quite a few years ago."

"Oh?"

Dale looked at Grant seriously. "I spent time in prison with your dad." His gaze locked with Grant's, whose eyes widened in surprise.

"My dad?" he asked incredulously. "You did? Wow." He took a step closer. "What can you tell me about him?"

Dale shrugged. "His name is Jeremy. I got to know him pretty well. I don't know what else to tell you... Would you like to meet him?"

Grant was taken aback. Right in front of him stood the missing key to finding his biological dad. Suddenly it felt important to meet him—but was he ready? He felt suddenly unsure. "Well, yes, I do, but I'm not sure I'm ready." New questions swirled through his mind. *Do I really want this? Would it change anything? What would my grandparents say?*

"Well, it's totally up to you," Dale assured him. "Just let me know when you're ready, and I'll put you in contact with him."

Grant went home and talked to Mamie. He wanted her blessing if he did go through with this. "Mom, the craziest thing happened today. I met a guy named Dale who works in maintenance. He used to be in prison with my birth dad. He still knows him, and he offered to put us in touch." He paused. "Should I accept his offer?"

Mamie was quiet for a long time. She knew of Grant's desire to meet his birth dad, but was this the time? Would he be strong enough to face this, or would it pull him down again?

"Your birth dad is a very important character in your life," she said at last. "If you really want to meet him, I think that is your right. I would give my blessing. But I'll warn you, it will be hard to relive that part of your past. It might also be hard for the rest of the family, especially for your grandpa and grandma."

Grant nodded. "Too many memories?"

"Yes, and a fear that you might want to leave us to be with your father," she said honestly.

Grant swallowed hard. There was certainly a part of him that badly wanted to find this man, but what might be the cost? Mamie was his mom in the truest sense of the word. He didn't want to hurt her or do anything to make his relatives uncomfortable. Now that LaVon was gone, he had a new sense of loyalty to his family.

After another year of pondering and praying, and after many conversations with his relatives, Grant felt it was time to move ahead. He would at least get a phone number for his birth dad from Dale. But due to varying job schedules, Grant and Dale seldom crossed paths at work anymore.

One Thursday morning as Grant headed to work, the thought of contacting his biological dad lay heavy on his mind. He would be doing pilot car work later that day for a shed delivery, so it wasn't likely he would run into Dale unless it was during the morning break. *Okay, God,* Grant prayed. *I would really like to talk to Dale in private. Could you please arrange it so we can meet somewhere besides the breakroom? I don't want to talk to him in there with all the other guys around.*

At work, Grant clocked in and forgot about his prayer. He worked hard until breaktime. As he was walking toward the breakroom, he was surprised to meet none other than Dale. No one else was nearby, and Grant knew this was the time.

"Hi, Dale," Grant said nervously. "I haven't seen you around for a while."

Dale chuckled. "No, our paths don't cross much, do they?"

"Nope, they don't." Grant took a deep breath. "I think I'm ready to meet Jeremy whenever it works for you. Or maybe just get his phone number."

"Okay, that's great! Let me talk to him first and get back to you. When are you available? I'm sure he'll be anxious to see you."

"I'm flexible as far as schedule goes," Grant said. "Just let me know." He sounded calm, but his heart was thumping hard.

Dale moved on and Grant continued to the breakroom. He laughed and chatted with the other workers as usual, but his thoughts were far away.

Grant expected the answer could take some time, so he didn't feel prepared when Dale found him that very afternoon. "Will Saturday at 2:00 be all right?" Dale asked. "You can just come to my place. Jeremy agreed to meet you there."

Grant felt a sudden panic rising within him. Saturday? He had been thinking the meeting might be in a few weeks—that he would have more time to prepare himself.

"Uh," he wavered, swallowing hard. Then he nodded. "Sure. Why not?"

Saturday came all too quickly, and Grant climbed into his pickup to drive to Dale's house for the meeting. As he drove, his mind spun with possible scenarios.

I wonder what my dad will be driving? What if I pull in right behind him and he's sitting in his car and it's really awkward? He followed a little white van for a bit, afraid his fear might be coming true. When the van turned off, Grant sighed with relief.

Soon he turned in at Dale's driveway. A blue Ford van was parked beside

Dale's car. *That must be his van.* Grant put his pickup truck into park and turned off the key. He took a moment to still his racing heart. "It's now or never," he said, willing himself to get out of the pickup. Heart thumping, he approached the house and knocked.

Dale swung open the door. "Hey, Grant. Come in!"

"Hi, Dale," Grant grinned nervously. He saw a man standing behind Dale with a woman he assumed was his wife.

Grant walked over and shook their hands. "Hello."

Jeremy looked as scared as Grant felt. "This has been a long time in coming," Jeremy said.

Grant's soft heart went out to him. While it had taken Grant thirteen years to be ready for this time, Jeremy had waited much longer. Twenty-five long years had passed since his life had dramatically changed, with ten of those in prison.

"So tell me about yourself," Jeremy said once Grant was seated across from him at the table.

Grant told him about being adopted by his uncle and aunt. He talked about how hard it had been for him to learn about the situation surrounding his birth.

Jeremy's wife sat listening silently. Grant could see her looking at Jeremy, then at him, then back at Jeremy again. Finally she said, "You two look so much alike."

"We do?" Jeremy asked.

His wife smiled. "You do."

Grant tried to see a resemblance, but it wasn't easy for him, although Jeremy's dark hair matched his own, which had darkened as he matured. He did notice they shared a few similar facial features.

Finally Grant asked cautiously, "Would you be interested in meeting the rest of my family?" How would it feel for Jeremy to meet Faith's family after all these years?

"If they are willing to meet me, I'm fine with that," Jeremy said.

How will it feel for the others to meet Jeremy? Grant felt nervous about it. But in the meantime, there were more of Jeremy's family for him to meet. Several months after their first meeting, Jeremy sent Grant a text message: "My parents are coming to my apartment for my birthday. They would really like to meet you. Will you come?"

Grant did want to meet his other set of grandparents. "Sure," he texted back.

That evening, he knocked on Jeremy's apartment door. When Jeremy and his wife opened the door, Grant, who was over six feet tall, was surprised to see that Jeremy's dad was as tall as he was.

Grant shook his grandpa's hand. "I'm Grant."

He turned to his grandma, a short, motherly woman. He again stuck out his hand, but she brushed it aside. "Oh, just give me a hug," she said, so Grant stooped and hugged her. With that, they dropped all formalities. The five quickly found themselves at ease as they talked and enjoyed pizza and birthday cake. Stories flowed as the group became acquainted with each other. To Grant, it felt good to connect with these people who had not been part of his life until now.

The news that Grant's birth dad would like to meet the rest of his family was met with reserve and suspicion. "He's not Grant's dad," Phyllis bristled. "It takes more than an inappropriate fling to be a dad. He has no right to cause our family more pain." She felt that inviting this man into their lives might make things more difficult for all of them.

Carolyn, though reluctant, knew how much this family meeting meant to Grant and hated to discourage him. She assured him it wasn't unforgiveness that caused their opposition. "If you think we need to meet Jeremy so we can forgive him, that's not the case. We had to start forgiving him from the moment we knew you were conceived."

When Grant called Marilyn and asked if she wanted to meet his biological dad the next time they were in Kansas, her heart screamed, *No!* Outwardly, though, she heard herself say, "Yes, that would be all right."

The discussion dragged out over the next year. But by the next family gathering, they all reluctantly agreed. Grant arranged to meet with Jeremy at Dale's house again. Eldon and Mary Ellen, Carolyn, Mamie, Gareth and Phyllis, Dan and Marilyn, and Grant all went to the meeting. As they prepared to leave, Mamie tucked Grant's photo album in her bag, thinking Grant might want to show his birth father pictures of him at birth and as a boy growing up.

The meeting began formally, with everyone shaking Jeremy and his wife's hands and introducing themselves. Then they sat in the living room and made small talk for a while, the atmosphere stiff.

Finally Mamie started to worry that they would leave and not even discuss the subject that lay on all their minds. Pulling out the photo album, she offered it to Jeremy. "Here, would you like to look at some pictures of Grant when he was little?"

Jeremy walked across the room to pick up the book and carried it back to his chair. He sat and opened it, slowly and intently looking at each picture before moving on. When he got to the end, he flipped back to the first page and started over. Everyone watched him in silence.

Finally Marilyn spoke up. "Were you aware that Mom and Dad had two other handicapped girls?"

Jeremy looked up in surprise. "No, I wasn't."

"Taking care of them was very hard on my parents." Marilyn paused as she choked up, tears rolling down her cheeks. "But when Faith became pregnant, I think that was the hardest thing they ever faced. Is that right, Mom?"

Mary Ellen nodded silently as tears rolled down her face. In her mind, she recalled her heartbroken anguish at the news that her helpless daughter had been sinned against.

Marilyn wiped her eyes and continued. "We're very blessed to have Grant in our family. We all know we couldn't love Grant the way we do if we held bitterness toward you. God has forgiven us many times for our sins, and we would like you to know we extend that forgiveness to you."

As she spoke, Jeremy's head dropped lower and lower. He shook his head as the enormity of what he had done came upon him once again. Tears welled up in his eyes. "How can you forgive me?" he asked brokenly. "I don't deserve it. I have spent all my adult years trying to accept what I did back then."

Any remaining awkwardness and uncertainty in the room disappeared as tears rolled down everyone's cheeks. Compassion filled their hearts at the sight of Jeremy's obvious remorse. One by one they spoke, reassuring him of their forgiveness.

After more visiting, they got up to leave. Jeremy stepped over and put his arm around Marilyn. "I'm so, so sorry. I know you said you would forgive me, but I need to hear it again. Will you truly forgive me?"

Marilyn looked at Jeremy. His face was pleading for mercy. "Yes," she said simply, her voice filled with emotion.

Eldon cleared his throat and spoke for the first time. "More than anything, we want to be together in heaven someday."

Jeremy nodded. Even though the burden of guilt for his deeds felt somewhat lifted, he knew he didn't have the peace Grant's family had. He longed for that same peace in his heart.

One evening not long after that memorable meeting, Grant's phone buzzed. He pulled it out to find a text message from Jeremy.

"I thought I would let you know my wife and I became Christians," Grant read. "Your family's testimony spoke to me so strongly that I wanted what they had. I was miserable until I gave my heart to the Lord. I wanted to tell you myself."

Grant's heart warmed within him. He responded instantly: "I'm so happy to hear!"

Jeremy sent another message: "Thanks. Our pastor came to have a Bible study with us, and he wondered if we would like to be baptized. We are going to attend his church."

"That's wonderful!" Grant texted back. "I know this is a direct answer to our prayers."

Another message came immediately: "I would like you to come help baptize me. Would you do that?"

Grant texted back: "Sure! I would be honored. Let me know the details."

That Sunday, Grant took his friend Eli Yoder with him to the town pool where the baptism would be held. People were milling around with seemingly no order or plan. This was a different culture compared to the conservative Anabaptist services Grant was used to. It looked more like a swimming party or an ice cream social than a baptism.

Soon the pastor announced, "As far as I can tell, everyone is here. I think we'll get started." After a few brief comments, he invited Jeremy and Grant to come forward.

Grant followed the pastor and Jeremy into the pool. "Are you truly sorry for your sins?" the pastor asked.

"Yes," Jeremy replied simply.

"Are you willing to change your ways?"

"Yes."

"In the name of the Father, Son, and Holy Spirit, I baptize you." With the pastor on one side and Grant on the other, they dunked Jeremy under the water. Although the atmosphere was very different from Grant's own baptism, it was incredibly meaningful for him to be a part of his biological father's conversion experience. More and more, God was using Grant's life in ways he had never dreamed of. With joy in his heart, Grant ate ice cream and drank Kool-Aid to celebrate with the others who had gathered to support Jeremy Williams in his new life in Christ.

Several months later, Grant examined the address for his shed delivery with interest. "Winfield, Kansas," he mused. "That's where my story began." He followed the GPS to his destination, and as he expertly placed the storage shed on the property, he struck up a conversation with the homeowner. "So how long have you lived in Winfield?"

"Oh, let's see," the man mused. "Quite a while. I think it must be about thirty years now."

Grant gave him a slight smile. "Do you remember a situation here in Winfield State Hospital when a handicapped woman got pregnant?"

"Oh, yeah, I remember," the man said. "That was horrible news. And then that nurse turned himself in."

"Did you keep following the story?" Grant pressed.

"Nope, it was kept mum. I never heard another thing. I suppose the hospital was afraid of ruining their reputation." The man shook his head. "I often wondered what happened. But why are you asking me this? You look too young to remember."

"Yes, I am," Grant affirmed. "But I was the child of that woman."

"You aren't serious!" the homeowner exclaimed. He gaped at Grant, trying to process the thought.

"I am serious. That was my mom," Grant said simply.

"Well, I don't know what to say," the man stammered. "I guess I'm glad you were given the opportunity to live." He considered his words, looking at the strong, dynamic young man in front of him. "Yeah, your family made the right choice."

32

Not a Monster

Grant continued to find purpose and fulfillment in using his story to bring honor to God. He spoke here and there to youth groups and churches, but only occasionally. Should he look for more opportunities? What did God want?

As he grew into adulthood, he began taking his calling from God more seriously. A local newspaper had published an article about him and his family, and soon afterward a lady called from the LifeCare Pregnancy Center in Ottawa, Kansas. “We have a pro-life fundraiser every year that draws a big group of people. I read your story in the *Topeka Capital-Journal.* Would you be willing to talk at our event?”

Grant didn’t hesitate. “I feel strongly that the Lord has called me to tell my story. I would be delighted to speak at your event.”

Several weeks later, he got a text from Jeremy Williams: "Hey, I'd like to hear you tell your story sometime."

Grant texted back: "I'm planning to tell it next week in Ottawa. Shall we go together?"

"Yes, that sounds good," Jeremy replied.

The night of the fundraiser, Grant and Jeremy drove to the venue. A sea of people filled the banquet room, and Grant was a nervous wreck. This was the biggest crowd he had ever spoken to. How would he keep his thoughts together in front of so many eyes?

He felt the gentle reminder, *Remember, Grant, I've called you to tell your story. Just speak from your heart.*

The time came, and Grant was called up onto the huge stage. His knees trembled as he walked forward and took the microphone from the master of ceremonies.

Grant cleared his throat, and the microphone squawked. He chuckled nervously and grinned at the audience. "I hope this thing cooperates. I must say, this is the biggest crowd I've ever faced." As the crowd laughed understandingly, some of his nervousness went away. Grant paused and took a deep breath. He felt the Lord direct his thoughts with clarity, and the words spilled from his heart.

"November 21, 1991, was the day that forever changed the lives of a middle-aged Christian family. They were faced with an ordeal that would test their faith like nothing else they had ever experienced." He cleared his throat. "This family had eight children. Three of their daughters were severely mentally handicapped with cerebral palsy. The two oldest were in a state hospital, and the youngest lived at home. All three of them had never functioned at a higher level than a typical child does at three to six months of age." He paused to let his audience consider the reality his grandparents had faced.

"On that fateful day the presiding doctor of the state hospital where the two sisters had lived for the last twenty-five years called the parents and said he was coming out to discuss something very important. When he arrived, the doctor informed the family that the youngest of their two girls had been raped by a male nurse and was six months pregnant. The doctor told the parents that because of their daughter's extremely low body weight, the prescription drugs she was on, and the radiation from X-rays, there was almost no chance this child would live to see the light of day." Grant's voice broke. "But I want to tell you tonight that God has a plan for you—and for me. I was that baby."

The crowd sat still for a moment, then burst into applause.

Grant collected himself as he waited for the room to quiet down. "What the devil meant for evil, God has used for good. I was adopted by my uncle and aunt and have been blessed in many ways." He went on to tell the story of the little boy who was never expected to live.

As he neared the end of his speech, Grant felt his emotions rising within him. He paused to regain his composure, then went on. "There is someone here tonight that I would like for you all to meet. It is the first time he has heard me tell my story." He scanned the audience and beckoned to Jeremy. "May I introduce my birth dad to all of you tonight."

Jeremy slowly walked up to him. In front of the huge crowd, Grant embraced his dad as the crowd erupted with thunderous applause. "This man is not a monster. He is a forgiven human being—just like you and me. Yes, he made a shameful mistake, but that doesn't mean God can't use the mistake for His glory." With that, Grant led his dad down from the platform and they sat together at a table.

The master of ceremonies walked back up to the stage. He smiled through his tears. "Now I know why there were tissues on all the tables." The crowd applauded again. "Grant, your testimony is powerful. Use it to honor the life God gave to you."

Afterward, Grant was delighted to find that some of his aunts and uncles had attended the event to show their support. Myron, who had been unable to meet Jeremy with the rest of the family, took a moment to shake Jeremy's hand. "I thought I had forgiven you long ago, but this event has made my forgiveness complete."

The presentation at the LifeCare Pregnancy Center cemented a thought in Grant's mind: it was time he started searching for more people who needed to hear his story. One day a coworker approached him. "My brothers, cousin, and I play some instruments and would like to start a singing group. You have a pretty amazing story to tell. If we worked together, I think we could come up with a compelling presentation. We should go to Alabama and be a part of a prison ministry."

"That sounds like an awesome idea," Grant agreed. They started making plans to go.

When they arrived in Alabama, they worked through the prison ministry and began to visit prisons, singing and ministering to the inmates. The five young men experienced some powerful times on their tour. Every time complications came up, God came through for them in an unmistakable way.

One Friday evening, Grant and his friends headed into a prison to host a service. They had a lot going against them, as they were running late and one of them was sick—one of the key musicians. The group rushed through the doors, still needing to set up equipment and do a sound check. But when they entered the chapel, there were fifty men already there, waiting for them.

"Oh, no!" Grant moaned. There was nothing to do but set up anyway, knowing that their playing and singing would be a bit lacking. But on the second song, one of the inmates jumped to his feet and hurried up the aisle to fill in for the missing musician.

After the time of singing, Grant got up and began to speak. As he told his story, fifty pairs of eyes were riveted on him. "Bring your pain to Jesus," he told the men at the end of the story. "If you are tired of struggling with things that have hurt you, bring them to Jesus. If you come forward now, we will pray with you."

The men surged forward. Many had countless pains and hurts, and they weren't afraid to confess them. They wanted the healing Jesus brings. Grant and his friends spent hours with the inmates, counseling and praying.

After the men had gone back to their cells, a warden sought out Grant. "Young man, I've been here twenty years and I've never seen a response to an altar call like that. Those men connected with you and your story."

Grant broke down and wept. "If my story brings healing to these men, I give all the honor and glory to God. He has given me the burden of telling it to hurting people. Tonight was beautiful. I will never forget the response of those men."

33

Faith

As Grant's opportunities to share his story increased, the Bontrager family's attention swiveled back to Faith, whose health was taking a slow but definite downward turn. When she had turned fifty, her caretakers and Eldon and Mary Ellen had worked together to coordinate a birthday party. Most of the Bontrager family traveled to El Dorado Park to enjoy a big ice cream cake with her. Now fifty-three years old, Faith had outlived all her disabled sisters.

Eldon and Mary Ellen, and occasionally Carolyn, made a point of visiting Faith every few months. Their observations and the reports from her caretakers indicated that all was not well with her. She was showing signs of physical decline.

As Mamie and her children made plans for a family vacation in Montana, they kept uneasy ears on the updates. Although Faith was not doing very well, she had dipped and recovered so many times before that they decided to go ahead with their planned trip.

Once in Montana, Grant called Mary Ellen to find out how things were going. "Hey Grandma, what's up?"

"Oh, we're doing pretty good," her smiling voice answered. "How's Montana?"

"Oh, it's been good!" Grant replied. "But I keep worrying about Faith. What's the latest?"

Mary Ellen sobered. "She's not doing well at all. She hasn't eaten anything for a week."

Grant's heart sank. "Do you think I should come home? I really would like to be there when she passes away."

"Well, it's up to you," Mary Ellen replied. "But I don't know if this will lead to the end or not. She could easily snap out of it again. I'm guessing she will still be here when you come home."

"Do you think so?" Grant asked. "Well, that's good to know. I don't like being this far away, but we'll be home soon. Just let me know if I should come home early."

Grant thought he had made the right decision, but Faith's struggle to live was coming to an end. On Saturday morning, August 8, 2015, Grant's phone rang in his motel in Montana. "Good morning, Grant," Carolyn said, her voice thick with emotion. "Your mother died at around midnight last night. She passed away peacefully."

As Grant hung up his phone, he started to sob. He wept, not because he wished Faith back into her small, wasted body, but for the relationship he was never able to have with his birth mother.

Grant and the rest of the family immediately headed back to Kansas for the funeral. At Faith's viewing, the enormity of his mother's death washed over him. "I can hardly believe she's gone," he told Mamie. "She was my mother, but I never really knew her. It just really hurts." Mamie put her arms around him as he cried. "It makes me look forward to heaven, where

I can actually talk to her."

Many people began to stream into the church to view the woman most of them had never met, but whose child was such a part of their lives. Grant took his spot at the head of the casket. It was a deeply emotional time for him as he shook hands with those who had come to show support for him and his family. He was amazed again at how God had used this profoundly disabled woman to make such a huge impact on the community.

At the family service before the funeral, Marilyn's husband Dan Korver leaned forward on the podium, sharing his thoughts with the family. "In a lot of ways, this feels like the end of an era." Everyone nodded; he had put into words what they were all feeling. "For most of their married life, Eldon and Mary Ellen have been, to some degree, providing for handicapped children. They have sacrificed for these special girls, and they have taught their children to sacrifice. Dad and Mom, the example you have set is difficult to match. I think I speak for all of us when I say, 'Thank you.'

"Now here we are, with Faith being the last of the handicapped girls to pass away." Dan went on to share some memories—memories of a person they had never really known. Once again, the Bontragers mourned the many blessings Faith had never experienced, but they found joy in imagining her enjoying a perfect body.

Dan brought their attention to Faith's remaining legacy. "Grant, of all the people who support your ministry, I want you to know that your mom, Faith, is your number one supporter." Grant bowed his head as tears stung his eyes.

Slowly the family filed to the front of the church for the funeral service. After the singing, Arlen Mast, the bishop at Arlington Church, rose to open the service. His eyes swept over the Bontrager family. "Jesus loves me! this I know, for the Bible tells me so. Little ones to Him belong; they are weak, but He is strong." Arlen's voice was slow and deliberate as he quoted the familiar song. "I'm sure those words have been sung many times in our homes, but how many of you as parents really think about what you are saying when you sing this song? We tend to think that our children are ours, but I wonder if the phrase, 'Little ones to Him belong,' was more of a reality for the Bontrager family than for the rest of us. From the very beginning, it was apparent that Faith was the Lord's, and the Bontragers only got to take care of her for a while."

Arlen welcomed everyone who had gathered to take part in this special meeting, then he turned over the time to Delmar Bontrager, Faith's cousin from Kalona, Iowa.

"Faith lived her fifty-three years in complete innocence," Delmar began. "You could say that she is a soul who has been set free from a body that society would describe as handicapped. And we praise God for that deliverance. 'But Jesus hath cheered the dark valley of sorrow, and bade us immortal to heaven ascend.' " Delmar referenced the song they had just sung. "The Bible tells us that if in this life only we have hope, we are miserable people. The challenge to us today is—are we going where Faith is? When each of us is lying here in a casket, how is it going to be? Most of us here this morning have been given sound minds and healthy bodies, and we are able to make choices for ourselves. What are the choices we are making today? Where are they going to take us?" Delmar entreated the congregation to search their lives and analyze their hearts.

Then he turned to Grant. "Twenty-four years ago, what we initially considered a tragedy, God turned around and brought beauty out of ashes. LaVon and Mamie were so happy to have you placed in their arms, to be your mommy and daddy." Delmar's voice broke as he recalled the joy on his cousin LaVon's face. "Grant, I want to bless you for the man of God that you are today, and for the right choices you have made in life. We love you, Grant. Your family loves you."

Grant's shoulders shook as tears streamed down his face. The road he had walked had been long and dark, but he was so thankful for the peace and freedom he could experience now.

Delmar turned back to the congregation. "As a cousin in this family, I never knew Faith very well. But Eldon and Mary Ellen, as your nephew, I want to say your dedication and your commitment to your family has been a blessing to me. I know only a small portion, but to see you faithfully stand together through the journey of these past sixty years... You know, there are times when we want to say 'Why, Lord? Why?' But sometimes God says, 'Just give me your hand and trust me.' Today, four of your eight children are in heaven. We are grateful for the hope we have in our hearts today as we prepare for that moment when it's going to be you or me."

Delmar took his seat, then a group of special singers sang "The First Look," a song Mary Ellen had long held dear in her heart as she thought of her babies who never grew up. The lyrics spoke of pearly gates swinging open and Jesus standing with His arms opened wide to receive those who had been blind, crippled, and laden with cares.

After the song was over, David Yoder, the former bishop of Arlington Church and a cousin of Mary Ellen, rose for the last message. "What was just sung is one of those realities that is hard for us to grasp because most of us deal with some kind of infirmity. But the truth of what was sung—that there is a day and a place where infirmities will be gone—is a beautiful thought."

His quiet, thoughtful words probed the hearts of his audience. "Those of you who can understand the words that I say and take them to heart can only be God's child in one way. That is by choice. But Faith had no choice. She was incapable of choosing right and wrong. But for us, we must choose whom we serve."

He turned his Bible to Matthew 18:1-5. " 'At the same time came the disciples unto Jesus, saying, Who is the greatest in the kingdom of heaven? And Jesus called a little child unto him, and set him in the midst of them, and said, Verily I say unto you, except ye be converted, and become as little children, ye shall not enter into the kingdom of heaven. Whosoever therefore shall humble himself as this little child, the same is greatest in the kingdom of heaven. And whoso shall receive one such little child in my name receiveth me.'

"Jesus is speaking here about the value of a little child, and in this case we focus on Faith. Jesus makes it very clear that our regard for the helpless, our regard for the needy, is imperative if we are to be His children.

"For us to experience the kingdom of God, we must bend our hearts. We must bend our wills before God and become as little children. That is what the kingdom of God is made of. Unless we live with a childlike faith, we cannot be His." David's voice was kind but convicting as he explored the choices of man and the sovereignty of God.

Then David turned to the family, and Grant looked up as he heard his name. He would never forget the next words. "Grant, while the circumstances of your conception were outside of the intended perfection of God, never insult God by despising them. After all, it was God who chose to give you life. Although your conception was outside of His perfection, He has a purpose for your life. Here is a paraphrase of several verses from Psalm 139: 'God formed your inward parts. He covered you in your mother's womb. You are to praise God, for you are fearfully and wonderfully made. Marvelous are His works. May your soul be fully convinced of these truths.'

"God is a God of redemption, and you have confirmed that. And that is one of the reasons we are here this morning. There is not a person here this morning whom God does not want to redeem. There is no situation you face, hard as it may be, that He does not want to turn into something good. Let's never lose sight of that." David smiled at the congregation.

"Mamie, thank you for being the mother you are to Grant. May God bless you and LaVon for the ways you gifted your love to Grant.

"Greg and Angie, thank you for the love you poured into this energetic package." David's eyes twinkled. "And he's still got some of that energy left.

"Eldon and Mary Ellen, thank you for sparing a life when there was pressure to do otherwise. Thank you for caring for Faith with your love as parents. Those were difficult times, and only God can reward you for your faithfulness to your three handicapped daughters. Well done! One of the greater blessings is that you know where they all are now.

"Carolyn, Myron, Phyllis, and Marilyn, may God bless you and reward you for the ways you blessed your sisters. I am sure you learned many lessons some of us never did."

He lifted a paper. "I'd like to conclude by reading some of the lessons Phyllis cited that they learned as a family." Turning his eyes downward, David read:

> Dear Father in heaven,
>
> You are sovereign. We are so human. Yet you love us and desire to take us as your very own. But sometimes in our finite minds, we question you.
>
> Soon after she was born, it became apparent that Faith had the same health problems as Lynette. We had to resign our dreams again and accept God's plan.
>
> During her life, the lessons of endurance were nearly more than we could bear, like when Faith would cry for hours on end. But as we clung to you for comfort, you assured us your grace was sufficient.
>
> The lesson of hope and seeing the eternal was obvious when you gave Dad a glimpse of Faith standing on the portals of heaven.
>
> What guilt and helplessness and inadequacy we felt when Faith and Lynette needed to be moved to Winfield State Hospital. The lesson of letting go and trusting their care to strangers was much harder than the pain we feel today in parting.
>
> We all struggled with the heartrending lesson on forgiving ourselves when we weren't there to protect Faith in her darkest night. This came along with the severe test of forgiving others, which was not possible of ourselves.
>
> You have taught us that you make beauty out of ashes. You provided so much when you provided a pleasant group home for the girls to spend their last years in. Their caregivers treated them with compassion.

How could one person who never uttered a word teach us so many lessons? We thought Faith needed us, but now we see we really needed Faith. Help us never to forget the important things Faith taught us!

In Jesus' name. Amen!

Faith's family

David gathered his notes and took his seat as the ushers conducted a final viewing.

After the burial, the family stood in a small huddle around the grave. "I like to imagine all my daughters with their new bodies," Mary Ellen said, smiling through her tears. "I would never ask to have them back."

"Oh, it's so beautiful to imagine them up there." Phyllis's eyes shimmered with emotion.

Marilyn turned to Grant. "What would you have done if Faith's death would have happened when you were sixteen? Back when you were angry and searching for purpose?"

Grant looked down and slowly shook his head. "I don't really know. I'm afraid I would have been tempted to end my life. At that point life made no sense to me."

"Oh, Grant," Mamie said, shocked. "You wouldn't really have done that!"

"I'm not so sure, Mom," Grant returned. "I was one confused boy. I didn't think God had a plan for an accident like me."

"I don't know why God allowed Faith to live so much longer than her sisters," Myron mused. "But I'm so thankful He did. It gave Grant time to find peace with the circumstances of his birth."

Grant nodded. He would never again doubt his beginnings. He would strive to never look back again. But he would go on telling his story to a broken world—the story God put him on earth to tell. The story of a child of faith.

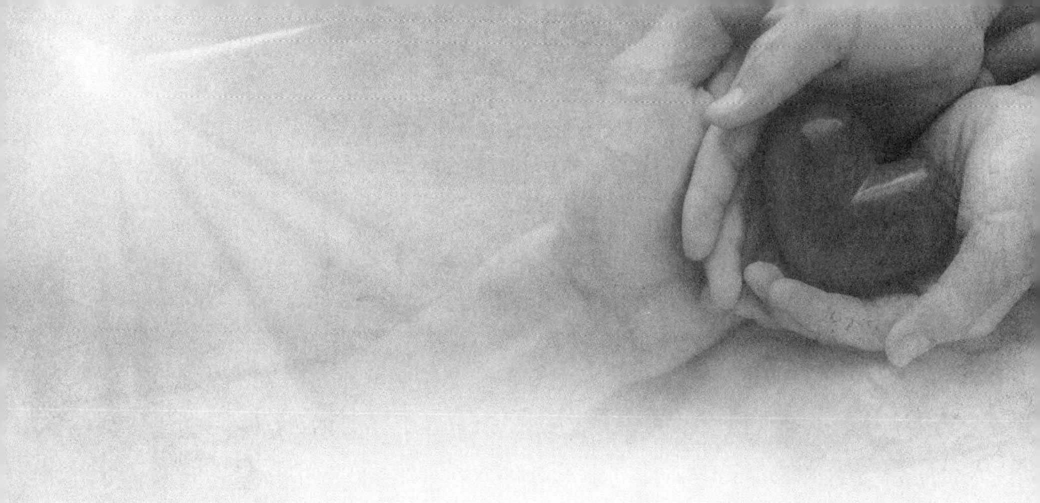

Epilogue

Pacing outside of the shack in Haiti where he was held hostage, Ryan Korver mused on the crisis faced by his grandparents nearly thirty years earlier. No one knew as well as Eldon and Mary Ellen did about what it took to care for a handicapped child. No one better knew the sleepless nights, the missed opportunities, the misunderstandings—and yet they never hesitated when faced with that unplanned baby. Ryan thought about his dear cousin Grant, who was a result of their decision. *Thank you, God! Thank you for grandparents who did the right thing, even when it was hard!*

As though written in the Haitian sky, words blazed back at him: "And *this* is what I want *you* to do!"

Ryan stopped pacing, his attention riveted. "God? What are you saying?"

"This is what I want you to do!" No one else heard an audible voice, but Ryan understood the message as clearly as if it had been shouted. "Take your family and leave this place."

"God," Ryan gasped. "Is this really on that scale?" His grandparents had acted in faith, regardless of the consequences. Would it take the same level of faith to dive into an escape attempt and trust God with the outcome?

The message came again: "This is what I want you to do!"

Ryan ceased praying. He understood. With the answer in his heart, he took his small son into the semi-privacy of the shack they all shared. As he fanned the feverish boy to sleep, Ryan wept like a child. God had spoken! Ryan finally knew what he needed to do. The relief was overwhelming.

"Ryan?" His wife Melodi's voice made him look up. "Are you okay?"

Ryan smiled through his tears—the sincerest smile he'd had since they were kidnapped. "I think I have my answer. I don't know what it will mean, but I know what we have to do."

"Really?" Melodi's eyes widened as she sank to the mattress beside him. "Tell me about it, please!"

"God told me..." Ryan's voice broke as he choked back another sob. Andre stirred restlessly in his sleep, and Melodi gently patted the child's back until he relaxed.

"Shall we move somewhere else so we don't disturb him?" Melodi whispered, nodding toward the doorway beside them. The mattress in the back room was farther from the sleeping Andre and not immediately visible to anyone passing the outside door.

Once seated on the mattress, Ryan started at the day's beginning. Choking back the tears, he told his wife everything he had been wrestling with. He ended with his dwelling on Grant's story, his little prayer, and God's immediate response. "I know what we have to do," Ryan said. "We need to leave, and it'll be up to the others if they will come with us."

Melodi buried her face in his shoulder as they wept together. "For so long, we've wanted to go home! And now it feels like we're almost there." The couple didn't know what lay ahead, but they knew they must step out in faith.

"Now we need to tell the others," Ryan whispered. "And I'm scared. I'm not good with words, and I'm afraid this will divide our group further." He blew his nose.

"It's not about you," Melodi replied, squeezing his hand. "It's about God. Just tell them what He told you. It's not our decision anymore."

"That's right," Ryan said as he stood. Even though they couldn't see the whole trail ahead, they knew without a doubt the next step God was asking of them. All they could do was follow in faith.

At 2:45 the next morning, the twelve captives—ten adults, with two small children in their arms—silently slipped out of the small shack and struck out through the Haitian countryside. Their journey was bathed in prayer, with faith that the great God of the universe would guide their steps.

Less than twenty-four hours after God's revelation to Ryan, he and his family burst through the door of their home on the Titanyen base. In three big strides, he crossed the kitchen and grabbed the telephone. In a moment, the whole Bontrager family would hear yet another testimony of how Grandpa and Grandma's faith—and Grant's story—continued to change lives.

When Grant heard how his story had brought the hostages together, he broke down and sobbed. *Can this be for real? Did God actually use this horrible story of sin and disrespect to bring about the miraculous escape we've been pleading for all these weeks?* The thought was overwhelming. Good out of evil. Beauty for ashes. Purpose in pain. Grant's mind spun as he struggled to grasp it.

Grabbing his phone, he called Ryan's mom. "Marilyn! Did you hear this? Did you hear what they said? God used Faith's story to lead them out of there!"

"Oh, Grant!" Marilyn's voice was filled with emotion. "Isn't it amazing? God used Faith's story to unite them and answer our prayers!"

"I can hardly wrap my mind around it." Grant found himself nearly speechless.

Marilyn was quiet for a time as they pondered the miraculous happening. "You know," she finally said, "a lot of people go through hard things and never see any good come out of it. It feels like such a gift from God to be allowed to see something that we once viewed as dark and ugly being used in such a specific and amazing way. Grant, I've always tried to be supportive of you sharing your story, but part of me would have been just as glad to see something so sad left in the past."

Grant could hear the deep emotion in her voice as she continued. "Oh, I felt like I had forgiven Jeremy Williams for what he did, and it was really beautiful to see you serving the Lord and finding purpose in life, but I didn't like to think how Faith had to suffer." Her voice broke. "But having God use this story in this way shows me His redemption. Grant, it brings value and purpose out of her pain like nothing I've ever experienced. I want you to know that our family is backing up your ministry all the way."

At the other end of the line, Grant nodded dumbly as tears streamed down his cheeks.

Ryan and Grant had always been close, and Grant couldn't wait to talk things over with him in person. He was thrilled to hear that Ryan was bringing his family to Kansas to share the story of their miraculous escape. A crowd gathered at the Pleasantview Activity Center, and Grant opened the service with a brief devotional before introducing Ryan.

Eldon was nearing ninety and didn't leave home much anymore, but an event like this was something he couldn't miss. He sat close to the front, listening intently as his grandson spoke. Silent tears rolled down his wrinkled cheeks. Thoughts and memories surged through his mind. Nobody but God could bring good out of this story of their lives.

In the footsteps of his grandparents' example of forgiveness toward those who had violated their loved one, Ryan concluded his testimony: "Those gang members need the Lord. We just heard from a reliable source that the fellow who brought us our food every day was killed last week in a gun battle with the police. It was a reminder that those men live violent lives, and they don't have a long life-expectancy. They are in desperate need of the Gospel. Let's remember to pray for them."

Although Mary Ellen had not braved the wintry weather that evening, she was waiting for Eldon when Carolyn dropped him off after the event. They stayed up late that night as he shared Ryan's story. Even though dementia had stolen much from her, Mary Ellen could still well remember the events of long ago. Her eyes grew moist as she and her husband discussed with humble awe how God had used their faithfulness during the darkest moment in their life to bring direction to their grandson during his trial.

"It really got me to thinking," Eldon confided to her. "There's no denying that we went through some really hard stuff during our life, and it was often hard for me to accept that God allowed some of the things He did. But you know, Mary Ellen, what if it would be possible to change all of that? Would we really want to change our story?"

Mary Ellen was quiet for a long time. Then she finally said, "No. It was very hard—too difficult to describe at times—but we learned so much."

Eldon nodded. "And we met so many wonderful people. So much good came out of our experience that it's hard to feel like it should have been different."

"I agree," Mary Ellen replied. "The older I get, the more I see that other people have hard stuff to work through too. It wasn't just us. This was just the story we were asked to live."

"As I sat there this evening listening to Ryan, I realized it all makes more sense now," Eldon said. "When we can see the whole story, we can see clearly how God was with us all the time."

He reached out and grasped Mary Ellen's gnarled hand. They sat in silence, thankful to have a God who had brought healing to their hearts. He had provided the grace they needed to keep going during both the good times and the hard times.

Afterword

Grant went on to tell his story many times over the next years. In 2020, he met a lovely girl named Jen who had recently moved from Missouri to Kansas. After dating for a short time, they were married on June 14, 2021. Mr. and Mrs. Grant Bontrager and their children, Spencer Gage and Zayla Faith, now live in Kansas near the place where he grew up.

Eldon Bontrager died on August 22, 2023, at the age of ninety-one, having lived his long life well. Mary Ellen joined him in paradise a little over a year later, on November 4, 2024. She was also ninety-one years old when she died.

Their legacy lives on in the lives of their descendants.

Historical Resources

https://www.hutchnews.com/story/news/2018/09/27/throwback-thursday/9843810007/.

Roads Taken: The Great Jewish Migrations to the New World and the Peddlers Who Forged the Way, by Hasia R. Diner. New Haven: Yale University Press, 2015, and Peddler.pdf (gregorylefever.com) "Era of the American Peddler."

"Foreign affairs: The Khrushchev Visit" | JFK Library, and "Khrushchev arrives in Washington" | September 15, 1959 | HISTORY.

"Winfield State Hospital." —Kansas Historical Society Pages 1-14 Flip PDF Download | FlipHTML5.

https://www.weather.gov/top/1966TopekaTornado.

Blizzard 1971 Archives – Harvey County Historical Society (hchm.org).

https://www.weather.gov/ddc/Top25HistoricalWeatherEvents.

"Works Progress Administration: WPA & New Deal" —HISTORY.

"The Education for All Handicapped Children Act of 1975" | U.S. GAO.

https://www.cjonline.com/story/news/2017/01/30/kansas-son-family-forgive-father-s-unspeakable-crime/16558111007/.

About Laura Smucker

Laura grew up in the state of Oregon, with its rocky coastline and diverse natural beauty. Growing up in a family of writers, she learned to love words at a young age. In fourth grade she took a writing course, which she enjoyed from start to finish. The course taught Laura how to put together words, and soon she discovered how much she loved to express herself on paper. She learned to write journals and create poetry and prose.

Laura got married at a young age, and moved with her husband John to the various communities where he taught school. After ten years had passed, during which four children were added to the family, they moved to Poland to serve in mission work. During those ten years, Laura wrote her first book: *Strands of Gold.*

After returning to the States in 2011, Laura wrote the books *A Reason to Hope* and *Prejudice and Pardon.* A year after their return, a fifth child joined the family. Amid children getting married, the sudden death of a grandson, and a son getting kidnapped in Haiti, the following years were intense and often beyond John and Laura's ability to understand God's plan for their lives. But through it all, they experienced His unfailing love and constant presence and care.

The Smucker family now lives in Madras, Oregon, where they are part of an outreach. Laura enjoys making candles, writing, having coffee with friends, and babysitting her grandbabies.

You may write to her at laurasmucker@gmail.com or in care of CAM Books, P. O. Box 355, Berlin, Ohio 44610.

About Kaylene (Bontrager) Stoltzfus

Kaylene grew up in Arlington, Kansas—a land of beautiful skies and wonderful people. She was born to a family who saw much to appreciate in a well-told story, and some of her first memories are of her grandma—with tears of laughter streaming down her face—sharing a story to lighten the weariness of a sticky corn day. Kaylene was taught by example how even the small eccentricities of life can be enhanced in the telling thereof by using carefully chosen and descriptive words.

She spent her teenage years babysitting and working at her aunt's restaurant. At the age of twenty, she moved to Virginia, where she worked at Faith Mission Home for over three years. This was a time of growth, ultimately changing the course of her life when she married a fellow staff member named Jay Stoltzfus.

Jay and Kaylene were quickly blessed with five children, and much of their life is spent guiding them into the ways of wisdom and truth. Currently the Stoltzfus family lives in the town of Millersburg, Ohio. Their small-town lot is home to beehives, chickens, ducks, produce gardens, and an ever-revolving series of pets. Over-climbed trees and a threadbare lawn bear testimony to their active tribe. Jay and Kaylene share a love of homesteading, and their hobbies include buying and reading good books, soil improvement, exploring fermentation, and cooking ethnic dishes. Their bucket list is long enough for several lifespans! Jay and Kaylene's life together has not always been easy, but they thank God for each other and for His tremendous power and grace that has guided them this far.

You may write to Kaylene at jaynkaystoltz@gmail.com or in care of CAM Books, P. O. Box 355, Berlin, Ohio 44610.

About Christian Aid Ministries

Christian Aid Ministries was founded in 1981 as a nonprofit, tax-exempt 501(c)(3) organization. Its primary purpose is to provide a trustworthy and efficient channel for Amish, Mennonite, and other conservative Anabaptist groups and individuals to minister to physical and spiritual needs around the world. This is in response to the command to "Do good unto all men, especially unto them who are of the household of faith" (Galatians 6:10).

CAM supporters provide millions of pounds of food, clothing, Bibles, medicines, and other aid each year. Supporters' funds also help victims of disasters in the U.S. and abroad, put up Gospel billboards in the U.S., and provide Biblical teaching and self-help resources. CAM's main purposes for providing aid are to help and encourage God's people and bring the Gospel to a lost and dying world.

The Way to God and Peace

We live in a world contaminated by sin. Sin is anything that goes against God's holy standards. When we do not follow the guidelines that God our Creator gave us, we are guilty of sin. Sin separates us from God, the source of life.

Since the time when the first man and woman, Adam and Eve, sinned in the Garden of Eden, sin has been universal. The Bible says that we all have "sinned and come short of the glory of God" (Romans 3:23). It also says that the natural consequence for that sin is eternal death, or punishment in an eternal hell: "Then when lust hath conceived, it bringeth forth sin: and sin, when it is finished, bringeth forth death" (James 1:15).

But we do not have to suffer eternal death in hell. God provided forgiveness for our sins through the death of His only Son, Jesus Christ. Because

Jesus was perfect and without sin, He could die in our place. "For God so loved the world that he gave his only begotten Son, that whosoever believeth in him should not perish, but have everlasting life" (John 3:16).

A sacrifice is something given to benefit someone else. It costs the giver greatly. Jesus was God's sacrifice. Jesus' death takes away the penalty of sin for all those who accept this sacrifice and truly repent of their sins. To repent of sins means to be truly sorry for and turn away from the things we have done that have violated God's standards (Acts 2:38; 3:19).

Jesus died, but He did not remain dead. After three days, God's Spirit miraculously raised Him to life again. God's Spirit does something similar in us. When we receive Jesus as our sacrifice and repent of our sins, our hearts are changed. We become spiritually alive! We develop new desires and attitudes (2 Corinthians 5:17). We begin to make choices that please God (1 John 3:9). If we do fail and commit sins, we can ask God for forgiveness. "If we confess our sins, he is faithful and just to forgive us our sins, and to cleanse us from all unrighteousness" (1 John 1:9).

Once our hearts have been changed, we want to continue growing spiritually. We will be happy to let Jesus be the Master of our lives and will want to become more like Him. To do this, we must meditate on God's Word and commune with God in prayer. We will testify to others of this change by being baptized and sharing the good news of God's victory over sin and death. Fellowship with a faithful group of believers will strengthen our walk with God (1 John 1:7).